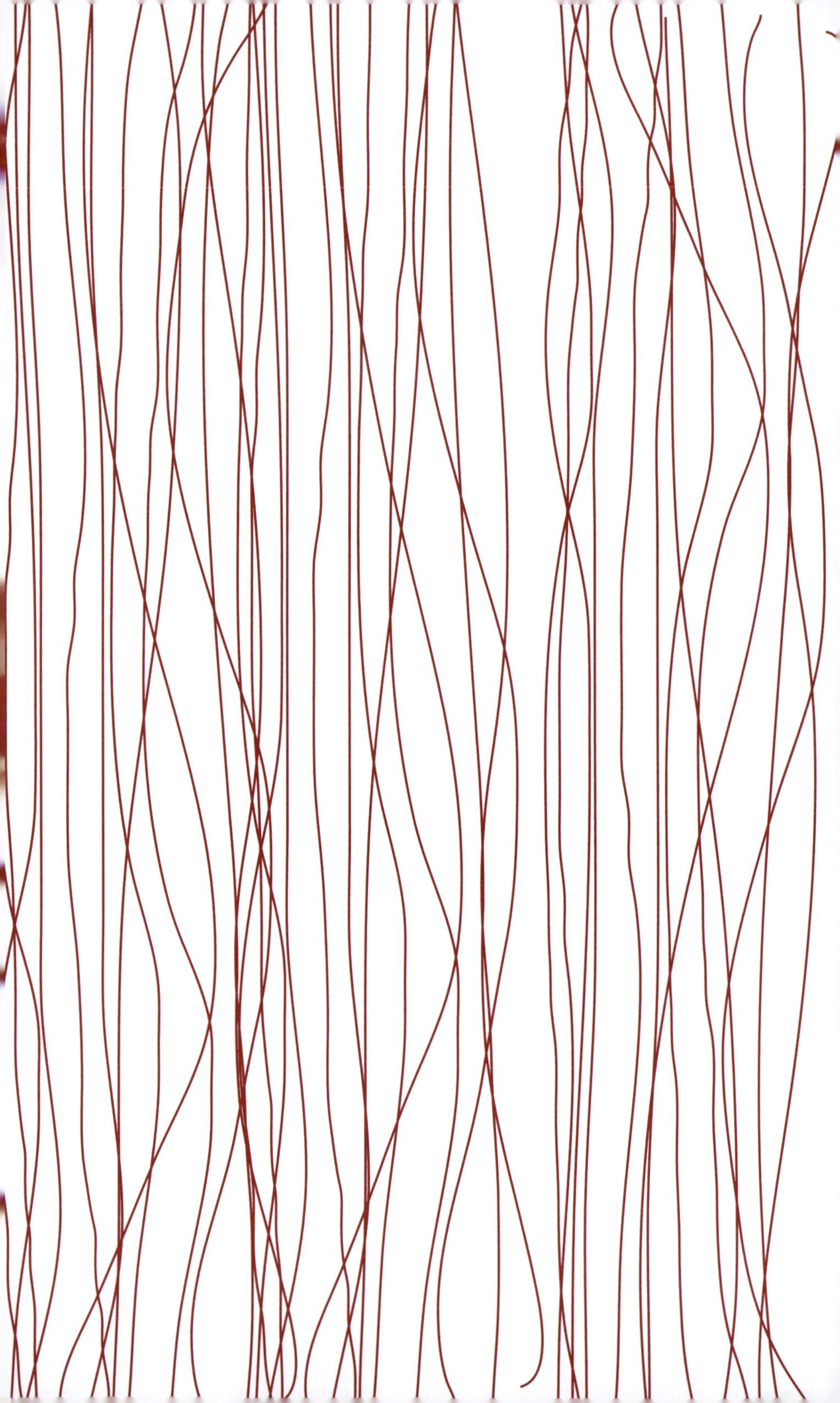

Portrait of a Serial Killer.

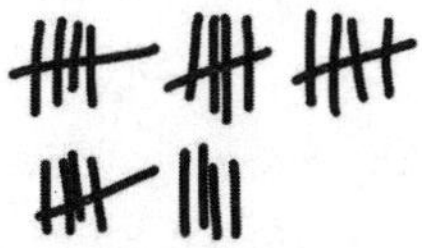

Also by Khushwant Singh

FICTION

Train to Pakistan
I Shall Not Hear the Nightingale
Delhi: A Novel
The Company of Women
Burial at Sea
The Sunset Club
The Portrait of a Lady: Collected Stories

NON-FICTION

Truth, Love & a Little Malice: An Autobiography
Nature Watch
Indira Gandhi Returns
A History of the Sikhs
Ranjit Singh: Maharaja of the Punjab

ANTHOLOGIES

The Freethinker's Prayer Book
99: Unforgettable Fiction, Non-fiction, Poetry & Humour

TRANSLATIONS

Land of Five Rivers
Umrao Jan Ada (with M. A. Husaini)
Shikwa and Jawab-i-Shikwa
Celebrating the Best of Urdu Poetry (with Kamna Prasad)

Portrait of a Serial Killer.

UNCOLLECTED WRITINGS

KHUSHWANT SINGH

edited by Mala Dayal

ALEPH

ALEPH

ALEPH BOOK COMPANY
An independent publishing firm
promoted by ***Rupa Publications India***

Published in India in 2015 by
Aleph Book Company
7/16 Ansari Road, Daryaganj
New Delhi 110 002

ISBN: 978-93-82277-76-7

1 3 5 7 9 10 8 6 4 2

Printed and bound in India by Replika Press Pvt. Ltd.

The marble plaque installed in Khushwant Singh's first school in Hadali, Punjab (now in Pakistan)

Fakir Aijazuddin, a family friend, had taken his ashes by train to Pakistan and had them interred and grouted permanently behind the plaque.

This book is dedicated to
Nandini Mehta in gratitude for the gift of friendship.

Contents

Introduction

This book will be published on the hundredth anniversary of my father's birth, and a little over a year after he passed away. In death, as in life, my father cast a long shadow, especially when it came to those of his friends and fans who admired his honesty and courage as a journalist, and his forthrightness and lucid style as a writer. This was evident from the obituaries written at his death, not only in India and the UK, but perhaps even more so in Pakistani newspapers, both English and Urdu. Article after article mentioned his strong advocacy of Indo-Pak friendship and cited incidents of how he stuck his neck out for his beliefs.

The affection he commanded in Pakistan was also evident at a special session held in his honour at a literary festival I attended in Lahore in February 2015. The hall was packed with perhaps a thousand people. The panel discussion was chaired by Fakir Aijazuddin, who had taken some of my father's ashes by train to Pakistan and interred them at Hadali, where my father was born. My father's warm welcome to visitors from Pakistan, his love of Urdu poetry and scholarship were mentioned by all the panellists. One of them recounted an incident that occurred after the 1971 war: My father went to see Mrs Indira Gandhi and pleaded for the release of the 93,000 prisoners of war. He told her that holding these prisoners was morally wrong. She snubbed him, saying, 'Thanks for lecturing me on morality.' He was undeterred and continued to ask that they be released. Nor was he bothered when he was referred to as an unpaid agent of Pakistan.

The audience clapped and cheered.

I returned to Pakistan two months later for the Islamabad Literary Festival. This time my brother and I were able to go to Hadali. The village came out to welcome us, overwhelming us with warmth and hospitality. We saw the place where my father was born; the house was now just a pile of bricks, but the government school where he studied, though dilapidated, was still functioning. Our friends Shahnaz and Aijazuddin accompanied us on this trip and showed us where my father's ashes has been mixed with cement and placed behind the marble plaque so that he could rest where his roots were. They had brought rose petals to put on the ledge of the plaque and, like my father had done some thirty years before, I was overcome and broke down.

◆

As is to be expected, this collection has more than one piece on Pakistan. But it also has pieces on a number of other subjects that my father was interested in. Throughout his very long career as a writer, editor, journalist and columnist, his work had a few distinguishing characteristics that made it impossible to mistake it for that of any other writer—most noticeably a dislike for humbug, flowery phrases and hyperbole. He usually wrote several drafts of every piece that was eventually published. Each of these drafts was diligently typed out by Mr Lachman Das, his long-time assistant, on a manual typewriter, and delivered to my father, who would then correct and revise the piece for it to be typed out again by Mr Das. When I was going through his manuscripts and papers to put together this book I often found more than one draft of a piece. In such cases, I chose to include the version that seemed to be the most distinctive and polished. Several of the pieces have been lightly edited. To the extent possible, the pieces are chronologically arranged within the sections in which they appear. The multiple drafts of a number of the pieces also made it difficult to accurately date them and identify the magazine or newspaper in which they eventually appeared. It would, however, be safe to say that versions of the majority of the pieces in the book appeared in *Yojana*, *The Statesman*, the *New York Times*, *New Delhi*, the *Hindustan Times*, the *Illustrated Weekly of India* and *The Tribune*. To the best of my knowledge, most of these pieces, or at any rate these versions of these pieces, have never been collected in book form before. A few of the pieces have never been published before.

The book is divided into four sections: 'Unforgettable People', 'Memorable Places', 'The Indian Way' and 'A Matter of Politics'. The first section contains character sketches of people as diverse as the serial killer Raman Raghav who terrorized Bombay before he was caught; the pre-eminent biographer of Mother Teresa, British journalist Malcolm Muggeridge; and one of India's most popular singers, Lata Mangeshkar. Included in this section is 'An Evening with Dev Anand' whose photograph with my father has been put up at Government College, Lahore, with the heading 'Pride of Subcontinent'.

During the first phase of his career as a journalist, when he edited and wrote for magazines and newspapers like *Yojana*, the *Illustrated Weekly of India*, *New Delhi* and the *Hindustan Times*, he was an indefatigable traveller, making trips to some of the most far-flung places in the subcontinent, and overseas. The journeys he made when working for *Yojana* generated some of his finest work, transforming what could have been dreary reports on steel plants and dams into lyrical prose. These essays appear in the section 'Memorable Places'.

In his later years, my father became an entertaining, erudite guide to the way we as a people comport ourselves. In the section 'The Indian Way' the reader will find insightful and amusing pieces on matters like VIP culture, birthdays and fame, and serious commentaries on subjects he felt passionately about—the measures that needed to be taken to prevent violence against women, root out corruption and combat communalism.

Due to the vast readership of his editorials and observations on the Indian political scene, my father was wooed and flattered by politicians throughout his career. At times, his impassioned defence of those he espoused (examples being 'The Persecution of Indira Gandhi' and 'In Defence of Sanjay Gandhi') would not only anger friends and admirers but also get him into trouble—this was most noticeable in his vexed relationships with some members of the Gandhi-Nehru family, notably Indira, Sanjay and Maneka. He respected upright, incorruptible political figures like Jayaprakash Narayan, and his profile of JP in the section 'A Matter of Politics' is a good example of his political journalism at its finest. Other noteworthy pieces in this section include his poignant and graphic account of the Bangladesh War.

◆

To end on a personal note, in my father's sunset years, the evening gatherings at his home got shorter and he no longer enjoyed company, even that of women. But the one thing that never changed was his commitment to his work. He continued to wake up at 4.30 a.m. and get down to work. He continued to read, review books and write his columns till the end.

As I was reading the essays, I was struck by the many facets of my father I was aware of but had not given much thought to—his contempt for namak harams, his fierce loyalties, his occasional political naiveté, his sensitivity to the beauty of nature, his involvement with and love for his country, and his courageous denunciation of 'fundoos' of every religion. In short, he was not just an excellent writer and journalist but a man of integrity with an unshakeable belief in doing what was right. An unusual human being, he was not just a nice man to know but a fine man to know. As he wrote, 'You can't take anything with you, but you can leave behind things better than a bank balance for your wife and children. You can leave something worthwhile of yourself for the times to come.'

New Delhi
April 2015

Mala Dayal

UNFORGETTABLE PEOPLE

BABA KHARAK SINGH

The life of Baba Kharak Singh illustrates the theme of the conflict between absolute integrity and compromise. It could be summed up in the statement that while compromise is the essence of success, uncompromising integrity is the essence of immortality. The Baba did not succeed in any worldly sense but he did win for himself a reputation for uprightness that will never die. He was known as the betaj badshah—the uncrowned emperor—of the Sikhs. The actual crown, i.e. the fruits of his endeavour went to people who were more worldly-wise and knew the art of give and take. While Kharak Singh went into the political wilderness, his younger colleagues in the Akali movement reaped a bumper harvest of political power. Master Tara Singh gained control of Sikh organizations; Giani Kartar Singh was many times minister of the state government; Partap Singh Kairon became chief minister of East Punjab. And there were many others.

Kharak Singh's childhood was not in any way spectacular or indicative of his future career. He was born in Sialkot in 1868. His father was a contractor who made a profitable living in British army cantonments. The family were Ahluwalias by caste—a consideration of some importance even in the professedly casteless Sikh society, the majority of whom were Jat agriculturists.

The Singh Sabha which started in the 1890s was in some respects a movement of Sikh resurgence; it claimed the adherence of most educated Sikhs. The Singh Sabha stood for the teaching of Punjabi in the Gurmukhi script; for Sikh schools and colleges where the traditions of the hirsute Khalsa were instilled into young men; for resistance towards the absorptive tendencies of Hinduism; for separate electorates and privileges for the Sikhs; and above all, for loyalty towards the British Raj. Kharak Singh's family were ardent Singh Sabhaites.

The winds of change began to blow across the Punjab and assumed the violence of a gale during the First World War. The Ghadr Conspiracy of 1915 and the shooting at Jallianwala Bagh in April 1919 swept away all vestiges of loyalty towards an administration which supported butchers like General Dyer and the lieutenant governor of the Punjab, Sir Michael O'Dwyer. Amongst the most powerful converts to the freedom movement was young Kharak Singh.

The massacre at Jallianwala Bagh was followed by several weeks of aerial bombings of villages, floggings without trial and other indignities; it was an anarchical 'diarchy'—a word coined by Mahatma Gandhi. The Mahatma came to the Punjab and, inspired by him, a radical group of Sikhs broke away from the Singh Sabha to form the Central Sikh League. The League pledged itself to non-cooperation and soon became a part of the Indian National Congress. The moving spirit behind the League was Kharak Singh.

Kharak Singh was a devout Sikh. The misuse of Sikh shrines by mahants (priests who were as often Udasi Hindus as orthodox Sikhs) had begun to agitate the minds of the Sikhs—the most agitated person was Kharak Singh. He was amongst the pioneers of the Akali movement designed to oust these hereditary priests from the control of the gurudwaras and replace them with elected committees. The transfer of control went smoothly for some time till the flare-up at Nankana, the birthplace of Guru Nanak. At the Janamasthan (birthplace) the Udasi priest, Narain Das, hired a band of thugs and butchered in cold blood 131 Akalis who had come to take possession of the shrine.

The Nankana massacre gave a tremendous fillip to the movement. Bands of Akalis began to eject the priests and take possession of the gurudwaras. They were organized into committees under the overall control of the Shiromani Gurudwara Parbandhak Committee (SGPC) at Amritsar. The first office bearers of the SGPC were the old loyalists of the Singh Sabha. They were voted out within a few months and Kharak Singh became its president. He was also the moving spirit behind the paramilitary volunteer organization, the Shiromani Akali Dal.

The priests resisted being ejected by asking for police protection. The authorities decided to help them and began arresting Akali volunteers. In some places, as at Guru ka Bagh near Amritsar, Akali passive resisters were subjected to savage torture. The Akali movement continued with unabated force for almost five years. Kharak Singh and thousands of other Sikhs were imprisoned over and over again. The government yielded eventually and in 1925 passed the Sikh Gurudwaras Act, handing over control of all Sikh shrines to the SGPC. This was the year of Kharak Singh's triumph. He did indeed become the uncrowned king of the Sikhs.

Immediately after winning the battle of the gurudwaras, the Akalis split into different factions. Kharak Singh led the group which aligned itself with the Congress. He was again imprisoned in the civil disobedience movement. He won undying fame for his conduct in Dera Ghazi Khan Jail. To protest against the jailers' decision to forbid Congress prisoners from wearing Gandhi caps, the Baba refused to wear anything except his kachha. He spent four bitter Punjab winters without any covering on his person. His capacity to bear suffering was truly superhuman. In the Akali and Congress agitations, the Baba was imprisoned eighteen times and spent a total of twenty years in jail.

The Baba's break with the Congress came with the Nehru Report. He felt that the Congress had been unfair to the Sikhs and not only denounced the party but also Sikhs like Master Tara Singh who did not sever their connections with the Congress.

The word 'compromise' did not exist in Kharak Singh's dictionary. He found himself isolated and out of the stream of political movements. He had to suffer the adoration of the Sikh masses who yet refused to be guided by him. He saw lesser men climb to fame and popularity and his own following dwindle to a few unscrupulous men whose only interest was to exploit his great name towards their own ends.

Baba Kharak Singh's last many years were extremely lonely. He retreated into his shell, spending many hours of the day in prayer. His closest companion was his faithful Alsatian, Badal. The dog fetched the Baba's mail and his newspapers; it fetched the servants when the master was in need; and it kept away intruders. In the heart of the capital the Baba lived in virtual vanaprastha. He died as all Indians would like to die—a dedicated sanyasi.

(*1963*)

NEHRU AS A WRITER

Several years ago, Pandit Nehru happened to be in London to attend one of the Commonwealth Prime Ministers' Conferences. In accordance with his wishes, one afternoon was left free for him to browse around the bookshops. I was nominated to be Panditji's escort on this expedition.

I picked him up from his hotel. As soon as we were in the car I asked him, 'Sir, what kind of bookshops would you like to visit?' He looked a little startled at my question and retorted, 'Shops which have books in them.' I was snubbed. But I persisted with my enquiry—largely to show off my own knowledge of the variety of London's bookstores—'There are many shops here which specialize in Oriental books; some have large collections of books on India; there are others which go in for rare editions or specially bound volumes. There are yet others which—'

Panditji interrupted my catalogue of bookshops by speaking directly to the chauffeur: 'Driver, take me to Bumpus'.' (Bumpus was one of the largest popular bookshops in the centre of London.) I decided not to offer any more unsolicited advice.

SHAW AND WILDE

We spent about an hour in the store. In that hour, Panditji selected about twenty books. I took charge of the bill to pass it on to his personal private secretary. Back home I examined the bill. Of the twenty odd books, fifteen were on George Bernard Shaw, the other five on Oscar Wilde. The only conclusion I drew from this selection was that the prime minister was familiar with the works of Shaw and Wilde—because he had not bought a single book *by* them but all *on* them. Had Shaw or Wilde also affected his own writing? I turned the pages of his autobiography to see if I could find any clue to the authors who had influenced him.

It was a rewarding pursuit. The first to quicken the imagination of young Jawaharlal was a person—I cannot describe him as an author—

he was much more, a storyteller in the *Arabian Nights* tradition. This person was Munshi Mubarak Ali of Badaun. The munshi sahib told the boy Jawahar of the events of the Indian Mutiny of 1857. And obviously told them in a way that left a permanent impression on his listener's mind. Thereafter, Jawaharlal was put through a series of books by his Irish tutor, Ferdinand T. Brooks. He read Lewis Carroll, Rudyard Kipling, Cervantes, Scott, Dickens, Thackeray, H. G. Wells, Mark Twain and Conan Doyle. 'I was thrilled by *The Prisoner of Zenda*, and Jerome K. Jerome's *Three Men in a Boat* was for me the last word in humour', he wrote many years later. He continues: 'Another book stands out still in my memory, it was Du Maurier's *Trilby*, also *Peter Ibbetson*. I also developed a liking for poetry, a liking which has to some extent endured and survived the many other changes to which I have been subject.' His favourites were Walter de la Mare, Swinburne and some Chinese poets.

It was under Brooks's influence—Brooks was a Theosophist—that young Nehru was introduced to Buddhist and Hindu religious literature—the Dhammapada, the Upanishads and the Bhagavad Gita.

Later, at Cambridge University, where he studied science, Nehru's extra-curricular reading included the German philosopher Nietzsche, Bernard Shaw, Lewis Dickinson and Bertrand Russell. He also confesses to being influenced by Oscar Wilde and Walter Pater, and in matters of historical interpretation by Meredith Townsend's *Asia and Europe*.

NEHRU AND CHURCHILL

The man whose name immediately comes to mind for comparison with Nehru, both as a great statesman and a great spinner of sentiments, is of his contemporary—Sir Winston Churchill. In the writings of both Nehru and Churchill, their vast erudition comes through. Their pen portraits are like the caricatures by Charles Dickens: they are gently satirical; they bring a smile to one's lips without evoking vulgar or unkind laughter. Their patriotic exhortations rise to the sublime heights of the Greek classicists. If Churchill has an edge on Nehru in his ability to turn a phrase, Nehru has the better of Churchill as a 'painter of landscapes'.

I will try and illustrate these points from some of Nehru's books.

I have ten on my list. Of these ten, three are major works. We see Nehru at the height of his literary prowess in his autobiography (*An Autobiography*), which he started writing thirty years ago. *The Discovery of India* and *Glimpses of World History* exhibit his interest in, and a refreshingly different approach to, history. Most of the other works are of slender proportions. But in his letters to his daughter Indira, and more so in his prepared speeches delivered on important occasions, like on the eve of Independence, on Mahatma Gandhi's assassination, on the opening of the Bhakra Dam, we get Nehru at his emotional and exhortative best.

LANDSCAPE PAINTER

First let us see Nehru as a painter of beautiful landscapes of the mountains and valleys of his native Kashmir.

> Like some supremely beautiful woman, whose beauty is almost impersonal and above human desire such was Kashmir in all its feminine beauty of river and valley and lake and graceful trees. And then another aspect of this magic beauty would come to view, a masculine one, of hard mountains and precipices, and snow-capped peaks and glaciers, and cruel and fierce torrents rushing down to the valleys below. It had a hundred faces and innumerable aspects, ever-changing, sometimes smiling, sometimes sad and full of sorrow… As I gazed at it, it seemed to me dreamlike and unreal, like the hopes and desires that fill us and so seldom find fulfilment. It was like the face of the beloved that one sees in a dream and that fades away on awakening.

His sensitivity towards the beauty of nature was heightened when his contact with it was restricted—as in prison. This is how he described his days in the jail in Dehradun:

> Lying there in the open, I watched the skies and the clouds and I realized, better than I had ever done before, how amazingly beautiful were their changing hues.
>
> To watch the changing clouds, like clime in clime;
> Oh! sweet to lie and bless the luxury of time.

Time was not a luxury for us, it was more of a burden. But the time I spent in watching those ever-shifting monsoon clouds was filled with delight and a sense of relief.

One misses many things in prison, but perhaps most of all one misses the sound of women's voices and children's laughter. The sounds one usually hears are not of the pleasantest. The voices are harsh and minatory, and the language brutal and largely consisting of swearwords. Once I remember being struck by a new want. I was in the Lucknow District Gaol and I realized suddenly that I had not heard a dog bark for seven or eight months.

DEFT DESCRIPTIONS

Nehru's descriptions of people were very deft, particularly when he did not see eye-to-eye with them. His portrayal of Lord Linlithgow is truly amusing.

> Heavy of body and slow of mind, solid as a rock and with almost a rock's lack of awareness, possessing the qualities and failings of an old-fashioned British aristocrat, he sought with integrity and honesty of purpose to find a way out of the tangle. But his limitations were too many; his mind worked in the old groove and shrank back from any innovations; his vision was limited by the traditions of the ruling class out of which he came.

There are several references to Jinnah. Nehru explained Jinnah's bitter hostility to the national cause in the following words:

> Success came to Jinnah very late—when he was past sixty. The secret of his success has been to take up a permanently negative attitude.

He had earlier analysed Jinnah's break with the Indian National Congress:

> Sarojini Naidu had called him [M. A. Jinnah] the 'Ambassador of Hindu-Muslim unity', and he had been largely responsible in the past for bringing the Moslem League nearer to the Congress.

> But the new developments in the Congress—non-co-operation and the new constitution which made it more of a popular and mass organization—were thoroughly disapproved of by him. He disagreed on political grounds, but it was not politics in the main that kept him away. But temperamentally he did not fit in at all with the new Congress. He felt completely out of his element in the khadi-clad crowd demanding speeches in Hindustani. The enthusiasm of the people outside struck him as mob-hysteria. There was as much difference between him and the Indian masses as between Savile Row and Bond Street and the Indian village with its mud huts.

MEMORABLE DESCRIPTIONS

Nehru's descriptions of some of the revolutionary leaders—Shyamji Krishna Verma with his pockets bulging with newspapers, Raja Mahendra Pratap in tweeds and a coat with innumerable pockets crammed with letters, and the fierce Madam Bhikaji Cama are memorable.

Nehru was a devoted husband and father. His references to his daughter Indira are particularly full of tenderness. She was only four years old when her father wrote to her from prison: 'Priyadarshini [Indira's second name], dear to my sight, but dearer still when the sight is denied.' He tried to make up for his absence by writing educative letters to his daughter. Occasionally, he let the father in him get the better of the teacher. One such occasion was on her thirteenth birthday. The letter was written from Naini Jail and starts as follows:

> On your birthday you have been in the habit of receiving presents and good wishes. Good wishes you will still have in full measure, but what present can I give you from Naini prison? My presents cannot be very material or solid. They can only be of the air and of the mind and spirit, such as a good fairy might have bestowed on you—something that even the high walls of prison cannot stop.

We see Nehru at his fervent best in his exhortative speeches. It is here that he rises to Churchillian heights. What Winston achieved in his famous 'Blood, Sweat and Tears' speech after the disaster at Dunkirk—'We shall fight them on the beaches etc.'—Nehru did by appealing to sentiment. The most famous of this kind was the now too well-known 'Tryst with Destiny' speech delivered on the midnight of 14 and 15 August 1947. Lesser known, but more charged with pathos was the speech on the assassination of Bapu: 'The light has gone out of our lives and there is darkness everywhere.' Dealing with the same subject, he said:

> Even in his death there was a magnificence and complete artistry. It was from every point of view a fitting climax to the man and to the life he had lived. Indeed it heightened the lesson of his life. He died in the fullness of his power and as he would no doubt have liked to die, at the moment of prayer. He died a martyr to the cause of unity to which he had worked unceasingly, more especially during the past year or more. He died suddenly as all men should wish to die. There was no fading away of the body or a long illness or the forgetfulness of the mind that comes with age. Why then should we grieve for him? Our memories of him will be of the Master, whose step was light to the end, whose smile was infectious, and whose eyes were full of laughter.

SECRET OF SUCCESS

The secret of Nehru's success as a writer lay in the fact that he wrote with absolute candour. 'Whatever you might write', he used to advise his colleagues, 'never write out of fear'. This fearlessness gave his writing an everlasting vigour. Poet Rabindranath Tagore summed it up beautifully when he said that Nehru was like Rituraj—the spirit of spring which is the spirit of eternal youth.

(*1964*)

AMIR KHUSRAU

Scholar, swordsman, poet, composer of music, inventor of the sitar and chronicler of events—all in one was Abul Hasan Amir Khusrau. He could walk the razor's edge serving both God and Mammon: he was as at home in the court of the sultans as in a dervish hermitage, a flatterer of kings and the chosen disciple of a saint who avoided kings like the plague. Above all, although a first-generation Indian, he loved India and Indians more than any other country or people. Amir Khusrau is by all accounts one of the most fascinating characters of medieval Indian history. Abul Hasan's father, Saifuddin Mohammad, was a Turk of the Lachin tribe who fled from his hometown Kush in fear of the Mongols and sought asylum in Delhi, then ruled by a fellow Turk, Iltutmish. Saifuddin was a reputed swordsman. He was given employment and, in recognition of his services, granted a jagir in Patiala (Mominabad) in Uttar Pradesh. Saifuddin married the daughter of Nawab Imad-ul-Mulk, a convert from Hinduism. They had three sons, of whom the youngest, born in 1253 CE was named Abul Hasan.

According to legend, literary greatness was predicted for Abul Hasan on the day of his birth. It is said that the father carried the child in its swaddling clothes to a soothsayer who pronounced: He will be a greater poet than Khaqani (then the greatest literary figure in Persia).

Khusrau's father moved from Mominabad to Delhi and found employment in the court of Ghiyasuddin Balban. Delhi then consisted of two cities: one at the citadel of Rai Pithora at Mehrauli and the other at Kilokheri. Khusrau was eight years old when he was brought to Delhi and taken to pay his respects to the Sufi saint Nizamuddin. He refused to enter the khanqah and instead composed the following lines:

> Great king on whose palace walls pigeons into falcons turn
> When a seeker comes to thy door should he enter or must he return?

The saint, through his occult powers, knew what troubled young Khusrau and sent the following reply:

If thou art a true man, enter!
For a moment let us our secrets share
But if thou are a fool or a knave,
Go back, do not tarry here.

Khusrau became a disciple of Nizamuddin.

A year later Khusrau's father died. His maternal grandfather became his guardian. From his mother and her father, Khusrau imbibed a love for Hindi; from his paternal relatives he picked up Turkish, Arabic and Persian.

In the earlier days, he used Sultani as his nom de plume. Later he preferred Khusrau. To this name he added the family title Amir and came to be known as Amir Khusrau.

Khusrau did not take on an ustad. Instead he studied Persian classics. Firdausi, Khaqani and Saadi (his works had begun to circulate in India) were his masters. But more than these he learnt by association with a very close friend—Amir Hasan Dehlavi, who had made a name for himself in the capital.

Khusrau spent most of his time at the saint's khanqah at Ghiaspur on the Yamuna. Thus began his dual life. His soul was claimed by the Sufi mystics; his body by his rich patrons.

It was no easy matter to serve a saint and a sultan at the same time—particularly a saint like Nizamuddin who forbade his followers from entering government service and openly spurned the authority of the king. It was a tribute to Khusrau's genius that he remained the closest of Nizamuddin's disciples and the highest paid poet laureate of his time. Khusrau knew the art of durbardari, the art, as he said himself, 'of weaving a false story in every reign'.

Khusrau took his first job when he was twenty years old. His patron was a nephew of Balban known popularly as Malik Chajju—a brave soldier, a lover of poetry and as generous as Hatim Tai. Khusrau flattered Chajju's vanity.

I asked the dawn: the sun thou promised where is it?
Up came Chajju's face and the heavens were lit.

'For two years', wrote Khusrau, 'I was in that cypress garden and refreshed his [Chajju's] court with the soft breezes that blew from the lily of my tongue'. Khusrau was not a very modest man.

His downfall came over a trivial lapse of form. The emperor's second son, Bughra Khan, who was the governor of Multan, called on Chajju. He heard Khusrau recite and was so pleased that he had a platterful of silver presented to the poet. Chajju expected his protégé to refuse the gift. Khusrau accepted it—and was promptly fired.

Khusrau did no more than describe Chajju as bad ahad (breaker of promises). He went over to Bughra Khan and began to ply both his pen and his sword in the service of his new patron. For a while he lived at Samana and then accompanied Bughra on his victorious campaign to Bengal. There he composed the *Fateh Nama*—epistle of victory.

The climate of Bengal did not suit Khusrau and he obtained leave to return to Delhi. But not for very long. His next patron was the heir-apparent Prince Mohammed, governor of Multan. Multan became the centre of culture. Poets from all over the Middle East and India flocked to the prince's court. Khusrau became the royal 'pen bearer' and then the custodian of the royal Quran. His friend, Amir Hasan Dehlavi, was appointed 'custodian of the royal inkpot'. The prince sent an invitation to Sheikh Saadi along with some poems of Khusrau whom he described as Saadi-i-Hind. The sheikh praised Khusrau's work but regretted his inability to come to India.

Khusrau spent five years in Multan, 'watering the city's five rivers' as he said with characteristic immodesty with the 'seas of my delectable verses'.

In a skirmish with the Mongols, Prince Mohammed fell: his father, Emperor Balban, died of grief. Khusrau and Amir Hasan Dehlavi were taken prisoners. For the next two years Khusrau and his friend suffered the indignities of slavery in Herat and Balkh. But Khusrau continued to write. Amongst the compositions of the time was an elegy (marsiah) on the death of Prince Mohammed. The marsiah became the most popular song of mourning amongst those who had lost their kin in battle.

Khusrau escaped to return home to Mominabad. There, says he, his aged mother's breasts filled with milk at the joy of reunion with her son.

Khusrau's next patron was a chieftain of Awadh. He was as generous as Khusrau liked his patrons to be.

I told the sea, 'You are open handed as my master.'
The sea trembling to its very soul protested 'No! No!
My miserable waves cast off flotsam and worthless weed.
Your master, proud and generous, scatters rubies.'

Neither munificence nor appreciation could keep Khusrau away too long from his beloved city, Delhi, where 'handsome youths flaunted turbans tilted at roguish angles'. So two years later Khusrau was back in Delhi writing fulsome eulogies in praise of the philistine, Sultan Kaikobad. He was rewarded with a khilaat and 2,000 pieces of silver. And once again Khusrau was at home at Nizamuddin's hermitage at Ghiaspur and the 'whore-packed city', as the chronicler Barani describes Delhi.

Kaikobad debauched himself to his grave in three years. Jalaluddin Khilji ousted the Turkish oligarchy and crowned himself Sultan of Delhi. Khusrau found it convenient to forget his Turkish paternity and emphasize instead the Indian half of his blood. He wrote in praise of the new sultan. Writes Barani: 'While wine-servers brought goblets and beautiful courtesans danced, verses of Khusrau were sung.'

During his service with Jalaluddin, Khusrau had many awkward moments. Once when his first patron Malik Chajju was brought in chains to court, and again when Nizamuddin flatly refused to receive the sultan. 'My hermitage has two doors,' replied the saint. 'If the sultan enters by one, I will leave by the other.' When Jalaluddin threatened to pay a surprise visit to the khanqah at Ghiaspur, Nizamuddin left Delhi for Pakpattan where his peer, Sheikh Farid, lived.

We do not know how Khusrau faced Malik Chajju, but when directly confronted with a choice between the sultan and the saint, he did not hesitate to cast his lot with the latter. 'If I disobeyed the sultan I would have lost my head, but if I am false to my peer I will lose my faith,' he said.

Jalaluddin forgave Khusrau. Khusrau complimented him with even greater praise. But no sooner had the sultan's nephew Alauddin Khilji succeeded in assassinating his uncle and usurping the throne, Khusrau tuned his honeyed tongue to sing praises of the new monarch: 'Was I not the first to felicitate you on your accession? Hearken to my prophetic words! Destiny itself has made you Sultan of Delhi.'

In Alauddin's regime Khusrau's unbounded genius for eulogy blossomed to its fullness. He remained as immodest as ever, 'sprinkling the royal carpet with my charming odes'. And well-calculated: 'grass grows only with rain and poetry with the generosity of kings'. But Khusrau was getting old and finding it very tedious to waste several hours of the day hanging about the court. 'I have to string pearls and have a fresh mind to coin subtle phrases. If I have to stand before you all day and all night, how can I write poetry? Before I find a pearl worthy of your royal ear my blood must come to the boil.'

Khusrau's best work in Alauddin's regime was on the romance (ashiqa) between Prince Khizr and Deval Rani. Khusrau did not like Alauddin's favourite, Malik Kafur, who later assassinated the king. For a short while Khusrau attended the durbar of the transvestite Mubarak Khilji. By then relations between the court and Nizamuddin had come to a breaking point; Khusrau attended on both.

He discreetly absented himself in the months of turmoil when Mubarak Khilji was murdered by Khusrau Khan—who in his turn was destroyed by Ghiasuddin Tughlaq. But as soon as the Tughlaqs had gained control of the empire, Khusrau was there to pay them homage.

Ghiasuddin Tughlaq resented Nizamuddin. Khusrau continued to serve both. He was with the king in Bengal when Tughlaq wrote a haughty note to Nizamuddin threatening to expel him when he returned to the capital. 'Hunooz Dilli door ast. (It's a long way to Delhi),' replied the saint with prophetic foresight. And for Ghiasuddin, Delhi did prove to be an impossible distance. He was crushed to death under an arched gateway.

A few days later Nizamuddin was himself laid to rest. His parting words to his followers included a message for Khusrau. The poet was not to be allowed to come too close to Nizamuddin's grave lest he (Nizamuddin) be tempted to rise to embrace him.

The grief-stricken Khusrau came to Ghiaspur and wept copious tears beside the kewra tree from where he watched his beloved saint's tomb.

On her bed sleeps she who was once so fair
Her face is now covered under her hair
O, Khusrau, 'tis time thou too the homeward path did tread
Shades of twilight over the land are spread.

A short while later (in 1325) Khusrau followed his saint into the other world. His body was buried a few metres away from the tomb of his spiritual mentor.

Khusrau loved India for its bananas, birds and betel. He also admired Indians. He enumerated ten reasons to prove the Indian's superiority over other people: Indians learn the sciences of other countries while other countries are ignorant of Indian sciences; Indians can speak foreign languages whereas foreigners never try to learn Indian languages; people come from all over the world to India to learn, but no Brahmin has to go anywhere else to educate himself; the Arab numerical system, especially the symbol zero, is of Indian origin. *Kalila wa Dimna* (Panchatantra in Arabic) was originally written in India; chess was invented in India; these three arts, the moral fable, mathematics and chess are India's contribution to universal civilization; Indian music is warm and moving and difficult to master; Indian music charms animals as well as human beings; and, finally, no other land can boast a poet like Khusrau.

However, Khusrau was not consistent in his admiration of India and Indians. He confessed that he loved India because 'the land has been saturated with the water of the sword and the vapours of infidelity have been dispersed'. Often his irritation with the people made him explode: 'Do not count Hindus among men for they venerate the cow, regard the crow superior to the parrot and read omens in the braying of an ass.'

(*1967*)

PORTRAIT OF A SERIAL KILLER

When one man kills another we look for motive; when one man kills many men we look into his mind. Raman Raghav has confessed to killing twenty-four men, women and children. He is charged with the killing of only the last two of his victims. He has pleaded guilty. The judge rejected the pleas of insanity put forward by his counsel. 'I am not mad,' says Raman angrily, 'you are all mad.'

What made Raman Raghav the way he is—by his own confession the most fiendish killer of our times? I pieced together his life story from his confessions and what he said to the doctor who kept him under observation.

Raman Raghav is one of a family of six from a village in Tirunelveli district of Tamil Nadu. He had little affection for his mother, but he says he loved his father. The reason he gives sounds odd. 'My father taught me to steal and commit murder. He was doing these things himself. He had gone to jail for theft.' The paternal influence was decisive. 'Theft is a good profession,' says Raman. He should know because, says he, 'I have been doing it since childhood.' He did not study much: 'Three books in two years.'

Raman Raghav's parents died early. His three sisters and the only brother (whom he loved and admired) are also dead. His only surviving relative is his sister, Parvati.

Hatred of women is a dominant aspect of Raman Raghav's character. How he came to despise and at the same time crave their company is not quite clear. However, his first real experience of them provides a clue. As is customary among certain castes in Tamil Nadu, a marriage was arranged for him with his sister's daughter, Guruamma. Before he could consummate the marriage he was arrested for theft and sent to prison. Meanwhile Guruamma became pregnant by another man—and died giving birth to a stillborn baby. This betrayal was followed by another. Village elders found him another woman. Raman discovered that the mate proposed for him had been discarded by another man and had children by him. He also found that he could get what he wanted without having to marry.

A boy he had befriended persuaded him to join him in Bombay. Here he had his third experience of feminine perfidy. The two friends were employed in a textile mill. Raman worked during the day, his friend on the night shift. One rainy night his friend's wife invited him to share her bed. He refused. Next morning the wife complained to her husband that Raman had tried to seduce her. Raman was thrown out of the chawl.

Thus was Raman Raghav betrayed, abandoned, abused. To his way of thinking, there was always a woman behind every episode. He became a confirmed misogynist and a lone wolf. If no one had any use for him, he in turn had no use for anyone. He became a mawali (vagabond). He was arrested for vagrancy and beaten by the police. He went in and out of jail on convictions of petty pilfering, robbery and violence. He apparently also killed a man or two but got away with it. Twice he was sent to mental institutions for observation as a borderline case; both times he was discharged as normal. He describes his life in Bombay. 'I used to visit prostitutes frequently. I used to steal because I got more money by stealing.'

Sex assumed the proportions of an obsession. 'Everybody needs his ration,' he told the doctor philosophically, 'just as a motor car requires petrol, so the body requires sexual satisfaction.'

Crime and sex became Raman Raghav's daily ration. Where he got his sex from we do not know—perhaps the caged red-light district of the city—but for his crime he chose the distant suburbs and for his victims the poor shanty dwellers, often separated from each other by marsh and scrub and swamp and foul-smelling sewers. There he robbed and killed and raped in the still hours of the night. He created absolute terror in the region; people were afraid to come out of their homes after dark. He struck them in their homes—the killing was often senseless, eliciting no more than ten paise. But each one was carefully planned and had characteristic features about it which made it clear that it was the work of one man. First, he used a blunt weapon, an ankada. Later, he used the sharp point of a heavy iron bar and stabbed his sleeping victims above the ear. People who saw him disappear in the dark said he wore his hair and beard long and carried a trishul and was therefore a sadhu. Some said the killer was able to change into a dog—or just turn into vapour. Not till his confession was it known that the man was Raman Raghav.

The chronicle of killings will chill anyone's blood. A tea stall vendor who adulterated Raman's tea narrowly escaped having his skull bashed in. Others were not so lucky. 'I saw a bearded Muslim sleeping on his khat (bed),' states Raman in his confession. 'It was three o'clock at night… I dealt him a blow on the head with the iron bar. The bearded fellow died.' This yielded some money—Rs 262. But the next killing a few days later only produced ten paise and a little ghee. A few days later Raman struck again—this time a whole family. For some days he watched their movements. He says: 'On a khat in the said hut were asleep a man, a woman and a child. They had fastened the door and gone to sleep. I climbed (in) from the rear and saw that the woman was feeding the child with powdered milk. I saw a chain on her neck. Up to three o'clock at night the woman did not sleep. I saw a black mani, one inch long, set on a gold chain. Hence I returned…. I kept watching the said hut for three to four days. Even then the woman was not asleep. On the fifth day she was asleep. I entered the hut by cutting with the rod the ropes that were used to close the front door. Standing in the open space between the two khats, I dealt the man two to three blows with the rod. He died. The woman started crying. Then the child also started crying. The child was about two months old. I gave two to three blows to the child with the rod. He died. The woman also died… I got inside and broke off the gold chain from the woman's neck. I put it in my pocket. I thought of sleeping with the woman. By the side of her head was a kerosene lamp. I put out the lamp, but someone switched on the electric light on the top… A woman ran up. She saw me and I saw her. She must (have been) aged about seventy years. She saw the blood and started crying out.'

The killings continued—all at night, all with the same kind of weapon, either smashing the skull or piercing it above the ear—and every time the killer mysteriously vanished into the swamps. The most fiendish of his deeds is recounted thus: 'At a distance of about half a furlong a woman and two children were asleep in a hut. The children were aged eight to nine years. The woman was asleep in the middle. I gave three to four blows to the woman. She died. She (was covered) with just a cloth. She was otherwise naked. I slept with the woman. I sucked the milk of her breast.'

◆

'Do you believe in God?' asked the doctor.

Raman replied: 'When I was a child I did. I do not do so now. I do not go to temples.'

'Why?' asked the doctor.

'Because,' replied Raman, 'God is partial to women.'

Raman's lust-hate relationship with women is best expressed in his sexual symbolism. When the jail barber shaved off his moustache, he was furious, and wanted to kill him. He did not speak to anyone for seven days. It was like someone cutting off his head with a sword (castration complex?). 'I do not want to look like a woman or a hijra,' he said. He explained his reaction to the doctor. 'If I slap your child won't you feel bad? That's how I feel about my moustache.'

Raman wants women. He made an offer to the administration. 'I should be let (out) on bail for one year. I will not do any theft or murder. I want a woman to stay with me for that one year. Not as my wife, only as a companion. The woman should be below thirty years of age. If a child is born, it is the responsibility of the government to look after my child. A prostitute would do. I want a woman for sexual intercourse and not only for preparing food…'

According to Raman he was beaten and given ganja to induce him to confess. He refused. Then his 'inner voice' ordered him to speak. 'I did not confess under coercion. I confessed at the command of the inner voice,' he says.

◆

Raman Raghav is dark, stocky and powerfully built. He is a dandy: short cropped hair, white nylon bush shirt and black trousers. (Police Commissioner Nadkarni told me that Raman presses his trousers under the pillow to keep their crease.) He has a scowl on his face and a look of contemptuous disdain for the world. He sways gently from side to side like a man at prayer. He is arrogant. He does not rise when the judge enters the courtroom. He just sits holding the rod connecting his leg-irons like an emperor holding a sceptre. He surveys the scene in the court—the comings and goings of lawyers, policemen, sightseers as would a king surveying his durbar. And people's eyes are always fixed on him. When they go out they dare not turn their backs on him but retreat in awe and reverence. Only once, when a pretty girl caught his eye and smiled, did a wan smile appear on Raman's otherwise dour visage.

◆

When the charge of murder was read out to him, Raman pleaded guilty. 'Have you anything more to say?' asked the judge. 'Yes,' replied Raman, 'the government has given me a lawyer, but does not give me soap to wash nor a woman to sleep with.'

◆

Raman has his own notions of right and wrong and decorum. It is his kanoon. One must not smoke in the presence of an officer. An officer must not smoke while performing his duty. He refused a cigarette from the doctor examining him and refused to speak to him while the doctor's cigarette was lit. He is as finicky as a middle-class spinster when it comes to hygiene. He lost his temper with a waiter who had his thumb in his tumbler of drinking water. He chided a child for returning a handkerchief, in which he brought fish, without washing it. He has respect for the written word. Each time he was asked a question by the judge, he demanded to know what had been recorded earlier. 'I have admitted the crime,' he said 'but what goes on record must be correct.' So he checked names and addresses produced by the police. He counted notches on the weapons he was alleged to have used before admitting they were his. He also has his own notions of honouring debts. 'I always paid my dues,' he said proudly. How he paid them is another matter. 'I had no money so I committed murder and got it.'

Raman Raghav seems to be a man without fear. He is conscious of the fear he inspires in others. As he fondly inspected one of his weapons produced in court he noticed the consternation on the faces of the dozens of police officers and onlookers. 'Do not be afraid,' he assured them. Only once did I notice him flinch. A court official held out a photograph of the dead bodies of the two men for whose murder he is charged. 'Do you recognize the faces of these two men you killed?' asked the official. Raman Raghav quickly averted his glance. 'I cannot be sure. I have poor eyesight.'

(*1969*)

HUMAYUN KABIR

There are some men who are so much more alive than others that one finds it hard to accept news of their death. One such man was Humayun Kabir. I had begun to hero-worship him in my university days because he did everything I tried but failed to do. He got a string of firsts including one from Oxford. He spoke well, wrote beautifully. His booklet *Muslim Politics in Bengal* was the clearest exposition I had ever read of the party system of his community. Then came a veritable cascade of poems and short stories. These, however, were of no great calibre. I was a little disappointed on meeting him. I had visualized him as tall and fair. He was a small, dark man who blinked nervously through the thick lenses of his glasses. He was also very irritable and had no sense of humour. I recall his discomfiture at a UNESCO conference in Beirut where he had been provided with a tall, handsome Sikh as his stenographer. The delegates assumed that the Sardarji was the leader and Kabir the amanuensis. Kabir was not amused and vented his spleen on the poor stenographer. But what Kabir lacked in physical and social charm was more than compensated for by his enormous vitality and integrity.

If he had stuck to academic life, he would have made a first-rate professor. Alas, he chose to become a second-rate politician.

(*1969*)

THE ANGLO-INDIANS' DILEMMA

Forty-five years ago, Herbert A. Stark of the Bengal and Indian Educational Service wrote a series of articles for the *Anglo-Indian Citizens* tracing the history of his community from the sixteenth to the twentieth century. These articles were later published in a book, *Hostages to India*. Stark prefaced it with lines from Homer's *Iliad*:

> Wherefore set thy mind
> My race to know? The generations are
> As of the leaves, so also of mankind.
> As the leaves fall, now withering in the wind,
> And others are put forth and Spring descends,
> Such on the earth the race of men we find;
> Each in his order a set time attends;
> One generation rises, and another ends.

On the jacket is also imprinted an anguished cry for help—'O England! Who are these if not thy sons?' The quotations sum up the four problems of the Anglo Indians—definition, identity, loyalty and survival.

A host of expressions have been coined to describe persons of mixed parentage: country-born, Indo-Briton, East Indian, Eurasian, Domiciled European. The one common factor was that the change of nomenclature did not succeed for too long in concealing the pejorative that insinuated itself into the labelling of the offspring of mixed races. This was not unique to India—to wit: mulatto and mestizo which were equally tainted with the tar brush; and the none-too-delicate café au lait, which is the French metaphor for a half-caste. The need to define arose from the need to discriminate. But how can anyone define with any precision how much of milk and how much coffee has gone into his cup?

MENTAL ATTITUDE

The concept had remained fluid simply because people of the Anglo-

Indian race belonged to a baffling range of the 'pigmentary spectrum' extending from Nordic white to Negroid black with the two ends trying desperately to pass off as either pure white or pure black. The matter was further complicated by the fact that in India, not infrequently, some Christians of 'pure' Indian blood but reared in a Eurasian atmosphere successfully passed into the Anglo-Indian community. I recall at least one example. A Mr Ramachandra, a sallow-complexioned Punjabi Christian with a sizeable divorce practice in the Anglo-Indian community, changed his name to A. G. Maurice; he, his wife and children gained membership of the Anglo-Indian clubs. Mixed blood was never the sole consideration; the mental attitude was always of importance. Ultimately the need for political safeguards and privileges to ensure survival brought forth a very rough and ready definition. By the Government of India Act of 1935 the term Anglo-Indian included all persons of European descent in the male line whether of mixed or allegedly of unmixed blood. The Constitution of free India accepted this definition. How rough and ready this definition is will be presently noticed.

The dilemma of the Anglo-Indian arose from prejudice—of the 'pure' whites against the mixed, of the Anglo-Indian's desire to be white and the black's resentment that he should want to be so. These prejudices gave rise to false legends about miscegenation. It was too readily believed that Anglo-Indians were the product of the lowest strata of European and Indian society and not always born in wedlock. This was far from the truth. Earlier, Europeans, not infrequently themselves titled gentry, more often than not married women of the Indian aristocracy—many of them princesses of royal blood, both Muslim and Hindu. Even when they consorted with concubines they did not hesitate to acknowledge their offspring. The prominent Anglo-Indian leader Frank Anthony lists the names of eminent Europeans who raised Anglo-Indian families: Job Charnock, Eyre Coote, Major Hyder Hearsey, Colonel Kennedy, Walter Reinhardt, the American Elihu Yale (founder of Yale University) and many others.

Nevertheless, the stigma of class and illegitimacy continued. The Europeans' attitude towards their own children born of Indian women became discriminatory. They were not allowed to go to England for higher studies or to hold senior posts either in the civil or military services. The Eurasian child's desperate efforts to escape these sanctions produced ludicrous results. In one case twins who offered themselves as recruits for the army found themselves in two different regiments. One who was light-skinned got a King's Commission; the other a Viceroy's Commission in the Indian army. In their anxiety to be accepted as English, Anglo-Indians agreed to do all the dirty jobs the imperialist English wanted them to do to maintain their empire in India. Thus while the commissioners of police, most of whom were pure English, remained in their khus-cooled offices, the Anglo-Indian inspectors and sergeants had to disperse Indian agitators with pistol, tear gas and lathi. They had to be more British than the British themselves. They spurned mixing with Indians, refused to learn Indian languages or live as the Indians lived. Even so, Britain would not recognize these sons. They were at best stepsons, only fit to be in the lower rungs of the army, police, railways and postal services.

Too late in the course of history did it occur to the Anglo-Indians that they would have got a better deal from the Indians. Whatever other prejudices Indians may have had—and they have always had many—discrimination against offspring of their blood because of race or colour was not one of them. Indian resentment against the Anglo-Indian was not because of what he was, but because of what he did or was made to do by the English.

It was only in the 1930s, under the leadership of Sir Henry Gidney, that Anglo-Indians began to turn to the Indians for recognition of their special status. Dual loyalties with priority for England, however, continued. Cursing the British for letting them down (the titles of the books—*Hostages to India* and *Britain's Betrayal of India*—themselves tell the tale), Herbert Stark made an impassioned appeal to the English and the Indians:

> In the days when our forefathers insecurely owned but a few acres of Indian soil, we stood by them in the hour of storm and stress. We took our place at their side when they were defending themselves behind mud walls which weakly protected their warehouses and settlements. We fought for them against Indian

chiefs and ambitious rivals. We contributed to their victories. We shared in their disasters. When European wars on the continent claimed every available recruit for the forces, we augmented their depleted armies in India. We explored the markets which swelled their trade and expanded their commerce.

When they entered upon the consolidation of their empire in India, we formed the wheels, the cranks, the levers of their machinery for government. Through our agency, revenue and settlement operations, land surveys and road-making became possible. But for us the telegraph and postal systems, river navigation and railway construction would not have been feasible. We were the first missionaries of the Christian religion, the earliest teachers in Indian schools, the pioneers of Western arts, industries and science. In truth, we took a leading part in every project that tended to advance the moral, material and intellectual prosperity of the land—our land—and its peoples.

And yet we are of those who have come out of great tribulation. We have trod the thorny path of repression. We have struggled through wrongs, sufficient to crush out of existence most races. That we today retain the essential traits, instincts and culture of our forefathers, is remarkable testimony to the virility of the British nation. If England is the land of our fathers, India is the land of our mothers. If to us England is a hallowed memory, India is a living verity. If England is the land of our pilgrimage, India is the land of our homes. If England is dear as a land of inspiring traditions, India is loved for all that she means to us in our daily life.

SPECIAL STATUS

Sir Henry Gidney in an address to his kinsmen in Bangalore urged them to face up to the reality of their station: 'Deny the fact that you are sons and citizens of India, disclaim it, conceal it in your efforts to ape what you are not, and you will soon be the "not wanted at all". The opportunity is yours today to more closely associate yourselves, from early school life, with the rest of India, to realize that you with all other communities, have a right to live in this, your country, and that you are first and last sons of India...But if there is one thing which you must completely eradicate from yourselves it is the retention of "superiority" and "inferiority" complexes; and you should bring about their replacement with a complex of equality.'

Frank Anthony, who succeeded Gidney as the leader of the Anglo Indians in the crucial years preceding the transfer of power, was equally explicit: 'We are Anglo-Indians by community. Of that fact we have every reason to be proud. We have forged a history, in many ways notable, of which any much larger community anywhere in the world could be justifiably proud. Let us cling and cling tenaciously to all that we hold dear, our language, our way of life and our distinctive culture. But let us always remember that we are Indians. The community is Indian. It has always been Indian. Above all, it has an inalienable Indian birthright. The more we love and are loyal to India, the more will India love and be loyal to us.'

A majority of the Anglo-Indians however continued to harp on the same old tune: 'Britishers we are. Britishers we will always remain.' This attitude was not overlooked by the Indians. If only the Gidneys and Anthonys had spoken earlier and carried the community with them, the story of the Anglo-Indians would have been less tragic.

Once the Anglo-Indians turned to the Indians and unequivocally expressed their Indian identity, things began to change. At first there were some doubts. Once Gidney was asked, 'Are you not an Indian?' Gidney replied, 'Yes.' He was then asked, 'Are you not a Christian?' Again Gidney said, 'Yes.' 'Then you are an Indian Christian.' While indignantly repudiating the suggestion the usually quick-witted Gidney for once had no rational answer. Prime Minister Nehru was also not quite clear in his mind who exactly the Anglo-Indians were. Frank Anthony records that at his first meeting Nehru asked him whether the children of his cousin B. K. Nehru through his European wife were Anglo-Indians. Perhaps, biologically, replied Anthony, but not legally since the statute mentioned only 'European descent on the male line'.

Anthony's meeting with Sardar Patel deserves to be quoted as a deft pen-portrait of our departed leader. 'As I sat down, I scrutinized the Sardar. His heavy-lidded, half-closed eyes and sphinx-like manner did not help in my assessment. I stated the case of the community before him rather fully, setting out the historical and political position and also the special economic needs of the community. Beyond a few non-committal, monosyllabic grunts he did not interrupt me. I wondered how much he had taken in. To my surprise he then put to me a series of staccato questions which no other leader had asked. I realized then, what further contacts and subsequently increasing close association only helped to confirm. Here was a man with a crystal clear mind who could see the core of a problem within the shortest possible time.'

A soupçon of confusion and prejudice can be discerned in the attitude of Krishna Menon in a memorable exchange with Frank Anthony. They met in the lobby of Parliament. The defence minister told Anthony that he had just promoted Henderson-Brooks to the rank of lieutenant general and added, 'But the fellow has not one but two European names.' Anthony was ready with the reply: 'Do you expect him to have two Hindu names?'

Indian leaders gave the Anglo-Indians most of what they asked for. Nevertheless a large number felt insecure in the Indian climate and emigrated to England, Australia and other dominions—leaving only about 250,000 in their motherland. The reason, says Anthony, is the resurgence of Hindi-Hindu chauvinism in India making the Anglo-Indian feel that India is not his home. This is too simple and one-sided an explanation of the continuing ambivalence of the Anglo-Indian himself.

TRAGIC SYMPHONY

The saga of the Anglo-Indian can be likened to a tragic symphony now reaching its finale. They have much to be proud of: a nobly conceived race of men and women, finer looking than their parents and physically fitter than either. Look at their record in hockey, boxing and athletics! Serving the Empire with unparalleled devotion, contributing more than their share to education and the arts (Derozio, Anthony de Mello, Ruskin Bond), they are now on the verge of extinction. Frank Anthony has recorded all this in his book, but like most of his race he also takes a longing, lingering nostalgic look at the fatherland and the white countries of the Commonwealth. His book is the anguished cry of a child deserted by his sire whom he loved more than his poorer, humbler mother. In their newfound fatherland and the white countries of the Commonwealth, the fairer Anglo-Indian is fast disappearing as a separate community. He does not want to be different. The same process is taking place in India. The Anglo is fast becoming a historic anachronism. In a few decades this handsome and virile breed will have disappeared in the loving embrace of its Indian mother. Thus will the sponge of oblivion be passed over the slate of Anglo-Indian history.

(*1969*)

LATA MANGESHKAR

The voice on the telephone is masculine, asthmatic, bossy. It must belong to a big, bosomy, dominating woman. She turns out to be small, mousy, scatterbrained. The voice on the telephone is dulcet, hesitant. It must belong to a petite, cuddlesome sweetie-pie. She turns out to be an Amazonian no-nonsense woman.

Aural fantasies persist. Lata Mangeshkar! I am middlebrow and for years I have woven around that voice fantasies that would make her blush. Then another voice almost exactly like hers makes itself heard. A twin voice! I am not far wrong—it's her sister Asha Bhosle. Then another and another. A quartet: Lata, Asha, Meena, Usha! And all four, singers! However, only Lata's voice has that je ne sais quoi.

Then came the breathless moment of truth. I met them! All the four sisters and their composer-brother Hriday.

Lata is beautiful. Not in the conventional, vulgar film star sense of the word, but what the word means to *me.* She is slight, dark, faintly pockmarked. She radiates an aura of goodness, gentleness, humility. Her namaskar is a distant bow. Her eyes never rise to meet yours. What does one say to Lata? You have the most wonderful voice in the world? I've worshipped you for a quarter of a century? It would sound inane, naive, stupid.

'I got your place of birth wrong,' I tell her. 'I thought it was Mangesh in Goa. I got many letters telling me it was Indore.'

'Yes, I read that. My father was born in Mangesh. We never lived there.'

I am flattered she has read something I had written. I am emboldened to quote myself. As I wrote: 'I went to the temple, not to pay homage to Lord Mangesh, but on a sort of pilgrimage to see the place where you were born.'

A slight blush spreads over her face. She looks down and twiddles her fingers. I notice she has lovely hands. 'Where were you educated?'

'Educated? Nowhere. My father taught me all I know: Marathi,

Hindi, a little Urdu... and music. We were always travelling. He was in the theatre business—Indore, Kolhapur, Poona, Bombay. I was just thirteen when he died.' An oil-painting of a young man is brought in. It reminds me of the picture of Swami Vivekananda taken on his American tour. 'A very handsome man!' I remark. Lata turns wistful, stares a long while at her father's portrait and sighs: 'Yes, he was handsome.'

Another large portrait is produced. This is her mother's. Also a very attractive lady, in the traditional Marathi-style sari, earrings, nose ring, bangles. Then more pictures. They've been painted by Lata's youngest sister, Usha, a demure girl with curly hair and glasses. There are other pictures by Usha—of Shivaji paying homage to Guru Ramdas, some landscapes...

I look around the room. Signs of prosperity are evident. A glass case full of ivory figurines, solid mahogany furniture, a jhoola in the veranda, the spread on the table. Prosperity but no Western sophistication. 'Have you ever known poverty?' I ask.

Lata smiles and nods her head. 'Indeed I have! My father had no head for business. And he died so young. I was the eldest of the family.'

My friend Raju Bharatan, who knows just about everything known about playback singers, recordings, films, etc., butts in to say: 'Lata had to look after her mother, sisters and brother. For quite some time, she was the mainstay of the family, you see.'

'When did you get your first break?' I ask Lata.

Lata looks up at the ceiling to recall. Raju tells us precisely when, with which film and all that. She nods in agreement. 'Thereafter she's never looked back,' says Raju. 'You see, her only real competitor is her own sister, Asha. Others are a long way behind the Mangeshkars.'

Lata lets Raju take over. She knows he knows more about her than she does. He quotes J. G. Stanford, the then deputy chief executive of EMI, as listing Lata among their top ten sellers in the world. I express surprise that she is not at the very top. 'Indians do not buy many records; they are poor,' explains Lata. Raju continues the narrative: 'Up to date she's made some 16,000 discs. Probably a world record.'

'How many languages?'

Lata begins to list them: 'Marathi, Hindi, Gujarati, Tamil, Telugu...'

'It might be easier if you listed the languages you haven't sung in! English?'

She smiles. 'No—no foreign language. And I do not like all this westernization to our film music. I often refuse to sing if I find that the tune is too westernized or that the words are cheap and vulgar.'

'Which is your most popular record?'

'Among the private ones, my recitation of the Bhagavad Gita,' she replies. 'The music was composed by my brother Hriday here, of whom I think very highly.'

Raju tells us how many discs were sold. 'Of course you record two, sometimes even three, songs a day, don't you, Lataji?'

She nods.

She leaves her home for the recording studio at eleven. Usually there has been no rehearsal with the music director. In the studio, she listens to the tune for half an hour, familiarizes herself with the words—and sings! She's back home by 3 p.m.

'Now I do no more than one recording a day.'

I am tempted to ask her how much she gets for each recording, but better manners prevail. I know what some of the other playback singers get. Lata's earnings are in astronomical figures.

I ask if anyone has written about her family.

'I am writing my autobiography. I've brought it up to the 1940s. It's in Marathi.'

'Will you allow me to serialize it?'

She pauses for a while, looks at her brother and sisters for approval and then nods: 'If you like.'

I have the Mangeshkars in the bag. I beg permission to leave. By the sideboard are two Oscars—statuettes of a female figure in ebony black. Mini silk saris are draped round them to cover their nakedness. I make a facetious remark. Once again Lata blushes and continues to blush as she bows us out.

(*1970*)

Above the mantelpiece in the sitting room is a large painting which appears to be symbolic of the relationship between Fakhruddin Ali Ahmed and his begum. The message is conveyed through playing cards. On one side is a triumphant looking king of diamonds separated by a narrow strip of the ace of clubs from a somewhat discomfited queen of hearts. In the foreground is a large ace of diamonds on which the queen is placing the trump, the ace of hearts—except that the trump, instead of being red as a hearts sequence ought to be, is blue.

While waiting for the Ahmeds I made a rough sketch of this painting. Surely the queen of hearts must be Begum Abida trumping her diamond king (president to be) with a coldly calculated move!

Suddenly the Ahmeds entered. Begum sahiba was most amused at my interpretation. 'Nothing personal about it,' she exclaimed. 'It was painted by our daughter Sameena Shaheen.'

I turned to Mr Ahmed and asked him about his views on God and religion. 'My mother was very orthodox; till I had this trouble with my heart, I always fasted during Ramzan. And I am quite regular with my prayers, particularly on Fridays.' Fakhruddin is a Taurus. 'Do you believe in the stars or astrology?' I asked him. 'No,' he replied firmly, 'but I believe my father, who was something of a Sanskritist, had a horoscope made for me. I don't know what happened to it.' He doesn't remember whether the horoscope forecast his becoming rashtrapati.

'Do you do much reading? Have any books influenced your thinking?' I asked. 'Since I came into public life I have had little time to read anything apart from newspapers and magazines. But in my earlier days Spengler's *The Decline of the West* impressed me. Aldous Huxley has been my favourite novelist. I rate *Jesting Pilate* very high. And, of course, I read Urdu poetry, Ghalib, Momin, etc. Of the contemporary poets, I am particularly fond of Ali Sardar Jafri.'

'And Faiz?'

'Of course! Faiz is very good.'

We turned to politics. 'I met Jinnah sahib twice. The first time was in 1925 when he came to Cambridge to address the Indian Majlis. All I can recall is his beautiful Parsi wife. She asked me to get meat for her Persian cat. The next time was in 1945. He was with Liaquat Ali Khan, Saadullah and Shaheed Suhrawardy, canvassing for the Muslim League candidate against me. Somebody suggested that they should talk to me but Suhrawardy scotched the idea by saying that he would not shake hands with a kafir. My association with the Nehrus also began during my Cambridge days. I met Pandit Motilal, Jawaharlal and Kamala in 1925. I think Indira was with them—only six years old. I heard Jawaharlal again at the Indian Students' Union in London. In 1937 Jawaharlal stayed with me in Gauhati.'

'Did you ever suspect that Indira would one day become prime minister of India?'

'Suspect! I had no doubt she would do so. I still have a copy of the letter I wrote to her when she agreed to become minister for Information and Broadcasting in the Shastri cabinet. In the letter I said she was destined for higher things.'

Begum Abida asked: 'Do you read and write Urdu?'

'I have translated some Urdu into English. It was my ambition to translate Iqbal's *Shikwa,* but I don't think it can be done.'

'Why not? It is great poetry.'

'Precisely! The music in Iqbal's words would be gone.'

I quoted a few lines to illustrate the musical resonance produced by alliteration.

Ek hi saf mein kharey ho gaye Mahmud-o-ayaz
Na koi banda raha aur na koi banda nawaz

Her eyes glittered with excitement. She took up the lines and began to recite this beautiful poem—one that is among the most powerful of all the works of the Urdu language. When the begum's memory faltered, Fakhruddin came to her help.

(*1971*)

MOHAMMAD SLEEM

I was distressed to note that neither All India Radio nor any Indian newspaper carried the news of the death in Lahore of Mohammad Sleem. He was one of the greatest tennis players that India produced. For more than fifteen years he was recognized as India's number one. In addition, he had not only the largest criminal law practice in the Lahore High Court but enjoyed a well-deserved reputation for integrity that bordered on crackpottery.

It was not easy to make friends with Sleem. He was a bachelor who treasured his privacy as a miser guards his gold. He rarely accepted hospitality or entertained people. I broke into his charmed small circle of friends through his nephew, Manzur Qadir. After court hours, Sleem would drop in at the Qadirs' to have tea before going on to the tennis club. Afterwards, he changed into a dinner jacket and went to dine at Stiffles Restaurant. He ate early and alone—at the same table served by the same waiter. He was a gourmet. He discussed the menu for the next night with the chef, examined the bird he was going to eat and chose the wine to go with it. He lit his Rs 15 Havana cigar and strolled back home.

The Partition left Sleem lonelier than ever. His few friends came to India. For some years he made it a point to spend his Christmas vacation with them in Delhi. Then the two governments put so many restrictions on travel that he gave up. He also complained of a change in his Indian friends' attitude towards him.

Sleem used to spend his summer holidays in Europe. It's there I met him many years after Partition.

I found myself standing next to him in a urinal in the Piccadilly underground. We were both overcome—but in the situation we found ourselves in, we had to postpone falling into each other's arms. Thereafter we were together every evening. I asked him if he still played tennis— he was sixty-six. 'Of course!' he snapped. 'You want a game?' I smiled somewhat patronizingly. I was still in my thirties and playing better than I had done as a University Blue. He challenged me: 'I'll take you on for one set any time, any place. Dinner on the loser.' Next day he took me to Ranelagh Club (very exclusive; he was the only non-white member). He beat me without dropping a single point in the set.

Sleem was meticulously organized and punctual. Every time he left London he would open his diary and make a date for the next year: '23 June, Piccadilly Circus, Men's Lavatory, 7 p.m.' And sure as ever, on the dot of seven, I would see him stroll along in his grey suit, carnation in buttonhole, Havana cigar in mouth and wrapped in the fragrance of cologne and goodwill.

The world is the poorer for the passing of this great gentleman.

(*1972*)

'Movie-making is great fun,' he said, bending over the table towards me. 'You are never sure if a film will succeed. It's a gamble. One you think will be a box-office hit turns out a flop; another you think nothing of hits the jackpot.' He leant back in his chair and snapped his thumb and finger to emphasize his point.

He continued talking at rapid, machine-gun-fire speed. 'There was my film, *Prem Pujari*.' He paused to see if the title meant anything to me. 'You didn't see it? Never mind! It was anti-Pakistani. Here, the Muslims made it out to be anti-Muslim. Demonstrations, theatres set on fire, hullarbazi—film withdrawn. Rs 26 lakh gone down the drain!' he said, plunging his right hand down to the carpet. 'The same *Prem Pujari* is put back in circulation after Bangladesh. It is a hit!' His hand went up again and he snapped his thumb and finger. His face beamed with triumph. 'The Rs 26 lakh back in one night!'

Dev Anand does not believe in breathers, and continued at his breathless pace. 'Then I went on to *Hare Rama*... How did I get the idea? I am always on the lookout for ideas. One film over, another hatching in my brain,' he explained, tapping his tousled hair scattered untidily over most of his forehead. 'I was on location in Nepal. Ran into an Indian girl. Jasbir. Yes, must be Sikh. Broken home. Father in Montreal, mother in Moga, Jasbir in Kathmandu, mixed up with hippies, smoking charas, ganja, pot. It was a ready-made story. I wrote the synopsis, had a team of writers to turn it into a screenplay—*Hare Rama Hare Krishna*!'

Once more he snapped his thumb and finger to tell me how successful the venture had been. Also, the making of Zeenat Aman.

'I shot the whole thing in nine weeks working day and night. Zeenat should have joined us for dinner but she is down with fever, 102 degrees.'

The telephone rang. His secretary, a demure, polite, self-effacing youngster called Khanna, put his hand on the mouthpiece and, in a hushed tone, pronounced the sacred name, Zeenat. Dev leapt off the chair, brushed back the hair from his forehead and began talking in conspiratorial undertones. His eyes continued to beam at me, but his mind was on Malabar Hill. He put down the phone. 'She's sorry she's unable to come. Now coming back to films...'

'Do you read much?'

'All geared to films, nothing else. Newspapers and magazines and that sort of thing. Films are my life. When I am making a film on the mountains, I read up all I can find on mountaineering—Kohli's *Nine Atop Everest,* Hunt, Hillary. What equipment they take, about Sherpas, everything. Next May there will be the coronation of the King of Bhutan. I'll read all I can about Bhutan. Maybe there will be a story there. Maybe...'

'What are you working on right now?' One has to plunge into Dev's torrent of words to get him to change the topic.

'Just finished *Heera Panna.* I am working on a musical—not just a film with songs but a real musical—*Ishq Ishq Ishq.* The location will be in Nepal—either Namche Bazaar or Pokhara. You come and be my guest. One week, one month. See how we go about it. You can do your work. I really mean it. Be my guest.'

I waved my hands in despair. 'How can I...'

'I really mean it. Make it four days... First time I asked you to come over, you said: No Amritsari invitations, fix the day and the time. So here it is, *you* name the day!'

I had been exposed to film stars' effusive invitations before and knew how little they meant. Dev had met me many times and each time it was: 'You must come and spend an evening with us at home; I'll ring you up.' It took four years for the invitation to materialize. And that after my matter-of-fact response: 'Name the date, time and place and I'll be there.'

I had met Dev's wife, Mona (Kalpana Kartik). She was not so elusive. She had agreed to an old man's desire to eat early and not have too many guests. But she avoided talk of her private life and I made no attempt to probe into it. She was lovely and vivacious enough to hold my attention. She was full of fun, laughter and gay abandon—telling me Sardarji jokes in rustic Punjabi and going into fits of laughter when I told her some she had not heard.

I had intended asking her what it felt like being the wife of Dev Anand; on meeting her I was more curious to find out what it meant to be the husband of Kalpana Kartik. But when I sat facing Dev Anand, I was sure that the question would be irrelevant as neither was the shadow of the other; both had strong personalities of their own.

Let us return to Dev Anand. It was hard to keep pace with him or to match his effusive warmth. He is unlike other film stars in being utterly single-minded in his pursuit to remain on top of the film world. The Gregory Peck image of yesteryears is gone; the swashbuckling, athletic do-gooder is visibly fading; a new image of a maker of films who has his feet as well as his ears firmly on the ground and knows what the people want has begun to emerge. He has a hunch for the topical. 'People want to know how their fellow Indians are doing abroad. They want to see how people in foreign countries live. So I asked Manohar Malgonkar to give me a story. He gave me *The Charcoal Burners*. It is not exactly what I wanted but it has all the ingredients. I am turning it...'

'Is it based on colour prejudice?'

'Some of it, yes, but what I...'

'Mixed marriages?'

'Also mixed marriages, but not quite the angle I had in mind. I told Malgonkar he is...'

'I believe you had some trouble with R. K. Narayan over the film version of *The Guide*.'

For the first time a shadow passed over his face. 'You know I made it in collaboration with Pearl Buck. She liked it. Narayan himself wrote to me saying he was pleased with it. Then he went and wrote that thing in *Life* magazine. I don't think...'

'I believe the Hindi version was a great success.'

The smile returned to his face. 'Of course!'

Could one ask anyone like him whether he had made any flops? His enthusiasm is so contagious, his single-mindedness to pursue the path of success so overpowering! His vision to reach beyond the horizons of his own country to the big world beyond so convincing. To what purpose? Does he have any values beyond worldly success?

'Do you believe in God or religion?'

He is not used to answering abstract questions. 'Well, yes and no. No particular kind of God. I don't go to temples, pray… But I can't say I don't believe in God. All my time is taken up with making films, dreaming films, acting, directing. I have little time for anything else.'

'Ever thought of death?'

'What do you mean? Everyone has to die.'

'André Gide wrote that one thing all creative people have in common is an obsession with death. You are a creative person.'

He didn't want to miss being creative but obviously he had not given much thought to the subject. 'I have little time to...'

'Have you ever been close to death?'

'Oh yes—in 1952. I was driving back from Kolhapur to Poona. I crashed into a tree. Three ribs broken. I spent twenty-one days in hospital.'

'Did you think of it at the time?'

'I said to myself: Let's face it; if I have to die, I have to die. That's that.'

'No more filmmaking!'

'That's right, no more filmmaking,' he replied, beaming with delight.

The séance was over. An array of soda-water bottles and the almost full bottle of Black Dog was evidence that the Scotch had not been drunk. Dev had nursed his own chhota in his hand, waiting for me to finish my quota of three. Then he put away his tumbler with the whisky still in it. He nibbled at the food, waved away the pudding and awaited a signal from me to release him. I had heard of film stars' bacchanalian feasts where they drink away into the early hours to combine supper with breakfast. With Dev the evening was over by 9.30 p.m.

I hauled myself up from the sofa. Dev, only a few years younger than I, leapt up like a coiled spring. His fight against age is a little pathetic. The garishly coloured shirt, broad silver-buckled belt and tight-fitting powder-blue jeans appear a little too mod for a man of his years. But then that is his image—the image of eternal youth. That's how the people recognize him. He strode ahead of me, his pace of walking as fast as his speech. I trailed behind, watching the admiring glances of waiters, room-girls, lift boys and heard the hallowed name 'Dev Anand' intoned as if it really meant 'the God of Bliss'.

His chauffeur had gone off to get a bite. We sat in the lobby of Oberoi Sheraton to await his return. Clusters of people collected at a respectable distance to gaze at their idol. All I could hear was a hum of 'Dev Anands'. Then someone asked somewhat loudly: 'Who is the Sardar with him?'

And someone else replied: 'Don't know. Must be one of his chamchas.'

(*1973*)

BEING UNTRUE TO ONE'S SALT

Does the name M. O. Mathai mean anything to you? Refresh your memory.

Till 1946 no one beyond the small circle of his family, fellow workers and friends had heard of him. For the next thirteen years he was known to everyone, because for those thirteen years he was Pandit Jawaharlal Nehru's special assistant—the power behind the throne... the deputy prime minister.

Then, as suddenly as he had emerged on the scene, he disappeared into oblivion. People may be pardoned if they thought he was dead. He is not. He has just published his memoirs.

M. O. Mathai does not see himself as others saw him. His view of himself approaches the Hindu ideal of a jeevanmukta—one who has achieved salvation while living. According to him, he had no personal ambitions when he joined Jawaharlal Nehru. All he wanted was to serve him and, through him, his people. He was a karmayogi who regarded work as his dharma. When his father, and a few days later his mother, died, in distant Kerala, he told no one and continued to work as if nothing had happened.

He didn't want any money or position. It was nishkamakarma (work without expectation of reward). He knew that the task he was undertaking had its hazards, but he was prepared to live dangerously. And so he did: he rescued a Muslim maiden from the hands of a villainous Sikh armed with a kirpan. He was nirbhay—without fear. He didn't give a damn for cabinet ministers and politicians because they were a contemptible lot, a bunch of mediocrities or worse. He didn't want anything of them but they wanted much of him; he made and unmade ministers, governors and ambassadors.

Everything the prime minister had to do was done through him; not a file went to Nehru without first being signed by him, nor left the PM's office till it had been okayed by him. No wonder people began to refer to him as the most powerful man next to Nehru. Actually, when it came to the nitty-gritty he did not really care what Nehru or anyone else thought of him as long as he was true to himself. In short, he looked upon himself as an Indian version of Sir Galahad:

> My good blade carves the casques of men,
> My tough lance thrusteth sure
> My strength is as the strength of ten,
> Because my heart is pure.

A thousand pities if foolish people do not see Mathai as he saw himself. At the time he joined Nehru (early 1946), it was abundantly clear to any nincompoop that Nehru would soon become the prime minister of India. And being his man Friday would give him backdoor entry into the corridors of power. Power gave Mathai more than money could have ever bought him. He drew (albeit reluctantly) a salary of Rs 1,500 per month with free board and lodging in the PM's house.

He travelled all over the world, stayed in the best of hotels, mingled with the mighty, and in due course became overbearing, arrogant and rude. After thirteen years of this 'selfless' service, Nehru was constrained to sack him because he had begun to throw his weight about.

As is truly said, success does not change a man, it unmasks him. It is only a big man who can resist being inebriated by power. Mathai was not a big man. Permit me another trite little verse somewhat altered by me:

> No more of your proud acquaintances boast
> Nor in what lordly company you have been
> An insect is an insect at most
> Though it crawl in the arse of a queen.

Mathai claims to have had loyalty and affection for Nehru. This does not inhibit him from maligning Nehru as a lecher who, unknown to the world, even sired a bastard. Can there be a better example of disloyalty to a master who is unable to answer such calumny? Does it not amount to being untrue to one's salt, of being a namak haram? Present also in the book, *Reminiscences of the Nehru Age,* is an element of blackmail. A chapter of precisely two-and-a-half lines is entitled 'She'. The publishers explain that this was withdrawn by the author at the last moment because it was 'on an intensely personal experience of the author's, written without inhibition in the D. K. Lawrence style'. The reference is quite clearly to Indira Gandhi and the novel, *Lady Chatterley's Lover,* based on the theme of a gardener's affair with the mistress of the house. At the same time, Mathai has announced that he is working on 'a companion volume to this work'. Seeing the sort of loyalty he has displayed towards the man who raised him from oblivion to importance, I have little doubt that 'She' will find publication in the sequel to come—unless by then Mathai's conscience, if he has one, makes him hold his hand.

It is significant that despite much chest thumping about how fearless he is, Mathai waited till Indira Gandhi was out of power to publish his memoirs 'for the sake of history'. Also, when it comes to maligning living people, he takes good care to avoid naming them lest he be hauled up for libel.

They are easy enough to recognize. The Rajmata of Patiala, Raghuramaiah, Panini, Nayantara Sahgal, Kamala Jaspal, Shastri and quite a few others. I fear none of them will have the courage to put Mathai in the dock he deserves to be in. For the living and currently powerful, like Morarji Desai, Mathai has only praise.

Mathai's book is a jumble of events and incidents and pompous pronouncements with no logical or chronological sequence. Arrogance and conceit ooze out of every line. He is riled by Kuldip Nayar because he described him as a stenographer; by Janardhan Thakur (*All The Prime Minister's Men)* and Minoo Masani (*Bliss Was It In That Dawn*) for daring to pronounce on subjects connected with his domain. Mathai is the sab jaanta wallah; other scribes a bunch of ignoramuses.

(*1977*)

FOOTPRINTS ON THE SANDS OF TIME

Within a short fortnight I lost two friends: Baldoon Dhingra and Meherban Singh Dhupia. It is the sharp contrast between the careers of these two men that induces me to write about them as lessons to those who are still alive. One started life with enormous promise that he did not fulfil. The other started his with many handicaps and yet came to the top.

Baldoon Dhingra's death in Paris was announced in only one paper; that too at the bottom of an inside page. All it said about him was that he had been a prominent member of the Indian community in France. Meherban Singh Dhupia's passing made the front pages of many daily papers, bazaars closed as a mark of respect and his cortège was followed by thousands of citizens, including several Members of Parliament. I will tell you why.

I got to know Baldoon Dhingra in the 1940s, soon after he returned from Cambridge and was appointed lecturer of English at Government College, Lahore. Everyone talked about him as a man with a very bright future. A good degree from a prestigious university, remarkable fluency in French, awards for poetry and enormous savoir faire. He had inherited considerable wealth from his father, Sir Bihari Lal Dhingra; he was a dapper, handsome man; married to vivacious Kamla Sehgal, he lived in style in his own double-storeyed bungalow in Model Town: cut glass, vintage wines, European classical music and a large library of books. Soirees with poetry readings at Dhingra's house became an important part of the cultural life of Lahore. He was a generous host, self-assured and bubbling with life. Anyone would have taken a safe bet that Baldoon's name (odd sounding though it was) would be worth dropping in years to come.

The Partition hit the Dhingras harder than it did millions of others who had likewise been uprooted and rendered destitute. He lost his effervescence and went as flat as soda water left overnight in an open bottle. Financial insecurity gnawed at him and robbed him of his creative faculties. His energies were thereafter consumed by an unending quest for security. He took a measly job with UNESCO in Paris. He did not like the job and did little to justify renewals of contract. He was soured because people with lesser qualifications got higher posts. However, he hung on as long as he could by getting round people who mattered until even his patrons could help him no more. He lived in a single-room apartment and when his daughters came home for their vacations, they often slept in the car parked on the street outside. Unkind stories of Dhingra's techniques of sponging became common currency in Indian circles. It was pathetic. A man who had so much to give ended up giving so little. An anthology of quotations and perhaps a few tracts are all he has left behind.

Baldoon Dhingra's life should be an object lesson to people with creative ambitions. Life is far too short to be wasted in pursuit of material security. You never know when it will end—so reckon it will end tomorrow. You can't take anything with you, but you can leave behind things better than a bank balance for your wife and children. You can leave something worthwhile of yourself for the times to come. I repeat these nasty platitudes because Baldoon's death made me sit down and add up all the hours that I had myself killed doing things that didn't matter. The grand total came to a staggering figure—more than half of my life.

Meherban Singh started life with everything against him: he had very little education, his means were extremely modest and his appearance unprepossessing—even as a boy he was short and enormously fat. When I met him first in the 1920s, he was working as a clerk in the railways. In his spare time he used to organize ping-pong (not yet elevated to the status of table tennis) and badminton tournaments in which he seldom made the second round. From organizing sports he turned to organizing clubs and societies. His success as a man who could get things done was phenomenal. From the President of the Republic down to sub-inspectors of police, he knew everyone who was anyone. He could have been described as a fixer because he could fix just about any job anyone wanted from that of an ambassador to a chaprasi. The number of people he put under obligation was legion. He never asked for anything for himself.

He never said 'no' to anybody so no one ever said 'no' to him. So many things came to him unasked. He had never been a scout but he represented India at an International Scout Jamboree in Holland. He was never much of a politician and had very poor command of English, but he led a delegation of Akalis (none of whom could speak English) to London in 1947 to plead the case of the Sikhs. He took on the Chelmsford Club and made it the most popular and profitable institution in the capital. Then he organized Punjabis scattered over the globe and arranged annual get-togethers in the poshest hotels of Europe and the United States. I have little doubt that if there was a public opinion poll to select the most popular Punjabi in the world, Meherban Singh Dhupia would emerge the easy winner. Dhupia's life is a lesson of another kind. No matter what the handicaps against you, with willpower and determination you can propel yourself to triumphal heights.

(*1979*)

MALCOLM MUGGERIDGE

I first met Malcolm Muggeridge sometime in 1952 or 1953. He was editor of *Punch*, I the public relations officer in the Indian High Commission in London. I had been a regular reader of *Punch*, and had seen how under Muggeridge's stewardship it had brightened up. It now had cartoonists Andre Francois and Ronald Searle, new writers of the calibre of Anthony Powell, Claud Cockburn and the poet John Betjeman. He was perhaps the first English editor to lampoon the nation's hero and the then prime minister, Winston Churchill, through an Illingworth cartoon, as a senile old man puffing outsized Havana cigars. I knew he had been with *The Statesman* in Calcutta and had a soft corner for Indians, particularly the Sikhs. I discovered why on our first meeting.

I rang him up and invited him to lunch at a well-known fish restaurant in the West End near the Savoy. He readily accepted. I ordered two dry sherries while we examined the menu and the wine list. He didn't know much about vintage wines and left the choice to me. 'If we are going to have fish, order any kind of white wine you like. Should not be too sweet,' he said. I ordered a bottle of Riesling and awaited our meal.

'I know you were with *The Statesman*,' I said to get the conversation going. 'Was that your first exposure to India?'

'Indeed, no,' replied he. 'I had been with Christian College, Alwaye, in Kerala. Taught English for some time. Didn't like it very much. Too much religion for my liking. But I did meet Gandhi and started wearing khadi. Actually it was at Alwaye that I started writing for English papers. I realized my real métier was journalism not teaching.'

Like most Englishmen, Muggeridge was reluctant to talk about himself. I had to ply him with direct questions to get reluctant answers. He told me of his two years in Selwyn College, Cambridge. He had got there on a scholarship but had not done too well in his final examination. He also abominated sport of any kind. He was later to describe Cambridge as 'a place of infinite tedium....with a bizarre collection of aged and incompetent teachers…from which I emerged unscathed and largely unlettered'. A surprising denunciation by a man from a lower-middle class background who owed much of his future career to friends he made at the university.

I turned to his days with *The Statesman,* which he later wrote of as 'easily the most melancholy of my life'. There was nothing very melancholy about the way he described them to me. He stopped nibbling at the fish but helped himself to more wine out of the ice bucket. He emptied the bottle into our glasses and shook it to see if there was any left. I ordered a second bottle of Riesling. The wine loosened his tongue and I experienced something of Muggeridge the compulsive talker and portrayer of vivid pictures in words. 'The best thing that happened to me in my *Statesman* days was meeting Amrita Sher-Gil. Did you know Amrita?'

I nodded. I told him that I was amongst the handful who were present at her funeral in Lahore. I had also seen her portrait of Muggeridge: she was in the habit of making portraits of her lovers, male or female. Had Muggeridge been her lover? I led him on. He didn't need much leading. 'She had lots of lovers,' I told him. 'I knew at least a dozen in Lahore who claimed to have bedded her.'

'For sure!' he exclaimed. 'She had quite an appetite for sex. I should know.'

Thereafter there was no stopping him. They had run into each other somewhere in Calcutta or Delhi where Amrita was exhibiting her paintings. Rapport was established. They became lovers. Amrita invited Malcolm to spend some days with her in her parents' home in Summer Hill close to Simla. Muggeridge spent a week with them. Old Sardar Umrao Singh Majithia and his fiery Hungarian wife were most understanding about the physical needs of their talented daughter. Muggeridge was at the time in the prime of his youth and proud of his physical prowess. He admitted that he was no match for the Indo-Hungarian lass nearly ten years younger than him. There were apparently no emotional overtones in the liaison. Muggeridge's description of how it ended remains in my mind. 'At the end of the week, I was thoroughly exhausted, like a wet rag which has been put through a wringer. She came to see me off at the Summer Hill railway station. As she waved goodbye to me when my railcar began to move, she had a triumphant smile on her face.'

It was an amazing confession from a man who claimed to have been happily married to an English beauty, Kitty Dobbs, the niece of the communist Bea Webb. He was by then the father of three children. The lunch stretched on. The restaurant was empty and the waiters impatiently awaited our departure. We left at 4 p.m.

I saw quite a bit of Malcolm Muggeridge and we entertained each other at lunches. He was certainly a most engaging conversationalist who held your attention and rarely gave anyone else the chance to talk. He was by no means a handsome man—balding, beady-eyed, with high cheekbones and an oversized chin—but his wit and the outrageous comments he made on celebrities kept his audience amused. He wrote the way he talked—poking fun at the high and mighty like Bertrand Russell, Churchill ('disaster'), John Kennedy ('a fraud'), Ronald Reagan ('not such a fool as people say'), Eisenhower ('a meandering old president') and the British monarchy ('a royal soap opera').

He had done so many things and been to so many places that he was never short of topics. At Cambridge, he had been a Fabian Socialist (his father was a Labour Member of Parliament). Soon after he came out of the university, he became so enamoured of the Soviet Union that he decided to spend the rest of his life in Russia. A six-month stay in Moscow and a visit to famine-stricken Ukraine cured him of his leaning towards communism and he became a very bitter critic of the Stalinist regime. He taught English in India and Egypt. He worked for British intelligence in Africa, he was in Paris when the Allies liberated it and extended support to P. G. Wodehouse, who had been detained for having collaborated with the Nazis. He denounced the charge against Wodehouse (he was accused of being a German spy) as 'absurd and degrading'.

Back home in England he settled down in Robertsbridge in Sussex growing his own vegetables and keeping bees for honey and eating yoghurt. He turned vegetarian, teetotaller and quit smoking. He had by then become a television personality; he stopped watching TV and told his friends proudly that he had his aerial removed.

Malcolm Muggeridge never kept the same job for too long or stayed at one place for any length of time. Though a bit of a grasshopper, two things abided with him throughout his life of eighty-seven years: an interest in religion and journalism. He wrote for a variety of papers: the *Manchester Guardian, Statesman and Nation, Evening Standard* and *Daily Telegraph,* of which he was assistant editor for some time. And of course *Punch*. Out of his journalism, broadcasting and travels came many books: *Tread Softly for You Tread on My Jokes, Chronicles of Wasted Time, Conversion: A Spiritual Journey*, and many others.

I couldn't take Muggeridge's religiosity very seriously. He was an Anglican but to the best of my knowledge, rarely went to church. Apparently turning towards religion was a phenomenon of later life. And when he did turn religious he took to one which did not allow any doubting or reasoning. The decisive moment came when he returned to India when he was more than eighty years old to make a film on Mother Teresa for the BBC. He was completely bowled over. He relates some miracles he witnessed in the company of Mother Teresa: in the twilight gloom of Nirmal Hriday movie cameras were able to record due to some divine light; and large sums of money miraculously arrived to help Mother Teresa continue her good works. It was this encounter that finally convinced him to join the Roman Catholic Church. His book on Mother Teresa, *Something Beautiful for God*, is the least readable of all his books. He called himself 'a Jesus freak'; others named him St Muggs. To me he remains Amrita Sher-Gil's defeated lover.

(*Undated*)

JOHN MASTERS

The interview began and ended with *Bhowani Junction.*

'Where is Bhowani Junction?'

'Jhansi.'

'I thought it was Jubbulpore.'

'No. Jubbulpore was the location of *The Deceivers.*'

Precise, direct and without any affectation whatsoever. That was the impression John Masters made. His manner was that of a soldier—a soldier who has to answer questions standing at attention.

'When did you take to writing?'

'In 1947 when I resigned my commission in the Indian army. My first book was *Bugles and a Tiger*. It was rejected by eight publishers in succession. I put it away in a drawer and started writing *Nightrunners of Bengal.* That too was rejected by eight publishers and then accepted by the ninth. Thereafter I had no difficulty. Once *Bhowani Junction* was filmed, anything I wrote was taken—even *Bugles and a Tiger.*'

◆

Masters refused to admit that he had favourites amongst his own books. 'I hate to look at them once they are finished,' he said emphatically. But it was obvious that *Bugles* ranked high in his own estimation. It is the first in a series of biographical works and starts with the period which was perhaps the happiest in his life—the years he spent as a subaltern in a Gurkha regiment.

Bugles has all the qualities which Masters admires most in his favourite book on India, Kipling's *Kim*. It reproduces the sights, sounds and smells of this country vividly. In addition, it has delightfully humorous touches on the ways of the Punjabis, Pathans and Gurkhas. Both Kipling and Masters know India, but only Masters knows Indians. If the next two volumes of his biography, *Mercenary Calling* and *Pilgrim Son*, achieve any of the excellence of *Bugles and a Tiger*, Masters will undoubtedly take the first place amongst English writers on India.

(He dismissed Forster's *A Passage to India* as 'Too neat. Too donnish'. Perhaps Forster's fans will dismiss Masters as 'Too earthy. Too vulgar'.)

Masters is now engaged in writing a novel on Spain and a musical drama with an Indian background. The theme of the drama is the conflict in the mind of an Indian engineer—a woman—in charge of the construction of the dam which will submerge a temple held sacred by her people.

'Are you collecting material for a new novel on India?' I asked him.

'Not this time. I have only seven days and so much to do. I propose coming back in two years with my son and daughter to do a long trek in the Himalayas—in Kashmir, Ladakh and Kullu. Then I will collect material for something new. But I have enough to go on with. My family has been in India since 1790. I am Calcutta-born and lived in the country for fourteen years. That provides plenty of material for biography and fiction.'

◆

There were many questions I wanted to ask him about *Bhowani Junction*, but other visitors had come in to meet him. So I put the one which was on the top of my list.

'Mr Masters, in *Bhowani Junction*, one of your main characters is a Sikh who refuses to kiss his girlfriend because they are not married. Have you ever met a Sikh who was cramped by such inhibitions?"

He roared with laughter 'Indeed not. But *Bhowani Junction* is fiction. There could be fictitious Sikhs—sweet, gentle and reluctant to kiss.'

(*Undated*)

A TRUE BRIDGE-BUILDER

It was a grievous blow to those who strove to build bridges between Pakistan and India to hear that Minoo Bhandara, ex-member of the Pakistan National Assembly, had died.

Apparently, while on a visit to China, he met with a car accident and was seriously injured. He was flown back to Islamabad. Amongst those to call on him in hospital were President Musharraf and his wife, Sehba. He seemed to be recovering, but on 15 June he gave up the battle. He was barely seventy.

I don't recall when and where I first met Minoo. We had a common friend and role model in Manzur Qadir. He shared my opinion that Manzur was the paradigm of goodness and rectitude. It was this admiration for Manzur that created a bond between us. I do remember that at our first meeting I asked him, 'Are you a Bawaji?' He was nonplussed as he did not know what the word meant. I had to tell him that in India, we refer to Parsis as Bawajis behind their backs.

'And what are you doing in Pakistan?' was my next question. He explained he ran the Murree Brewery and was also a member of the National Assembly. We became friends and whenever he was in Delhi, which was often, he spent a couple of evenings with me. He was proud of his products, notably the single malt whisky, which he brought for me. He was invariably accompanied by a pretty Pakistani girl, usually a painter, poet or a novelist.

I also discovered that Pakistan's leading novelist in English, Bapsi Sidhwa, was his sister. Bapsi stayed with me when she was in Delhi. When I visited Pakistan, I stayed with Minoo in his beautifully laid out bungalow in Rawalpindi. It was next door to his distillery. He had built a mosque alongside for his Muslim employees. I asked him how Pakistanis took to his brewing liquor—forbidden as haraam. He smiled and replied, 'You know how things are in our countries: say one thing, do another. My products are only meant for export. But behind closed doors, the elite of Pakistan, when they can't get imported stuff, make do with the indigenous.'

Needless to say, among the richest who made their fortune legally in Pakistan was Minoo Bhandara, who had the monopoly of brewing beer and distilling whisky. Minoo's main interest was not politics but literature. He would patiently answer all the questions about political affairs in Pakistan that I fired at him and then turn to books, novels, anthologies of poetry or whatever. In Delhi he usually stayed at the India International Centre and spent his afternoons doing the rounds of bookstores in Khan Market. Invariably, our evening sessions would end with him asking what I was working on. At one time I was busy translating selections of Urdu poetry into English. I was facing a lot of difficulties with Ghalib.

I didn't agree with any of the interpretations of the opening lines of his *Diwan*.

Naqsh faryadi hai kis ki shokhi-i-tehreer ka
Kaagzhi hai pairahan har paikar-i-tasveer ka
(A painting speaks for itself. It needs no learned explanation in detail.
On paper it is painted. Itself it tells its tale.)

I told him that there was nothing to suggest that Ghalib had alluded to the practice of petitioners having to wear robes when they appeared before the shah. He simply meant to say that a picture tells its own tale, it does not need learned interpretation to explain its purport. Minoo disagreed and said, 'At the time we (i.e. Zoroastrians) ruled Iran, that was accepted practice.' We had an animated (never heated) argument over it.

Another time it was Faiz's oft-quoted lines:

Raat yoon dil mein teri khoi hui yaad aayi
Jaise veerane mein chupke say bahar aajaae
Jaise sehraon mein haule say chale baad-i-naseem
Jaise beemar ko bevajhe qaraar aajae
(At night your lost memory stole into my heart
As in barren wastes, silently spring comes
As in glades the zephyr begins to blow
As in one sick without hope, hope begins to grow.)

We argued over my translation. I conceded to the suggestions he made.

Every time Minoo came to India, it was to attend a conference or seminar on Indo-Pakistan relations. He put the Pakistani point of view to Indian audiences. Back in Pakistan, he described reactions of Indians in articles he wrote for Pakistani journals. He was a true bridge-builder between the two nations. With his going that bridge has fallen.

For me Minoo's death has been a personal loss. With all my Pakistani friends from my Lahore days now resting in their graves, he was my last remaining link with a country I call my watan—my homeland. That link has been snapped.

(*2008*)

MEMORABLE PLACES

MOONLIGHT IN BOKARO

I have never ceased to wonder at the way some people get absorbed in their work and forget the world about them. An interesting example of a one-track mind is Mr Guglani, the Damodar Valley Corporation (DVC) engineer at the Bokaro thermal plant. I must go back a little and provide the background to my meeting with him.

I left Hazaribagh in the morning and made brief halts at Jamunia and Konar dams. I stopped several times on the way to admire the scenery or examine wild flowers I had not seen before. The country through which the Damodar and its tributaries flow is rugged and wild. It is mountainous and densely wooded in parts. A fortnight ago, the flame of the forest was in full bloom so every now and then a blaze of orange would meet the eye. As we got nearer our destination this tree became more and more common. As we came around a hill overlooking Bokaro, we saw a notice telling people to look out for a breathtaking sight. And truly breathtaking it was. Below us stretched a valley—a vivid mass of orange. In the centre was the thermal plant alongside the Bokaro River.

'Mr Guglani, you are a lucky man to live in such a beautiful place.'

Mr Guglani agreed. 'Once a person has been to Bokaro, he wants to come again'. He named Mr Nehru and Mr B. C. Roy amongst the many who had fallen victim to the charms of the place. Apparently Marshal Bulganin and Mr Khrushchev were also meant to visit Bokaro, and only failed to do so because of their tight schedule. 'But you should see it at night, then it is more beautiful.'

'But at night you couldn't see the dhak,' I protested.

'Dhak? What is that?'

'Palas, flame of the forest, *Butea frondosa*—this orange flower all over the valley. Surely it is that which makes the place beautiful!'

Mr Guglani hadn't noticed the flower. But he was right about Bokaro at night. The station is floodlit and, being painted in silver, glistens like a jewel box. From a distance it is a very pretty sight, particularly if it is a moonlit night and the surroundings are also visible. Mr Guglani became lyrical about the moon over Bokaro.

'From my house I can see the moon come up over the factory. When it is between the chimneys of the thermal plant, it is really wonderful.'

Mr Guglani has bought a new camera to take photographs of the full moon between the smoke-belching factory funnels. To him it is not the moon that makes Bokaro beautiful, but Bokaro that lends lustre to the moon.

(*1957*)

LESSON FROM JAPAN

I got into a crowded third-class compartment of the train proceeding from Mysore to Bangalore. It was hot and there was nothing except coffee or tea to quench our thirst—and somehow a hot drink was not a particularly pleasing idea in that weather.

At Srirangapatna, a sugarcane seller made a welcome appearance. All of us bought a long piece each. In half an hour everyone had finished with the sugarcane and thrown out the husk—all except one, a Japanese gentleman sitting quietly in a corner.

I watched him examining the beauty of the colour on the outer surface of the sugarcane. He began carefully cutting the thick outer edge with a sharp knife and laying out the long flat strips on a towel. When this was over, he began chewing the contents—but with one difference. He stored the husk as well. Then he began working on the husk and the strips with the true skill of an artist.

'What are you doing with this waste matter? Why don't you throw it out?' I asked at last when my patience ran out.

He smiled. 'It is raw material for something useful and beautiful.'

When the train reached Mandya, I saw him deeply absorbed in fixing the soft sugarcane husk between the long flat pieces of the cane's bark already cut into equal lengths. He pulled out a needle and thread from his pocket and started sewing the husk to the strips. Soon, the waste product began taking on a distinct shape—the shape of a fan. The job was not over yet. He got out brushes and paints and painted the fan in gaudy colours. In a few minutes a lovely Japanese landscape had appeared on it.

The train came to a halt at Channapatna where I had to get down. I complimented the Japanese gentleman for using both time and skill for a worthwhile purpose and said goodbye. He smiled, bowed and gave me the fan.

(*1957*)

There were two questions to which I wanted answers when I went to Madhya Pradesh. First: how is it that in this modern age and with all the resources at our command, a medieval menace like banditry is allowed to continue? Second: why do so many people have a sneaking admiration for cut-throats and common prostitutes—the Man Singhs and Putlis—whose record has little of the heroism or love for the underdog one associates with lovable outlaws of the Robin Hood type?

I spent one day on the outer fringes of the dacoit country and met many villagers living in the area. It gave me a sort of bird's-eye view of the landscape in which the outlaws operate and the difficulties faced by the police. I got an idea of the fears of the local population and why they did not cooperate fully with the administration in wiping out the dacoits. I also saw something of the work being done in the villages and its impact on the problem of outlawry.

ABUL FAZL'S INTESTINES

We left Gwalior early in the morning. My companions were Kanhaya Lal Neema, the Block Development Officer of Dabra and his colleague Miss Hemlata Singh, an American-trained Social Education Officer. Within a few minutes we were in a country of low hills and dense thorny jungles. These hills and forests with their many ravines made by monsoon streams provide the outlaw with his hideouts. The poor quality of land undoubtedly provides him with the temptation to give up honest but unrewarding labour and take to the dishonest but more paying professions of thieving, robbery and murder. This is the economic content of the problem and its core. It has been there for many centuries and a sort of tradition of brigandage has grown up in these parts. We saw one monument to it about thrity kilometres from Gwalior when we turned off the main road towards village Antri. The village had been so named because Abul Fazl—the brightest of the nine gems of Akbar's court and the chief sponsor of the universal faith Din-i-Ilahi—was brutally murdered here by Vir Singh Bundela.

The crime was committed on the orders of Prince Salim (later Emperor Jahangir). To prove the success of his mission, Vir Singh cut off Abul Fazl's head and sent it to Salim. Only his intestines—antri—were buried at the spot where he died.

Antri now has an Extension Training School run by a vigorous old man, Mata Din Trivedi, and a centre for training gram sevikas under Mrs Nigam. Mr Trivedi told me a charming anecdote. Abul Fazl's elephant was deeply devoted to its master and took the assassination to heart. It killed itself by battering its head on the spot where Abul Fazl had fallen. An iron spike marks the site of the suicide.

ONE MILE OF ROAD BUILT IN ONE DAY

It was a Sunday, so I was not able to see either the school or the training centre at work. But I did have a word with the heads of the two institutions about their activities. Mr Trivedi was very excited about two items: a one-mile road made by the villagers of Sandalpur to connect it with Antri, and the work done in village Jirasia, which had sheltered dacoits for many years. The Sandalpur road was built in one day—on 15 August 1955. Prior to that there had been one track passing through a narrow ravine and each time a bullock cart left Sandalpur a man had first to go up to Antri to see that the 'line' was clear. Sometimes the valuable cargo of betel leaves, which are Sandalpur's chief produce, perished because of the time taken by a cart to retrace its steps to give way to one coming from the opposite direction. The road is not so much an example of shramdan (voluntary labour service) as that of gramdan (village grant). It had been held up for centuries because neighbouring landowners had refused to give an inch of land. This they did after a little persuasion by Mr Trivedi and his boys.

Jirasia is a tiny hamlet at the foot of a hill and became the haunt of dacoits needing rest and food. What the police failed to achieve with guns, unarmed community project workers have done with patient advice and timely assistance. Farmers were given better seed, taught newer methods of cultivation and persuaded to send their children to school. They became prosperous. From having nothing to lose by their association with dacoits, they became men of means with a personal stake in the maintenance of law and order. Some have acquired arms to defend the hamlet. Dacoits now give it a wide berth.

The Boys' Extension School is in the centre of Antri; the Gram Sevikas' Centre is on the outskirts with only a barbed wire fence to protect it. 'Aren't you and your girls scared of dacoits?' I asked Mrs Nigam. 'Not at all,' she replied with a smile. 'Dacoits never molest social workers. As a matter of fact, the safest thing to carry in these regions is a book. They do not bother anyone who is either teaching or learning to read.'

HARIJANS ALWAYS BEST

From Antri, we proceeded on the main Gwalior-Jhansi road and stopped at Samoodan—the prize village of Dabra block. Like most of the prize villages I had seen, this too was inhabited by Harijans. They are undoubtedly very progressive. Miss Singh confirmed this when I asked her whether Harijan women were as forthcoming as the men. 'Of course,' she replied warmly. 'But these caste people are an absolute nuisance. It won't be long now when the Harijans will take the lead. It will teach the Brahmins and others a good lesson.' Samoodan certainly was an attractive little village. It had all that an Indian village should have—a school, paved streets, pucca wells, compost pits and luscious vegetation all round. It had a general air of cleanliness and good living. I met the two leaders of the village—Radhey Lal and Chuni Ram—and heard them talk with pride of their achievements within the year. The womenfolk came out to talk to Hemlata Singh and show what progress they had made in the little things she had taught them. There was the young and attractive Rambai knitting a sweater for her child. She had got to knitting straight pieces. How was she to make the sleeves? Hemlata told her while the others watched. Our next call was at Chandpur.

It was an old fortress town with battlements sadly battered by time. This town had also widened its single-track road to a wide double-track pucca one. It had paved its streets, bricked its wells, organized its panchayat, mahila mandal, maternity centre and schools. An old lady I met in Chandpur deserves to be mentioned. Raja Beti is a widowed grandmother who not only runs her late husband's sweetmeat shop, educates her sons and runs her home, but also organizes women's activities in Chandpur. She is the one woman member of the panchayat and from what I saw of her, she probably leads the men by their noses. As soon as we got to her home, she got hold of Hemlata and began to discuss her problems. She seemed a bossy sort of a woman—somewhat different from one's notion of a Hindu widow. I thought she would not mind my taking her photograph. I took one without her noticing me. Then she saw me, drew her veil and spoke angrily.

We turned back from Chandpur to Gwalior. We had one last person to meet. Those who talk despondently of the unchanging east should meet this man. So also should all the young men who sit sipping cups of coffee and sighing that they can find no suitable employment. This was the sixty-five-year-old Amar Singh—a World War I veteran who later became a truck driver. When he lost his trucks and money in the Partition riots, he borrowed money from the government and, for the first time in his life, took to farming. This old man cleared a sixteen-hectare tract of thorny bush and kans, dug a well, ploughed it, sowed the seeds and harvested it—single-handedly. Now he earns Rs 2,500 every month from his land. It just shows that even the poor soil of Madhya Pradesh can yield to the honest and manly toil of a determined man. If Amar Singh can do it, so can others. Such labour builds a breed of men who can face dacoits without fear. Amar Singh lives alone in the jungle with nothing better than a shotgun which can kill nothing bigger than partridges. When I asked him about dacoits, he made the most convincing reply—he spat on the ground.

(1957)

THE ADIVASI ON THE IRON HILL

This year the summer has set in unusually early. At Jamshedpur, I heard the koel call in the first week of February. I drove over the wooded hills which lie along the border of Bihar and Orissa and saw a vast variety of wild trees which are normally in full bloom in March. There was the flaming red of the simul, the bright orange of the dhak and soft mauve of the bauhinia. On mango trees there were clusters of honeybees and the koels were calling like mad. I asked a young Adivasi if spring always came early in these parts. 'No,' he replied, 'this year it is earlier than before and I am sure it will be hotter. It is always much hotter here than the neighbouring districts.'

'I didn't know hills could be hotter than the plains,' I remarked.

'These are no ordinary hills,' he went on with a superior air. 'These are made of iron—solid iron.'

I looked a little puzzled. He picked up a dark brown rock and handed it to me. 'See how heavy it is. It is all iron. All these hills, as far as your eyes can see, are like this. I know because my people have, for many generations, made steel for swords, shields, spears and arrowheads. The Hos and Kols were the best steel makers of India.'

'What do your people do now?'

'We work for Tatakumpunee. We dig up the ore. There are 6,000 of us in the mines.'

'With these new machines being installed, there will be little work left for people like you.'

'But work is increasing at such a rate with steel plants going up at Durgapur, Bhilai and Rourkela that no one is thrown out of a job. And now young Adivasis are being taught how to handle the big machines. Lots of them are working as skilled hands in Jamshedpur.'

'Do you get enough to live on?'

He raised his hands to the heavens. 'God is merciful. We leave our children in the crèche and both my wife and I work. We get enough to fill our bellies. What more can one want?'

‘Mahua wine and rice beer,’ I answered, poking him in the ribs.

‘God gives us these also,’ he replied, roaring with laughter.

THE MISSING OFFICIAL

I left the young Adivasi and went up the hill to the rest house. The ground was hard and the rocks glistened in the sunlight. I recalled the words of Dorabji Tata. ‘Our footsteps rang beneath us’, he had recorded. He and his men had spent many weary months in the wilderness looking for iron. They had given up the quest and returned to Nagpur to hand over the prospecting licence. The official they went to see was not in his office. So they had gone to idle away the hours in a museum across the road. Their eyes fell upon an old geological map marking a range on the Bihar-Orissa border with a faded brown dot. They got out a report by an Indian geologist P. N. Bose which confirmed the dot on the map. Instead of returning the licence to the official, they went in quest of the dot, located it and struck iron. They also found other ingredients which go into making steel—limestone and coal—in the neighbourhood. Near the confluence of the two rivers, Kharkai and Subarnarekha, was a tiny hamlet, Sakchi. This they chose to make their home and the home of Indian steel. They cleared the jungle and put up the steel city. In the winter of 1911 when pig iron flowed down in streams of molten gold, the unknown hamlet of Sakchi had become one of India’s big cities. A few years later they renamed it Jamshedpur—in honour of the great Jamsetji who had dreamt it all. There is something to be said for bureaucrats who are busy keeping out of their offices.

Tata’s rest house at Noamundi—the site of one of the mines—is on the crest of a hill. From the balcony one can see a forest of sal trees stretching for many miles. About thirty kilometres away as the crow flies, is Joda from where they mine ferro-manganese. Although Noamundi is in the wilderness, it hums with activity. All day long one can hear trains and trolleys collecting ore, taking it to the crushing plant and then taking it for washing, and onwards to Jamshedpur. On the slopes is the miners’ town with its rows of workers’ houses, hospitals, crèches, bazaars and the inevitable mahua and rice-beer shops. The countryside has a haunting beauty which the machines have fortunately failed to spoil. They have driven off the wild animals—elephants, tigers and boars—but the woods are still there with a vast variety of flowering trees.

THE BRICKLAYER

At the rest house I ran into an American—he looked every inch an American. He was tall and portly and was smoking a cigar. We mumbled our names and shook hands. I asked him whether he too was a visitor. No, he replied, he worked with the Tatas; he had worked with them for over thirty years.

'Thirty years!' I exclaimed. 'You must have been brought over as an expert.'

'No,' he replied modestly. 'I came as a bricklayer.' I dismissed him as a man of no importance. For the sake of politeness I asked him about the steelworks and future plans. He told me how he had seen it grow during the two World Wars, its ups and downs, and its present project of doubling its output from one to two million tonnes. I had heard all this before so I asked him about something which, as a worker, I thought would be closer to his heart—workers' participation in the industry. He explained the joint councils in which workers had begun to be associated at all levels at some length. Then the bearer came in and announced that the sahib's car had arrived. He shook hands with me and left. I was surprised that a bricklayer should have a chauffeur driven car.

'Who was that?' I asked the bearer.

'That was Mr Haley, general manager of the steelworks.'

◆

The moon came up late; a silver beam stole through the bedroom window. I looked out and saw it caught amongst the sal trees. It looked very pale and reduced in size. The night was very still; only the sound of distant drums came across the valley. I sat and listened in the dark for a long time. Then looked out of the window again. The moon had disentangled itself from the sal branches and looked brighter. A broad beam had lit up the opposite wall on which hung a photograph of a benign old man with a beard. I got up to see who it was. It was Jamsetji Nusserwanji Tata.

(*1958*)

THE DOOMED VILLAGE

'Koi hai?'

They were obviously the most appropriate words of command in Poona. I expected a liveried bearer with regimental insignia on his turban to come in through the wire-gauze door, and, in the tradition of native servants trained in the hard-boiled British school of Poona Blimps, come to attention and salute. I shouted 'Koi hai?' several times, but no one came. The Poona colonels had gone. So had their lackeys who answered to 'koi hai'. I rolled up my bedding and hoisted it onto my shoulder. On the way out I paused in front of the picture on the wall. It was a colour print of a scene in Scotland. Shaggy, long-horned cattle standing in the blue waters of Loch something or the other; purple heather in the foreground, blue hills in the distance. I stepped out of the old India of British colonels embalmed in the Poona Hotel into the India of today—torrid heat, dust devils spiralling across the lawn and miles and miles of tarmac road glistening in the scorching sun. My destination was Koyna—the India of tomorrow.

The sun set behind the Western Ghats and all became dark. It was a moonless night—one could see nothing except the stars and the dim outline of the hills. The smell of vegetation and the occasional sight of deer standing along the roadside hypnotized by the dazzle of the car headlights told us that we were passing through a jungle. We began to climb a gently winding road and suddenly turned a corner to face a hillside littered with electric lights. This was the new township of the builders of Koyna. We came to a halt at the dak bungalow on the crest of the hill.

The alarm sounded an hour before sunrise. It was the piercing cry of the demoiselle crane. Then the hillside across the valley became a medley of bird song—koels, barbets, orioles, thrushes, magpie robins and a variety of water birds. I came out on the veranda in the grey light. Our side of the valley was a series of terraces on which were the homes and offices of the dam builders. On the other side was a vast and luxuriant forest. In between was a silver trickle—the river Koyna.

I was not the only early riser. A south Indian gentleman stood a few metres away facing the rising sun and murmuring his prayers. When he had finished, I approached him. 'Have you come to see the project?' I asked by way of introduction.

'I live here,' he replied gently. 'My name is Murthy. I am the chief engineer.' We shook hands.

'Doesn't look much of a river, this Koyna of yours,' I remarked. 'It seems hardly worthwhile building a dam on this measly stream.'

'Measly stream! Come and see it two months from now and you will change your opinion. The local name for it is "the torrent that bears the hill trunks".'

'That may well be but the mills of Bombay don't need wood for their boilers; they need electric power and this hardly seems to be adequate.'

Mr Murthy smiled. 'The Koyna is the toughest little river that India has and the most eccentric. It is less than 130 kilometres long—half of it runs north to south between two ranges of hills of the Western Ghats. Then it suddenly turns eastwards—a little above where we are damming it—and forty-eight kilometres lower down it ends its course in the Krishna.'

'That's all right, but there is hardly any water in it.'

'Very little now,' he conceded, 'but you come and see it during the monsoon.' He pointed to the range of mountains to the west. 'That wall is over 600 metres high. Beyond it is the sea. It catches the monsoon clouds and makes them give up their water before they go any further. It is hard to believe that in the narrow basin of the Koyna, the rainfall can be as heavy as 762 centimetres. In the neighbouring valley a couple of miles further eastwards, it is less than 51 centimetres. You have no idea what 762 centimetres of rain is like! Once our dam is up we will store it all in this valley instead of letting it run into the Krishna and back into the sea without making any use of it. We have already bored a four-kilometre tunnel through the hill on the left to take the water and drop it over a thousand feet onto the turbines in the bowels of the mountain. We will have the biggest underground powerhouse in the world. We will be producing 240,000 kilowatts of electric power from this sixty-four-kilometre river. The city of Bombay will get all it wants for its new industries, and there will be some to spare for the smaller towns of Maharashtra.'

I had heard this sort of thing before: rainfall averages, heights and lengths of dams, kilowatts of energy, kilometres of canal, acres of irrigation etc. But every dam has so much in common with others and something which is unique to itself. Three features make Koyna unique. Its four-kilometre tunnel through a mountain, and the 4,267-metre drop (all within the mountain) is one. Its underground powerhouse, the largest in the world, is another. Its setting is the third. Without doubt it is located in the most beautiful countryside I have hitherto seen. And when the dam is up next year, the expanse of blue water (there is no silt or mud in the hill torrent), the mountains and the lush green jungle, and the fresh sea breeze will make Koyna the most sought-after hill station in India.

◆

The next thing to do was to see the fabulous powerhouse and the tunnels. For these we had to drive round the mountain and drop to its base at a place called Pophali. Here huge caverns were being plastered to house the turbines and generators. From those we went up the mountain again to see a part of the four-kilometre tunnel which is practically completed. Here they explained why the powerhouse has not been built at the foot of the dam as in the case of other projects. The drop hill was not big enough. On the other side, the base of the mountain is at sea level and the water can be dropped several hundred metres more than the dam would allow. At a later stage however it is proposed to build a small powerhouse at the dam and use the water for irrigation.

◆

One thing still remained to be examined. That was to find out the reactions of the villagers whose lands and homes were to be submerged by the lake. I drove up to Kamargaon and asked the villagers, 'What do you think of the Koyna project?' 'We have been sentenced to death,' said Rakhnaji. 'All 600 of us—men, women and children.' Rakhnaji was old and wizened; his pessimism was perhaps due to a bad liver.

I picked on a younger man—tall and powerfully built. With him was a boy in his early teens. They were uncle and nephew. 'What do you think of all this?' I asked them.

The uncle—Ramchandra Chalke—remarked, 'Twenty-five years ago Tata Company wanted to make a dam here and the British tried to acquire land on their behalf. We launched a satyagraha and did not let them do anything. Now we are free, we don't mind. If the mills of Bombay want electric power to make things for India and our villages have to be drowned, we don't care. We will take whatever they give us—and we are happy with what has been promised.'

The assembly murmured assent.

'You are a strange people,' I said with exasperation. 'A few minutes ago you said the Koyna had passed a death sentence on Kamargaon and all of you. Now you say it is a good thing because it will bring riches to the country.'

Krishna Chalke explained away the contradiction with charming naiveté. He slapped his chest manfully and said 'We are Marathas, we like to die for our country.'

◆

We left Koyna a little before sunset. Within a few minutes we were back in the rugged hills with their Maratha forts and weird banyan trees. The shades of twilight gathered the countryside in its fold. A new moon looking like a finely pared fingernail came up over the crest of the hill. 'Look, the Id moon!' I announced excitedly to my companions in the jeep. 'We have no Muslims with us or we could greet them.'

'Our chauffeur is a Muslim,' replied my escort. I had not realized that. He looked a Maratha and spoke Marathi. I put out my hand to him. 'Id Mubarak.'

'Not like this,' he replied with a broad smile. He pulled over. Then in the light of the stars and the pale crescent moon, and under the ghostly watch of the hill fortresses where Mughal and Maratha had fought each other over the centuries, the Muslim chauffeur took each of us—Hindu, Sikh and Christian—in his embrace and pressed us to his heart. 'Id Mubarak, Id Mubarak.'

The new India of my dreams had at long last been born.

(*1958*)

THE MAID OF MAHI

I had never heard of Mahi till I got to Mahi. I did not even know whether it was the name of a man or a woman, a town or a mountain peak. I now know that it is the name of a river—a small but important river which pierces through the heart of the district of Kaira in Gujarat and runs into the Gulf of Cambay. What is more, I also know that the peasantry living about its banks is amongst the handsomest and the toughest I have seen in India. They have always been tough because the legend goes that anyone who drinks the waters of the Mahi takes to a career of violence. The word 'Mewasi', which stands for 'dacoit', is derived from 'Mahivasi'—inhabitants of the banks of the Mahi. The region has a long record of defiance of the law. During Mughal rule, state treasuries were looted here and most people gave the land of Mahi a wide berth. The Mahivasis were also the first people in India to launch a civil disobedience movement against the British.

Mahi will always remain etched in my memory, not because of the big canal they have made or the rugged scenery of scrub, sand and rock, but because of a chance meeting with sweet, unaffected and uncommonly attractive Lakhibehn. I named her the Maid of Mahi. Let me tell you how I met her and why I gave her that name.

It was the month of May, and the previous three days had been exceedingly hot. We left Nadiad in the early hours of the morning to get the day's touring done before it became unbearable. But by the time we got to Wanakbori, the sun was right overhead, blazing fiercely on the parched and dusty countryside. We saw neither man nor beast in the fields. At Wanakbori the executive engineer, Mr Padhye, gave me a long discourse on the project. His office was cooled with khus chiks on which water was splashed every few minutes. It was a much pleasanter way of learning about the Mahi canal than going out of doors and seeing it.

Mr Padhye told me about the Mahi rising from the Malwa Hills of the Aravalli range (on the other side of the Chambal) and running through barren desert country down to the sea. During the monsoon when the peasants did not need water, it had plenty to give; for the rest of the year when the land thirsted for every drop, the Mahi had nothing to offer. There had been floods and famines followed by much palaver about what ought to be done. But like many other projects, it did not go beyond discussions and blueprints till Independence. A pilot project was started in 1951. Investigations went on for another two years. Work was really started in 1954. And last June, the kilometre-long weir at Wanakbori had at long last diverted the water to the seventy-four-kilometre canal to feed 3,462 square kilometres of parched agricultural land. By the time Mr Padhye had finished, I was almost dozing in my chair breathing the cool air smelling of khus and the damp earth. 'Now I suppose you would like to see the weir and the canal,' said Mr Padhye abruptly rising from his chair. I did not. But there was no choice.

It was the hottest time of the day. The glare and the heat had shrivelled up everything. We came to the bridge over the canal. Bulldozers chugged away, eating up the sides to give it its sixteen and a half metre width and five metre depth. The sluice gates designed and made at Khadakwasla had been put in their places. The weir was practically up to its twenty-one metre height and waited for the river to fill it up. But there was little water in the river. Only the dry rock and the yellow earth which the sun had raised to scorching heat.

I wanted to get back to the office with its ceiling fan and splash of cool spray through the khus chiks. Then the sound of laughter attracted my attention. A group of young labourers was filling wheelbarrows with sand. They wore nothing except their loin cloths; the beads of sweat on their brown bodies shimmered like quicksilver. In their midst was a woman wielding her spade like a man and exhorting the menfolk to keep going. When we came closer to the party they stopped work to look at us. She was a young girl—barely seventeen. She smiled and laughed with the gay abandon of a child. And she was utterly unconscious of her dazzling beauty.

I asked her timidly if I could take a photograph. 'And why not,' she answered. She slung her spade across her shoulder like a soldier with his rifle. I took my photograph. 'Chalo apane kam pachhum sharu kariya (Come, let us resume work),' she shouted triumphantly to her mates and they went back to filling the wheelbarrows. The papers had been reporting the temperatures as 45 °C; there had been many deaths in the region from heat and sunstroke. At the Wanakbori weir there was no shade and yet instead of death, there was life and laughter and beauty.

I went across the bridge to visit one of the eight villages which had been shifted from the river bank to higher levels. This was a hamlet called Jhakoria where lived thirty-five families of Chauhan Rajputs. Here too there was life. Wedding celebrations were going on. Two young Jhakorians were being taken round the village by a group of women. They had a mobile awning spread over their heads which they kept up with a dagger. The headman informed me in a whisper that the families had done well in the exchange of land. What was true of Jhakoria was true of the 2,000 other peasants who had had to shift their villages.

I returned to the weir to have one more look at the girl working in the blazing sun. We had been away more than an hour. When we came back to the weir she was still there shouting to the boys to get on with the work. Her cheerful voice rose above the chug-chug of the bulldozers and the hammering of stonemasons. I stopped by her once more. 'Can I take another photograph?' I asked her.

She looked at me a little suspiciously. 'Why, isn't one enough?'

'I am a very bad photographer and the last one may be bad.'

The suspicion vanished. She smiled again and bared a row of pearly white teeth. 'All right, just one more.'

I clicked my camera and took out my notebook.

'What is your name?'

'Lakhibehn.'

'Are you married?'

She blushed deeply. The boys standing about her sniggered. She turned on them like a spitfire. 'Tame tamarun kaam ka (Mind your own business).' She did not answer my question. I tried to help her out.

'What is your father's name?'

She continued looking at the ground and turning awkwardly like an embarrassed child.

'Whose daughter shall I say you are in my paper?'

She looked up at last and smiled again. She pointed to the little silvery trickle going through the black rocks and answered in one word, 'Mahi.'

(*1958*)

REMAKING A VILLAGE

Last week I met two men as far apart from each other in their outlook and way of living as any two men living in the same village can be. One was a schoolmaster. He had a degree and, apart from a passionate love for Persian and Urdu poetry, his only other interest was social work. He spent all his spare time holding evening classes and getting the villagers to build a school and a community centre. He had a large family of ten children. He wanted each one of them to follow him in doing only social work. The schoolmaster had no land or private property of his own. What is more, he couldn't be more indifferent to money. He was Gandhian in his way of living, and extremely self-denying. This was Mahinder Singh, aged forty-four, known to Dulley and all the villages around as Masterji.

The other man was sixty-five-year-old Harnam Singh. He was completely illiterate and didn't think that knowledge of the alphabet was worth a brass button. He believed in making money. He tried to make it by running a taxi in Calcutta, and then another one on the Kalka-Simla road. That did not give him enough; so he opened a country liquor and opium stall near the famous Mughal Gardens at Pinjore, six and a half kilometres from Kalka on the Kalka-Delhi Road. He did better selling cheap alcohol and opium to innocent villagers. Then he took over the contract of Pinjore Garden fruit. The garden was owned by the Maharaja of Patiala and was looked after by a famous gardener called Mian Barkat. Mian Barkat was given to the bottle and soon became Harnam Singh's best customer. In a drunken stupor he spilt the secret art of mango-growing to Harnam Singh. Harnam Singh began to give him liquor free of charge and memorized all he could of Mian Barkat's instructions. After three years he closed the liquor and opium shop and returned to his village Dulley in the district of Ludhiana.

Harnam Singh gave up his good agricultural land in the consolidation and accepted a sandy pampas-infested tract outside the village. He went to Uttar Pradesh and bought a vast variety of mango cuttings. Within a few years the teaching of Mian Barkat bore fruit and Harnam Singh was growing 38 varieties of the succulent fruit amongst his 330 trees. He got 200 saplings from each tree, which he sold at Rs 2 each. He also planted orange, lemon, guava and pomegranate trees. When there was no more room for trees, he bought eggs from a breeder and started rearing Leghorns, Rhode Islands and Hampshires. Both the orchard and the poultry were reared with the most modern methods—fertilizers, insecticides, injections etc. Harnam Singh has achieved his goal—he has made the money he wanted to.

The only thing common between the idealist schoolmaster and the earthy Harnam Singh was that they belonged to the same village and both wanted to do something for it. Although the schoolmaster owned no land (a matter of considerable importance in a land-owning society) and was not even a Jat, he was the obvious choice as a leader. He was elected sarpanch. Under his guidance, Dulley paved its streets, put up street lamps at all corners, built a community centre with a reading room, set up a weaving centre, a primary school, a children's park and finally a large school for the girls of Dulley and thirteen neighbouring villages. The example set by Harnam Singh encouraged other villagers to follow in his footsteps. Agricultural production in the village shot up.

The attitude of the two men to this achievement is as different as it could be. I asked the schoolmaster what it felt like to have dedicated one's life for the betterment of others. He sighed and came out with an Urdu couplet: 'If I am spared the pangs of passion this time, I swear never to fall in love again,' he quoted. 'I should have made some money,' he continued, 'and given my family more comfort and a better education.'

The wealthy Harnam Singh was equally regretful about his past. 'If I had not wasted my time plying taxis and selling dope to stupid people, I would have seen my orchard in full bloom. (It takes a mango tree twenty years to come into its best.) But I wanted to make money for my son. I made it. Now I want to give it all away to the people.'

(*1958*)

SNAKES DOWN THE SPILLWAY

Early this summer a strange phenomenon was seen in some villages in the Himalayas. One night the people were disturbed in their sleep by a noise of hissing, and nightmares that their homes and fields were overrun with snakes. When they woke up, they discovered to their horror that the terrifying dreams of the night before had turned to reality. There were snakes everywhere: in the gutters, on the footpaths, around the wells, even hanging down from the trees. They asked the elders for an explanation. They had nothing to say. Then someone noticed another even stranger phenomenon down in the valley. The river Sutlej which ran through a narrow gorge—looking very much like a slender silver serpent—was bloated like a python which had swallowed a gazelle. The monsoon had not started nor was there any news of the sudden thawing of snows. How could the river suddenly be in spate within a few hours? They asked the elders again. Again the elders shook their heads. No, they had never known the Sutlej so swollen nor ever seen as many snakes.

'It's the dam!' shouted an excited youngster.

'Don't be silly, boy!' reprimanded an elder. 'What can the dam have to do with it? They have been building it for the last ten years but it made no difference to the Sutlej. And what have snakes to do with the dam?'

'I know it is the dam,' persisted the youngster. 'Up till now they had the river flowing through two tunnels. Now they have blocked the tunnels and the dam is blocking the Sutlej. For the last many days they have been evacuating villages along the river. They never came here because we are too high up.'

It was obvious the boy knew what he was talking about. And while the villagers sat on the crest of the hill they could see the Sutlej slowly getting bigger and bigger. Within a few hours, the river had become a lake; by the afternoon the lake had become a sea.

The snakes continued coming up in larger numbers than before.

Several parties of villagers living in the higher parts of the Naina Devi range armed themselves with lathis and decided to go down to the dam and see for themselves. Everyone had a friend or relation amongst the 8,000 men who worked on the dam.

It was true. The dam which had been talked of for over fifty years had at last become a reality—not the entire 239 metres, but more than half of it was ready and there were cranes running along its dizzy heights busy filling up the rest of the gap in the 'V' made by the two sides of the mountain. Now there was no argument. But how high would the Sutlej rise and would their village on the top of the mountain also be submerged?

They approached a tall young man who was explaining the dam to a party of visitors. 'Two of the largest diversion tunnels in the world...highest rolled fill dam in India...longest belt conveyor system in Asia....the most modern concrete production factory in the world.' It sounded very impressive but meant little to the villagers. All they wanted to know was what was going to happen to the neighbouring villages which were being submerged and was all this worthwhile? And, of course, about the snakes.

'Babuji,' began an old man, 'the Englishman used to say you cannot build a dam here because the mountains are not strong and the Sutlej is too powerful. The Englishman was wise. Why has our sarkar built a dam in such a hurry?'

'We are not only building a dam,' answered the young man pompously, 'we are also building the mountains. You know we have been injecting 400 tonnes of concrete every hour into the mountains to make them strong! When the Englishman saw this place, he knew nothing of these things. Now these mountains will be like walls of steel. The Sutlej will form a eighty-eight and a half-kilometre-long lake—the Gobind Sagar—which will have enough drinking water for the whole country for one year and enough fish to feed our state. Then there will be electricity for the whole of the Punjab and millions of tonnes more of rice and wheat from the new lands which will receive water all the year round from the Gobind Sagar.'

'Yes, babuji, but what about our fellow villagers whose homes and lands are being drowned? Thirty thousand will be homeless!'

'Oh no! No one will be homeless. Everyone has been provided with more than twice the amount of land he has and is being paid all the transport costs. We moved thousands of them yesterday by army trucks and lorries. We have been telling them for a year to clear out, but they didn't till the water was over their thresholds.'

The young man had all his answers ready. 'Sir,' faltered the old man, 'perhaps you could tell us why there are so many snakes all of a sudden.'

'They were like the villagers who didn't believe and were flooded out of their holes. Many got away, many more were less lucky. Look down below,' he said, pointing down to the river. They looked. A mass of water was cascading down two enormous spillways into a turbulent froth at the base. Then there were whirlpools before the river went back to its placid self—but littered with long white strands—these were snakes which had been drowned and crushed on their way down the concrete spillway. 'That is the fate of non-believers and cynics,' he said, as pompous as ever.

(*1958*)

WINTER RAIN

Sometime during the night it begins to rain. In my half-sleep I hear thunder followed by the gentle pitter-patter of raindrops on the roof of the bungalow. I recall the words of a Punjabi peasant: 'Winter rain is like ghee. It puts life into withered crops, it turns wheat into gold.' I rise from my bed and open the window. A fragrant smell of earth floods the room. It is cold and damp—but is exhilarating.

I get into my clothes as fast as I can, wrap a muffler around my neck and go out into the veranda. The village level worker introduces himself: 'I am the VLW.' I shake his hand and get into his jeep. He remarks cheerfully: 'By the grace of the great Guru we have rain. We will have a bumper crop.'

Drip-drip of raindrops and the swish-swish of the windscreen wiper; grinding of gears and the squelch of tyres in the mud. And the drone of the VLW's voice: 'This village is Hindu Rajput…lazy, opium-eaters! This one is Goojur…cattle raisers and cattle thieves!… We've made it a key village to train them in modern methods of cattle breeding…these are Labanas…these are Rai Sikhs…the one we are going to visit is Jat and Mazhabi (Sikh untouchables)…tractors, harvesters, threshers, fertilizers, insecticides… They will try anything. In five years they have doubled their crop. The Guru was right when he said every Sikh would be a sava lakh (equal to Rs 125,000).' The VLW is a Sikh.

'What about factions?' I ask him.

'Factionalism is in the Punjabi peasants' blood. That and drink and litigation,' he replies without much concern.

We press on in the rain and slush through narrow paths lined by prickly pear and flowering ipomoea. We pass fields of green corn and solid blocks of cane. The VLW tells me about the agricultural targets of the fourth Five Year Plan. He says, 'Cooperative credit, yes. Cooperative stores, yes. Cooperative marketing, maybe. Cooperative farming, no.'

I reply, 'It has stopped raining.' He puts out his hand to make sure and switches off the windscreen wiper. We drive on for another mile or so before he pulls up in an open patch beside a mound. He orders a peasant with him to go ahead and inform the villagers of our arrival.

We stand on the mound and survey the scene. Far to the north the mists roll away to unveil the Shivalik range which looks washed and blue. All around us are fields of mustard in flower; blocks of cane and villages rise like islands out of a sea of canary-yellow. The sun breaks through the clouds; raindrops on the mustard sparkle like crystal and gold. Larks rise from the earth, suspend themselves in the blue sky and pour down a shower of song. A black partridge calls. The VLW tells me that the partridge is saying: 'Subhan teri kudrat (Lord, how wonderful is thy creation)!'

We stand entranced till the villagers come to fetch us. We accompany them to Gobindgarh. We pass under an archway of banana trees and a red cloth with 'Welcome' printed on it in golden letters in English. The sarpanch puts a garland of marigold flowers around my neck. The headman of the Mazhabi section of Gobindgarh puts another. Many villagers are introduced to me; they take both my hands in theirs.

They seat me on a chair and place a brass tumbler of tea and a tray full of hard boiled eggs in my lap. I sip the over-sweetened tea and nibble at an egg. They help themselves to the rest, drink tea in noisy gulps, belch and brush their whiskers with the backs of their hands.

I am taken on a tour of inspection of Gobindgarh. All the men and children of the village accompany me. Women stand in their doorways and stare at us. The VLW draws my attention to the brick paving of the street, the covered drain, the electric lamp, the new panchayatghar and janjghar (for wedding receptions) and the school. They stand on stilts like the buildings in Chandigarh nearby.

'Every child attends school; 100 per cent literacy,' the VLW assures me. 'Isn't that so?' he demands from the crowd. There is an awkward silence. Then somebody ventures to reply: 'Everyone except Shanghara's son Balkar, Banta's daughter Dipo and…' The rest of the information is smothered in a chorus led by the sarpanch. 'No, no, now they all come to school.'

The VLW points out the latrines built for men and women and tells me of the changing habits of villagers. The latrines are clean and without odour. Nobody uses them.

We come to the poorer section of the village. We pass under another banana tree archway with 'Welcome' again in English. More marigold garlands and handshakes. Here the houses are smaller, some are made of mud instead of brick. They belong to Mazhabis. 'The Sikhs don't believe in caste and untouchability,' the VLW informs me. Nevertheless, the Mazhabi Sikhs have their own drinking water well and even their own temple. And the Mazhabis do not offer us anything to eat or drink lest we say, 'No, thank you'.

We call on a pensioner who is the oldest person in the village. Pala Singh is over ninety. His skin is black and glossy ('Because of the opium he takes everyday,' someone tells me.) His beard is parted in the middle of his chin, the sides curling into his turban. He wears thick bifocals. His shrivelled chest bears a row of medals. He straightens himself to give a military salute. He seats me beside him on his charpoy and begins to croak. I catch a few words, 'Sikh pioneers...Malika Biktoria (Queen Victoria)...Jaaraj Panjum (George V)...Mesopotamia.'

He goes on about the good old days of the British Raj, when men were men and rulers knew how to rule. Somebody yells in Pala Singh's ear to tell me of the letters he writes to Buckingham Palace. He knows they are making fun of him, but he tells me of the one-rupee notes he sent with the invitations to the weddings of his children, grandchildren and great grandchildren to his sovereign in London. They snigger, they laugh. Pala Singh takes off his glasses and with the end of his turban wipes a nostalgic tear running down his face into his beard.

We have been out some hours and I am hungry. I am escorted back to the sarpanch's house. A dozen elders join me in a repast of makki ki roti and sarson ka saag topped with butter. We eat with relish. We wash it down with tumblerfuls of buttermilk. The elders belch and take their leave. I feel like one drugged and crave permission to sleep it off. I stretch myself out on a charpoy.

It is warm. The sarpanch's mother brings out her spinning wheel.

The daughter-in-law grabs one of her children to pick lice out of his hair. The flour mill starts up; it sounds like the calls of a cuckoo. The hum of the spinning wheel and the monotone of the women's voices lull me to slumber. But even in my sleep I catch the smell of the mustard flower and cane juice being boiled into gur as it wafts into the sun-drenched courtyard.

A sudden chill awakens me. The sun has set. The sarpanch is milking his buffaloes; his wife is firing the oven with camel thorn to bake chapattis for the evening meal. Peacocks have come back from the fields and are screaming at each other across the rooftops. The jujube tree is alive with the twittering of sparrows. Children are shouting at each other; their mothers shout for them to come home. Dogs bark in the deepening twilight. From the gurudwara comes the chanting of the evening prayer followed by drumbeats. The congregation explodes with shouts of 'Sat Sri Akal'.

(*1968*)

THIS LITTLE VAIKUNTHA

When the pace of life becomes too hectic I recommend a long weekend in Haridwar. Here, although man has done his worst, he has mercifully failed to ruin the grandeur of the scene: the beautiful Shivalik Hills with the Ganga cavorting down the valleys. Crystal clear, blue and emerald green. In the daytime, sparkling in the sunshine, at night, reflecting the stars or the silver of the moonlight. In springtime the woods are bright with the red of the simul and flame of the forest. Only twelve kilometres upstream at Raiwala I've heard the tiger's mating call, woken to the crowing of the jungle fowl and seen fresh, steaming, cannon-ball-size blobs of dung left by wild elephants. It's Jim Corbett country.

Haridwar is at its best after sunset. And the best spot is Har ki Pauri. The ugly clock tower and uglier statuary (Madan Mohan Malaviya and a five-foot-nothing Netaji) are blurred. You cannot see the fat pandits rummaging in the water for the gold from the teeth of the dead whose ashes are immersed in the water. All you see are scores of tiny oil lamps floating down the dark stream. As dusk falls, temple bells begin to clang and conch shells trumpet to announce the time of worship of the holy Ganga. Clusters of flaming brass lamps are waved in aarti. The river glows. Hundreds of massive carp are attracted by the light. It is blissful beyond compare.

But Haridwar is, as the cliché goes, being fast put on the tourist map of India. Dak bungalows, rest houses, motels, cafeterias—all listed in the most hilariously worded brochures put out by the government of Uttar Pradesh. Every time I go to Haridwar I make a fervent prayer to Ganga Mai: 'Please let no one spoil this little Vaikuntha at least during my lifetime!'

(*1972*)

YANKS AT KHAJURAHO

The vast entourage of press, radio and tellymen that President Nixon took with him to Peking reminds me of my own brief encounter with the party that accompanied President Eisenhower on his visit to India. Our External Affairs Ministry arranged to fly them to Agra and Khajuraho. 'You know the Yanks,' said Somnath Chib, the then Director of Tourism. 'You be their guide for the day.' By the time I was able to round them up from their hotels, the day was well advanced. The pilot was in a bad temper and told me that I had to make up my mind between Agra and Khajuraho; we did not have time for both. I opted for Khajuraho. But I persuaded him to fly us over Agra so that they could at least have a glimpse of the Taj.

The Americans I know are academics. I have great respect for their knowledge and their general bonhomie. American pressmen are a different breed. This lot was not interested in anything outside their work. It was their day off and they were not going to be pumped full of stuff they could not file for their papers. I tried to speak to them many times over the microphone and tell them what we were going to see. They ignored me and continued to exchange reminiscences of their tour.

We circled over the Taj. They took out their cameras and clicked away for all they were worth. Even from a thousand feet in the sky it compelled attention. They took out their notebooks. 'Who did you say built it?'

'Shah Jahan. He was—'

'You mind spelling his name?'

I spelt out his name. 'Shah Jahan built it in memory—'

'How much did it cost?'

'I haven't a clue,' I replied, very exasperated, and gave up.

At Khajuraho the state director of archaeology took over the task of conducting the party. His attempt at presenting the history of the temples was no more successful than mine on the Taj. Then suddenly one of the boys spotted an erotic piece.

'Hey, Bawb! Look at that one!' he yelled, pointing to the panel. 'Jeezuz!'

They saw more, fixed telephoto lenses to take pictures and clamoured for information. The director got a captive audience. He explained the 'mystic' significance of sex and the many forms in which it found expression. Fellatio and...

'How do you spell that?'

The director spelt out the necessary words and proceeded to explain why the figure of a girl tossing a ball recurred on every panel. His learned exposition was lost in a guffaw of laughter; he did not know that the singular turned to a plural could change the meaning of an innocent English word into genitalia.

On the way back to Delhi, the man in the seat beside me handed me his visiting card and asked me if we worshipped 'all those sexy goings-on'.

'We certainly do not,' I replied emphatically.

'You try them at home?'

'No, do you?'

'Kreest! The missus would want to know where I'd picked up such crazy ideas,' he replied with a laugh. He fished out his wallet and showed me pictures of his missus and four smiling children. 'I sure am going to try them when we stop by in Paris!'

(*1972*)

GOD IS AN ITALIAN

God must be Northern Italian because Northern Italy is God's own country. The reason why I deify this part of the world is because here you see both the divine and the human at their best. The landscape consists of high mountains with snow on their peaks and the bluest of blue lakes in the embrace of their valleys. Villages built on the slopes blend into the hillside as if the Creator had himself raised them. Even modern towns that line the sides of the lakes—Maggiore, Como, Garda and innumerable small ones—have been fashioned by man in full awareness of the grandeur of the scenery.

Dr Samuel Johnson was of the opinion that a man who had not been to Italy would always be conscious of being an inferior person. I do not have to suffer from any such complex because I have just spent a three-week working vacation on the Como. The memory will abide with me for the rest of my days and perhaps even after. I could say with Browning: 'Open my heart and you will see, / Graved inside of it, "Italy".'

Villa Serbelloni on the Como was the estate of a wealthy American lady of the Rockefeller clan who married an indigent Italian nobleman. She left her mansion, hundreds of acres of vineyards, orchards and a vast dollop of dollars for the use of scholars, scientists, composers, poets and novelists. Her motive was to free them from the daily chores of housekeeping so that they could devote themselves solely to the pursuit of their disciplines. The director, Dr Olsen, an eminent professor, and his charming lady, Betsy, see to it that you have no excuse not to work. Everything—and by that I mean literally everything—is taken care of to give you the most luxuriant style of living you can find anywhere on the globe. 'What did you do to earn this kind of bounteous living?' ask my Indian friends. I have no answer except that it was in my karma. 'In my last life I saved the life of a Brahmin and a cow.'

Not all who came to the shores of the Como found it as paradisal as I. There was Benito Mussolini. Across the lake from Serbelloni is a plaque which marks the site where Il Duce was strung upside down and his mistress Clara Petacci had her mouth stuffed with the dictator's genitals. But then Mussolini was a cow-eater and a Jew-baiter.

It was in these sylvan surroundings that I spent my holidays struggling to finish a novel I have been working on for six long years. I closed my windows to the sunshine, the blue skies and the fragrance of honeysuckle to sit under the light of a table lamp, slogging from the time when church bells tolled for matins till I heard them peal the angelus. Who says writing is fun? Who says it must await the Muse? For me it's always been, as the cliché goes, 99 per cent perspiration and 1 per cent inspiration. And at the end, it hardly seems to have been worth the trouble. However, there is always the consolation that, although there is not much joy in the making and the publisher may well throw the manuscript into the wastepaper basket, I will be able to say to myself: 'Old chap, you had the best chance; you tried, you just haven't got it in you.'

From Como to Rome and into the arms of the comely Senorita Grazia Marciano, looking radiant in her saffron head scarf, kurta and lungi, with the picture of Acharya Rajneesh dangling from her necklace. Here's one person whose heart will always be graved with the word 'India'. She drove me round to the sights of her beautiful city—the Vatican, the Spanish steps, the Trevi and other fountains; she fed me pasta and Chianti—but all her talk was about India: meditation, yoga, Acharyaji. She waved her hand towards the animated bustle in the piazza and said in a tone of conviction: 'All this means nothing to me.'

(*1972*)

OPERATION TIGER

In a forest rest house lost in a densely wooded valley of the Aravalli range near Alwar, half a dozen naturalists foregather to devise ways to preserve what remains of our tigers. It is as good a place to meet as any. This is Sariska, a wildlife sanctuary. Within 500 square kilometres of hill and dale and boulder-strewn streams survive a few thousand head of blue bull, sambar, cheetal and wild pig. Of the hundreds of tigers that could be found here in the days of the Alwar Raj, barely fourteen remain. As far as wild animals are concerned, they were better off under the British and the maharajas than under the rulers of free India. Freedom gave Indians licence to kill off their country's fauna. It is abundantly clear that at the rate man continues to multiply and devour the earth, the only way that animals that do not serve him as food or pets can survive is to be put behind iron bars, as in zoos or sanctuaries, safe from his depredations.

Sariska is a good example of the problems facing game wardens charged with the duty of curbing man's ravenous appetite to destroy. The game sanctuary lies halfway between Delhi and Jaipur in hauntingly beautiful country. The volume of traffic increases every year—cars, trucks, buses, scooters, transistor radios, picnickers, boisterous school and college students whose notion of fun is making noise and litter. It is not the atmosphere in which animals can relax and multiply.

Jai Singh, game warden, tells me that his chief problem is human intrusion into the sanctuary. There are two tiny hamlets within the sanctuary with no more than thirty or forty families each. But these hamlets have completely upset the even, symbiotic pattern of wildlife. Men cut up wood, women cut grass, children graze buffaloes in pastures, buffaloes frighten off deer and make easy targets for tigers, who are then poisoned by villagers. The only way to save the tiger and other wildlife in sanctuaries, says Jai Singh, is to keep man out of them: 'Let them in at certain hours on a permit and then throw them out!'

Meanwhile, I almost saw my first live tiger in its near natural habitat. The bandobast was very pucca. The dialogue between Thakur Jai Singh and his men went in Rajasthani style as follows:

'You'll tie the bait near the pool by the watch tower.'

'Hukum.'

'You'll put the Sardarji in the watch tower and tuck him into bed.'

'Hukum.'

'When the tiger makes the kill, you'll awaken the Sardarji and flash the searchlight on the tiger.'

'Hukum.'

So a poor buffalo calf, with eyes as large and doleful as Padmini's was tied near the pool and I was tucked into a bed from which I could see it.

I could not get any sleep. I awaited the tiger's growl, Padmini's, bleat and the sound of her poor neck snapping. Many a time I got up and peered out. I could see grey forms of nilgai and sambar stag drinking at the pool. I could see the black blob of Padmini awaiting her doom. Once I stole out onto the balcony and saw my guide fast asleep in his quilt. Came the dawn with the crying of peacocks and the calling of langurs. I was relieved to see Padmini alive.

Later in the day, I heard the guide explain the absence of the tiger.

'He was there all right! I heard the cheetal give the warning cry. Even the buffalo smelt him and began to bleat. He prowled about, but when he heard human sounds he moved away. That Sardarji snored so loudly no animal would come near the place!'

(*1973*)

AMRITSAR

Our evening prayers always concluded with a short invocation to the Great Guru: 'Grant us the gift of thy holy name. Grant us ablution in the sacred pool of Amritsar.'

It was not the Great Guru who granted me the gift of his holy name but my grandmother who would not give me supper till I had said my prayers. And in his divine wisdom the Great Guru did not let me visit Amritsar till I was sixteen years old. Meanwhile my expectations were heightened by tales told by those who had been to the holy city. They said that lepers who bathed in the pool were cleansed of their loathsome disease; crows that dipped into it turned white; some even claimed to have seen the silver-white falcon of the last of our ten gurus (who had been murdered over 250 years ago) alight on the pinnacle of the temple dome and then disappear into the blue heavens. They brought back bottles full of water from the sacred pool; we received a few drops in the palms of our hands joined together, gulped them down, and then reverently smeared our eyes and foreheads with our damp hands. They brought a few morsels of dried chapattis and dal from the temple kitchen, which we ate as if it were manna. Some brought bracelets made of steel, combs made of ivory and small daggers—all emblems of the Sikh faith—and gave them to their favourite children.

Though only a little over 400 years old, Amritsar is to us Sikhs the mother of all cities. What Jerusalem is to the Jews, Rome to the Catholics and Mecca to the Muslims, Amritsar is to the Sikhs: it is their most important place of pilgrimage, the scene of many of the most important events in the 500 years of their troubled history, and the seat of authority from which religious and political encyclicals are issued.

I was in the first year at university when I first went to Amritsar. I cannot now recall whether it was what I had imagined it as a child to be. But the visit remains indelibly imprinted on the tablet of my memory.

I was escorting my mother, who wished to have prayers said for the soul of her father who had died a few weeks earlier. We emerged from the crowded railway station in the early hours of a winter morning. Those days there were no taxis in Amritsar; only pony-drawn two-wheeled tongas. There was a scuffle between tonga drivers till the victor herded us and the porters carrying our baggage to his vehicle. Before I could bargain with the driver the tonga was on the move. 'Where to?' the tonga wallah demanded.

'Durbar Sahib—the court of the holy one. How...?'

'That'll be four rupees,' he snapped, lashing his skinny horse on the flanks. 'Come on, son, like the wind.'

The pony broke into a gentle trot. We found ourselves going through narrow, serpentine bazaars with balconies almost touching each other above our heads. There was barely enough room for our tonga. We had to contend with other tongas, motor cars, pedestrians, cyclists and herds of cows and buffaloes. The driver perched himself on the beam of the tonga and stuck the wooden end of his whip into the spokes of the wheel to produce a rattle. His voice did the rest: 'Look out, babuji... Sister! Sister! See where you are going! Oi, you blind one, does the angel of death hover over you?' To the buffaloes: 'Durreh, durreh, may a snake bite you!' And then again to his pony: 'Shabash, son. Like the wind.'

The tortuous ride ended at a confluence of bazaars facing a clock tower. By the time I had paid off the tonga wallah we were surrounded by beggars and coolies. A blind woman held her bowl under my mother's chin: 'May the Guru grant you seven sons!' A leper dug his stump into my ribs: 'May the Guru grant all your wishes. May your pen write cheques of lakhs of rupees.'

The coolies who had grabbed our luggage pushed their way through the throng of beggars with us following on their heels. They dumped our trunks and bedding rolls outside an enclosure. We checked in our luggage with our shoes. My mother brought a leaf-cup full of rose petals and marigolds. We washed our feet in a cistern full of dirty, muddy water and gingerly walked over slippery marble slabs towards the entrance. Suddenly the temple burst into view. A few feet below us was a large, squarish pool of water; in the middle of this pool was an edifice of white marble topped with a large golden dome and minarets. It looked as if on a plate of lapis lazuli someone had placed a jewel box made of pearls, topped with nuggets of burnished gold. I gaped at it spellbound. My mother shut her eyes and mumbled her prayers. She went down on her knees and made obeisance, rubbing her forehead on the cold marble. When she rose, her eyes were brimming with tears.

We went down the marble steps and alongside the pool. There were several small shrines marking the site of some martyrdom or other event in the history of the temple. My mother made obeisance at each one and sprinkled a few rose petals. We came to another gate leading to the marble causeway which ran through the pool. At every threshold my mother ran her palms over the floor to take the dust of pilgrims' feet and put it across her forehead. And so we made our way to the sanctum sanctorum. It was packed with worshippers. In the centre under a gold canopy was the sacred scripture, the Granth Sahib; on one side a party of hymn singers singing to the accompaniment of harmoniums and tabla drums. Men and women sat facing each other separated by a passage through which a never-ending stream of worshippers came to make their obeisance and offerings of money and flowers before the sacred book. We could find no place to sit and allowed ourselves to be pushed along. We went up a short flight of stairs; on either side, the marble was festooned with floral designs embedded with semi-precious stones like carnelian and serpentine. The roof was studded with mirrors and the walls had frescoes depicting the lives of our gurus. At the rear of the inner shrine a few steps led into the pool: this was the Har ki pauri (steps of the Lord). Like other pilgrims, my mother filled her palms with the water, drank deep draughts and splashed it on her face. She filled the two bottles she had brought with her to take home. We retraced our steps over the marble causeway to circumambulate the pool. All along were men taking their ritual dip, their long hair knotted in buns and beards dripping with water. My mother went into the women's enclosure while I sat at a distance watching the grey shadows of the monstrous-sized carp in the pool. I saw my mother descend fully clothed into the icy cold water, hold her nostrils between her fingers and immerse herself. Once, twice, seven times—once each for her five children, once for her husband and lastly for herself. A few minutes later she came out radiant with a pink glow on her face, loudly chanting:

> In Ram Das's sacred pool
> have I bathed
> All my sins have been
> washed away

Ram Das (1534–81), the fourth of the ten gurus, acquired land in 1577 CE to build a new town. He started by excavating a tank and filling it with water from a canal that ran nearby. The place came to be known as Ram Daspura after him. Ram Das was succeeded by his son, Arjun, as the fifth guru. Arjun (1563–1606) invited merchants and tradesmen to settle at Ram Daspura. He built a temple in the middle of the tank and, having compiled the Granth, installed it in the temple. Thereafter Ram Daspura came to be known as Amritsar, the 'Pool of Immortality', and the temple as Durbar Sahib. This Sikh temple was unlike Hindu temples. Instead of being on a high plinth as Hindu temples were, Arjun built it at a low level, so that the worshippers would have to go down the steps to enter it. And, unlike Hindu temples, which had only one entrance, Arjun had the Harmandir open on all four sides. These architectural features were intended to be symbolic of the new faith which required the lowest of worshippers of God to go even lower and a temple whose doors were ever open to all who wished to enter. The four doors represented the four castes of Hindus. 'The teaching is for all the four castes, the Brahmin (priest), the Kshatriya (warrior), Vaishya (tradesman) and the Shudra (worker),' wrote Arjun.

The temple built by Arjun was destroyed by Muslim invaders and rebuilt many times over. When the Sikhs became the rulers of the Punjab, their maharaja, Ranjit Singh (1749–1839 CE), had it built in its present form—in marble and with domes and minarets of gilded copper. An inscription above the entrance of the central shrine reads:

> The Great Guru in his wisdom looked upon Maharaja Ranjit Singh as his chief servitor and Sikh. And in his benevolence, bestowed on him the privilege of serving the temple.

Amritsar, despite being the Mecca of the Sikhs, had few Sikh inhabitants. When the British annexed their kingdom in 1849 the Sikhs formed no more than 10 per cent of the population of the city; the rest were Hindus and Muslims in somewhat equal proportion. It was only in the bloody riots and arson at the time of the partition of the country into India and Pakistan in 1947 that the Muslims of the city were driven out to Pakistan to make way for Hindu and Sikh refugees streaming into India in their hundreds of thousands. Many bazaars had been burnt down. This proved to be a blessing in disguise: the roads were widened, the area surrounding the Golden Temple including the clock tower was levelled to provide space for an archive, a museum-cum-picture gallery and reception room for visitors. Since Sikhs now came to form almost half the population of the city, the traffic to the temple has increased manifold. Besides, Amritsar also became a frontier town, the Pakistan border being only thirty-two kilometres to the northwest. Its small cantonment became one of the biggest and most important in the country. A substantial proportion of the Indian army continues to be Sikh. Amritsar in fact became three cities in one: the old city around the Golden Temple contained within the remains of battlements of ancient Sikh times; adjoining it a garden city known as the civil lines comprising spacious bungalows for civilian officers, well-to-do businessmen, doctors and lawyers; and the cantonment.

◆

On a more recent visit I went to Amritsar by air. An hour after we took off from New Delhi the 'fasten seat belts' sign lit up on the panel above the front seat and the captain's voice came over the public address system to inform us that before landing he was going to fly over the city and give us a bird's-eye view of the Golden Temple.

The vast flat khaki plain that had stretched endlessly from Delhi was suddenly turned into lush emerald green paddy fields and blocks of sugarcane. There were several tanks of water linked to each other by a network of water-channels. Villages were dotted about everywhere. And suddenly we were flying over a densely packed mass of mud and brick, a veritable anthill of humanity. In the centre of this crazy huddle of houses and bazaars was the huge squarish pool of deep blue water and in its middle glittered the Golden Temple. The plane did not fly directly overhead—that would be disrespectful to Sikh sentiment—but circled round at an angle giving us an excellent view.

I had been invited to speak at the convocation of the newly set-up Guru Nanak University, named after the founder of Sikhism, Nanak. I spent the morning going round the campus, which is ten kilometres from the centre of the city. Thereafter I went to Khalsa College which is close by. Then, like any Sikh would, I drove up to the Golden Temple.

Prakash Singh, the public relations officer of the temple, was an old friend. Apart from conducting parties of tourists and handing out literature on Sikhism, he edited a Gurmukhi monthly dedicated to the exposition of Sikh history and religion. He was a somewhat unusual Sikh—young, erudite, sophisticated and yet devoutly religious. I entered unannounced and found him surrounded by a motley collection of European boys and girls, all very bronzed, and grubby in their leather jerkins and shorts. Most of the boys sported blond beards, and hair which could have done with some trimming. And all of them could have done with a good scrubbing in the sacred pool. Prakash Singh leapt up from his chair, made a gesture of touching my feet, then embraced me warmly. He introduced me to his 'Dutch and German friends' and then dismissed them. 'Remember to wash your feet before you go in; have your heads covered and on no account carry any tobacco. And when you've been around come back to my office and I'll take you to the Guru's kitchen for lunch. We feed several thousand pilgrims every day. It's quite a sight.' The boys and girls murmured words of thanks and obediently filed out of the room.

'Well,' he said, patting his beard, 'what brings you to Amritsar?'

'Spouting Sikhism to students who know more about it than I. I don't envy your job instructing foreigners who probably don't know the difference between a Sikh and a Sheikh.'

'Well,' he said pensively, 'there are many ways of looking at things. Without having to go abroad I meet people from all over the world. That can be fun. But I do get bored answering silly questions: practically everyone wants to know if the colour of the turban means anything and why all Sikhs are called Singhs. I give them the answers before they put the questions—'No, sir, the colour of the turban means nothing. Our tenth and last guru Guru Gobind Singh (1660–1708) converted the pacifist Sikhs into a militant brotherhood he called the Khalsa, or the pure. He made us swear never to cut our hair or beards and gave us all one surname—Singh—which means lion. But though all Khalsa Sikhs are Singhs, all Singhs are not Khalsa Sikhs. Lots of Hindus bear the same name. You must have had to answer such questions when you are abroad.'

'Most of the time girls want to know whether I sleep in my turban.'

'What do you say?'

'I invite them to come and find out for themselves.'

He roared with laughter. 'If I said anything like that, they'd fire me.'

Prakash Singh insisted that I visit the new picture gallery. 'I'll introduce you to Kirpal Singh, our artist. He has painted most of them. He will take you around.'

I followed him up the stairs of the picture gallery. The three rooms in which paintings and relics of the Sikh period were on display were jammed with peasants. Prakash Singh asked one of the keepers to fetch Kirpal Singh from his studio. Sikhs do not have a great reputation in the realm of arts ('The only culture they have is agriculture,' said a Sikh-baiter once). I was curious to meet the man through whose brush the vision of the past was recreated for a whole generation of Sikhs. Would he be a frail man with long, tapering fingers?

Kirpal Singh was a world away from my concept of a painter. Although he was a handsome man with a raven black beard and sparkling eyes, there was nothing artistically frail about him. His dress was eccentric. He sported a spotlessly white turban. The rest of his person was draped in funereal black. 'I have renounced the world,' he explained, somewhat naively. 'I will dedicate the rest of my life to telling the saga of Sikh heroism through my pictures. Some people wear saffron to indicate renunciation. I wear black because black is more symbolic of death...death in life.' It was the sort of irony Indians are fond of indulging in. Even more inexplicable was a massive axe which he carried in his hand. Its silver blade gleamed through the folds of his black gown. 'Oh that!' he said, baring a row of white teeth, 'I just like having it with me.'

We turned to view the paintings. An attendant made way for us through the throng. The first was a large portrait of the founder of the Sikh faith. He was portrayed as a man of sixty in a cotton skullcap, a flowing white beard and a mendicant's garb. He held a begging bowl in one hand (he was against beggary and exhorted men to work) and a rosary in the other. Above the frame was the legend 'Guru Nanak Devji 1469–1539'. Beneath the picture was an English translation of the opening lines of his morning prayer:

> There is one God
> He is the Supreme truth.
> He, the creator,
> Is without fear and without hate,
> He, the omnipresent,
> Pervades the universe.
> He is not born,
> Nor does He die to be born again.
> By His grace shalt thou worship
> Him.

Nanak's portrait attracted the largest crowd. Peasants touched the base of the frame and ran their palms across their foreheads. They shut their eyes and exclaimed loudly, 'Dhan Baba Nanak! (Saviour of the world).'

There were other paintings of Nanak's life. Amongst the many incidents of his life portrayed by Kirpal Singh I recognized two. One showed a crowd of people standing waist-deep in water offering water to the rising sun. Nanak was shown facing the opposite direction and throwing water into the air. This incident took place at Haridwar on the Ganga. Nanak wanted to demonstrate the absurdity of offering water to the dead in heaven. When the pilgrims had asked him why he was facing the opposite direction he had replied, 'I'm watering my fields in my village. Surely if you can send water to heaven, which is more than a million miles away, I can send it to my village that is only a few hundred miles from here.' The other picture showed a Muslim remonstrating with Nanak who was shown lying on the floor. On his way to Mecca Nanak had rested with his feet pointing towards the holy Kaaba. When a Muslim accused him of showing disrespect towards Islam, Nanak had replied, 'Brother, you turn my feet in some other direction where God does not dwell.' The series on Nanak's life ended with a painting of his cremation. On the funeral pyre instead of a corpse was a heap of flowers. On either side of the pyre were ranged his disciples—one side distinguishably Hindu by their dhotis and caste marks, the other equally identifiable by their fez caps and baggy trousers to be Muslims. They had contended for Nanak's body. The Hindus wanted to cremate him because they said he was a Hindu, the Muslims to bury him because they believed he was of their faith. It is said that Nanak's body mysteriously disappeared and flowers were found in its place, which the two groups divided between them.

Prakash Singh joined us for a while. We stood at the entrance of the Golden Temple and watched pilgrims come and go. 'The Sikh is as firm in his faith as he ever was!' exclaimed Prakash Singh. He was referring to a prophecy I had recklessly made in a history of the Sikhs I had published in 1959 that if the Sikhs continued to give up wearing their long hair and beard at the rate they were doing, by the turn of the century they would relapse into Hinduism. I had written (and still hold on to the view) that the only real dividing line between the Sikhs and the Hindus is the Sikhs' unshorn hair and beard; that there is no such thing as a clean-shaven Sikh, he is a Hindu believing in Sikhism. I had often quoted Dr Lorimer's remark that a Sikh is only a kind of vicious Hindu.

'But you do agree that whatever the Sikhs have achieved has been achieved by them as the bearded and hirsute Khalsa—their militancy and their conquests, their spirit of enterprise. The way they dominate life in India, it is hard to believe that they form under 2 per cent of the population of the country—a third of the defence services, half of any Indian athletic team, why, three of the four Indians who got to the top of the peak?'

'It would have been more appropriate if it had the name of Guru Gobind Singh on it.'

'Sure!' he laughed, 'but you know what Sikhs are! Have you heard any good Sikh jokes lately?' He put his arm round my shoulder. 'Have you heard of the Sikh minister of irrigation and power? Well, he was being shown round a hydroelectric power station. The engineer explained how electricity was produced by the turbines and then the water used for irrigation. 'No wonder our agricultural output is so poor,' remarked the honourable minister, 'what good is the water after power has been extracted from it!'

Prakash Singh laughed heartily at his own joke and slapped me on the back many times. 'But seriously,' he suddenly became grave, 'you've got this business of Sikhs dying out or relapsing into Hinduism all wrong.'

◆

There is more to Amritsar than the Golden Temple. The Hindus have built a replica known as the Durgiana Mandir (Temple of the Goddess Durga). There are historic havelis of the Sikh aristocracy of olden times, beautifully laid out gardens and a couple of forts. But its narrow bazaars remain the chief attraction. I was loitering about them when I found myself at the entrance of Jallianwala Bagh. Next to the Golden Temple, it is the most popular place of pilgrimage. Indians of all races and religions come here to pay homage to the 400 men and women who were killed on 13 April 1919 when General Dyer ordered his Gurkha troops to open fire on a crowd gathered in contravention of an order forbidding the assemblage of more than five persons. The massacre at Amritsar proved to be the turning point in the history of India's freedom movement. A group of die-hards acclaimed Dyer as the defender of the empire and presented him with a sword of honour. And although he was cashiered and severely criticized by many Englishmen including Winston Churchill, Indians never forgave the British for the foul deed. Thereafter moderate Indian nationalists who stood for cooperation with their English rulers were displaced by Gandhi who denounced British rule as satanic and demanded complete independence for India.

Jallianwala is not much of a bagh (garden). It is a squarish plot of land enclosed between the high walls of houses. At its centre is a well in which many people drowned while trying to flee from the hail of Dyer's bullets. Beside it is a platform and a red column designed like a flame to symbolize the torch of liberty. A marble plaque bears the names of the martyrs. Every evening there is a son et lumière programme narrating the sequence of events which led to the massacre.

◆

The people of Amritsar speak a dialect of their own and have lots of stories bearing on their character. An Amritsari does not greet another with 'Sat Sri Akal (God is Truth)' as other Sikhs do but says, 'I fall at your feet'. At times he makes a gesture by touching the other's knee. They are always inviting each other for a meal without specifying the date or the time. Such an offer of hospitality is referred to as an 'Amritsari invitation'.

It was such an invitation from an old friend, Dilbir Singh, a prosperous industrialist and prominent figure in society that took me to Amritsar during my latest visit. Dilbir Singh dresses in the smartest of Savile Row Suits and keeps a stock of premium brand Scotch. His wife wears the Punjabi salwar-kameez but his daughter wears jeans and his son indulges in rock and roll. Nevertheless they are orthodox Sikhs. He greets me with an embrace loudly chanting 'Wahe Guru Ji Ka Khalsa (The Sikhs are the chosen of God)'; I reply 'Wahe Guru Ji Ki Fateh (And victory to our God)'. After exchanging pleasantries with other members of his family we sit down to watch a programme beamed to India by Pakistani television in Lahore. 'Chivas Regal or Johnnie Walker Black Label?' Dilbir Singh asks me, opening his well-stocked drink cabinet. 'Any Scotch will do, I can't tell the difference,' I plead. 'I'll give you Something Special; it is smoother than any other Scotch.'

Pakistani television has a special programme meant for the Sikhs they drove out almost to a man not very long ago. It is designed to win the Sikhs over to their side in the event of future confrontation with India. It consists of singing of Sikh hymns recorded at the Golden Temple and highlighting the Indian government's discrimination against the Sikhs. It cuts no ice—but Sikhs enjoy being flattered by their erstwhile enemies.

'Why don't you shift your business to a safer place than Amritsar?' I asked Dilbir Singh. 'There will be more confrontations with Pakistan. One well-aimed bomb and this city will go up in flames.'

'Leave Amritsar?' he shouted back, excitedly. 'Never! I was born here; I will die here. If Amritsar dies, all the Sikhs will die with it.'

(*1978*)

IN HYDERABAD

Once upon a time, Hyderabad was a beautiful and clean city: lakes, massive boulders strewn about on rocky escarpments, palaces, mosques, mausoleums and fortresses. Winter winds did not chill your bones; the summer heat was cooled by a breeze pregnant with the promise of the monsoon. The well-to-do lived a life of gracious languor; everyone knew his place in the social hierarchy. At the apex was His Exalted Highness the Nizam, followed in descending order of importance by Dowlahs, Jahs, Jungs and the Musahibeen. Everything seemed to be divinely ordained: the muezzin's call from the minarets of Mecca Masjid ushered in the dawning of the day and the same call floated across the skies as the lengthening shadows of the twilight took the city in its embrace. It was a Muslim city with a Muslim ethos, presided over by a Muslim ruler residing in King Kothi. The Hindu lived in peace with his Muslim neighbour, copied his speech and mannerisms and was proud of his Deccani culture.

All this is gone. No one is exalted above any other; this is all for the good. But the number of Hyderabadis has more than trebled; this is not so good. The quiet, clean city that free India forcibly acquired has become a noisy, ill-kept, squalid metropolis. Only a couple of years ago the chief mode of transport was the man-powered cycle rickshaw with dancers' bells fixed to the axles of its wheels to warn jaywalkers. Now two-seater yellow autos splutter along like the caga fogos—fire-farting wasps. The municipality has fallen sadly behind in providing for the exploding population and the traffic. The roads are in sorry shape; pavements narrow, uneven and streaked with urine. The once elegant Banjara Hills have almost been eaten up by new houses. The citizens express their disillusionment with the municipality (baldiya) by castigating their city fathers with the saying: baldiya—khaya, piya, aur chaldiya. Hyderabad is also no longer a Muslim city. The Jahs and Jungs have been replaced by Raos and Reddys, Deccani Urdu by Telugu.

No longer is the Char Minar or the Mecca Masjid the focal point of the city's life; it is the white marble Sri Venkateshwara Temple on the highest hilltop overlooking the city. It is a splendorous sight when floodlit at night but during the day it is as garish as the temple bestowed by the same Birla family in Delhi. To the visitor, Hyderabad may still appear mysteriously attractive, but no longer to the locals. They say Hyderabad nageena (gem): ooper gachi andar choona—gilded on top but rotten underneath.

The Hyderabadis speak an endearing dialect of Deccani Urdu with Telugu overtones. An exaggerated version of this patois can be heard in Babban Khan's *Adrak ke Panje*. But it has been there since the time of Sultan Mohammad Quli Qutab Shah who founded Hyderabad in 1592 CE and wrote a lot of verse in Telugu, Urdu and Persian. And it is there in the works of contemporary writers and poets, notably Sulaiman Khatib. Two of the commonest oddities in currency are hao (yes) and nako (no). A northerner, irritated by these sounds, asked a Deccani scholar for an explanation. He replied: 'Hao and nako are only used by poor illiterates; no man of culture and learning uses them.' The northerner asked again. 'Nawab sahib, you surely are a highly educated man?'

'Hao'.

(*1979*)

STAYING ON

Beside the portico of the Darjeeling Planters' Club stands a beige Mercedes-Benz with four flat tyres and a rust-eaten chassis. It has been there for the last six years without anyone doing anything about it. Its owner, an Englishman named Geoffrey Ower-Johnston left it there after he returned from Calcutta with an injunction from the high court to prevent the Indian government acquiring his tea estates in Rungmook and Cedars. He had evidently celebrated his victory and fortified himself with spirits before facing his workers who, having not received wages for several years, had agitated in support of the government takeover. He left his car at the club and took a lift from a friend to his factory at Sonada eleven kilometres downhill on the Darjeeling-Calcutta road (now named Tenzing Norgay Marg after the first conqueror of Mount Everest). Ower-Johnston never returned to the club. He was murdered by his workers on the evening of 28 April 1981. His story sums up the tragedy of many Englishmen who had made India their home and decided to stay on after it attained independence in August 1947.

No one is quite sure exactly how Ower-Johnston met his end. He had lived on his tea estate for most of his life with his English wife, Janet, an attractive but somewhat strait-laced Englishwoman ten years younger than him. She had borne him no children. Meanwhile, Geoffrey was captivated by a winsome Nepalese clerk working in his office. He installed her in a cottage some distance away from his bungalow. She bore him a son and a daughter. He took Janet to the Darjeeling Club and to other social functions. But for sex and family life he went to his Nepalese mistress and her children.

Ower-Johnston was a big man, over six feet tall. He was also a kind master much loved by his workers. His estate's expenses on the health and welfare of labourers were much higher than that of any other estate in the region. But he was a poor manager, a poorer businessman and chronically short of money. He was never able to pay pickers and workers their wages on time. For years he persuaded them that he was ploughing his profits back into the estate to improve the quality of his tea and would soon be able to clear their arrears as well as give them handsome bonuses. This went on for many years till the workers' patience ran out and they told him to get out and let the government manage his business. They were happy when the notice of acquisition was posted on the factory premises underwriting their past dues. Ower-Johnston secured an injunction against the order and thought he could talk to his workers into giving him another chance. If they remained recalcitrant he was prepared to face their wrath. In his pocket he carried a fully-loaded Mauser pistol.

Tea pickers and workers make very clear distinctions between the manager's bungalow and the factory. The bungalow is considered akin to the king's palace or a temple where nothing untoward should take place. But in the factory and the office they may yell slogans, bandy angry words with the senior staff and, if necessary, go on strike. Ower-Johnston made the mistake of meeting them in the factory. 'You call yourself our elder brother and come to meet us with a loaded pistol. What kind of elder brother are you?' shouted the workers' leaders. Ower-Johnston took out his Mauser and handed it over to them. It did not soothe their tempers. Angry words led to blows. Ower-Johnston was a powerful man but he could hardly stand up to a mob of Nepalese, many of whom carry khukuris. He was beaten to death and carved up.

The news reached Darjeeling late in the night. The police informed the secretary of the Darjeeling Club, an Englishwoman named Marigold Wisden—another of the flotsam-jetsam abandoned by the English when they left India. Marigold drove down to the Ower-Johnstons' bungalow in Sonada to break the news to his wife. She reached there two hours after midnight. The servants who let her in told her that their memsahib had had a migraine attack the evening before and was sleeping it off. Marigold decided not to disturb her and spent the night smoking cigarettes till the memsahib rang the bell for her chhota haazri (bed tea). Janet took the news with the phlegmatic calm for which the British are famous. Breaking down and crying is not pucca and regarded as infra dig for the master race. That evening

Ower-Johnston's remains were buried in the Anglican cemetery. The mourners consisted of two groups: Janet's English and Indian friends on one side; the Nepalese mistress, her two children and their relatives on the other. Everyone noticed that the coffin was far too small for a man of the size of Ower-Johnston. His remains had been packed in a child-sized box. The Englishman had literally been cut to size by his Indian servants.

To this day Geoffrey Ower-Johnston's grave remains unmarked. His wife, Janet, left for England a few days after the burial; the Nepalese mistress had no locus standi in the eyes of the church, which controls the cemetery. His planter friends still talk of raising funds to put a marble slab and a cross with the date of Ower-Johnston's demise over his grave.

◆

British clubs in India, like the Darjeeling Club, were extensions of the English pub on Indian soil. The main feature of these institutions was the bar where the British spent their evenings drinking Scotch or stout, playing darts and gossiping. With more prosperity came ballrooms, billiards rooms, card rooms, dining rooms, squash and tennis courts. Since many Britons were posted in outlying districts and there were few hotels in the cities, clubs had residential accommodation as well. The interiors were remarkably alike. Normally, the main sitting rooms would have large paintings of past presidents, viceroys (occasionally of an Indian prince), old country maps, trophy heads of wild animals—horses, panthers, stags, bison, etc.—mounted on wooden shields. The furniture usually had leather upholstery and was imported from England.

The Planters' Club in Darjeeling is typical of British and Indian clubs. It is over a hundred years old, having been founded in 1868. Its present site, right above a noisy bazaar, was gifted to it in 1890 by the Maharaja of Cooch-Behar in the full knowledge that this club, like all others of its kind at the time was meant 'for whites only'. Till shortly before India became independent, Indians were not even allowed as guests. Then a few princes and those knighted by the British were grudgingly admitted as members.

Today, the Darjeeling Planters' Club has barely 300 members, of whom only half a dozen are Europeans. The decline of the Darjeeling Club began when British planters as well as civil and military officers left for England. The club fell upon such hard times that it could no longer afford to have a retired military officer as its secretary and accepted Marigold Wisden, who was willing to serve for board, lodging and a little pocket money.

Not much is known about Marigold Wisden. Everything I was able to find out about her was courtesy her friend, the pretty, petite Indrani Gyaltsen, a Bengali poetess and writer, and the wife of a local landowner who manages the Glenburn Tea Estate. Marigold was born in Darjeeling; no one knows exactly in which year. 'For ten years we celebrated her sixty-fourth birthday,' says Indrani. She was the daughter of a ne'er-do-well called Weatherall. Her mother ran a boarding house which paid for the education of her three children—Marigold and her brothers. The family was Catholic but never went to church. Sometime in the 1930s Marigold married an Anglo-Indian businessman living in Bombay… and deserted him on the first night of her marriage because he dared to appear naked before her. The story she told some other friends was different. She said she had borne stillborn twins to her first husband. 'Just as well,' she told them, 'I did not have the means to support them.' Then she 'married' someone called Karl. He was either killed in Kohima in World War II, or divorced her, or is still alive somewhere. Marigold named her favourite Tibetan dog Karl. After Karl's exit from her life, Marigold married a Colonel Wisden who took her and her mother to Kenya. Then one morning Colonel Wisden walked out on them never to return. Marigold stayed in Kenya for some years simply because of her dogs, cats and other pets, till they died. Then she returned to Darjeeling without a penny in her pocket. She was lucky to get the job of secretary of the Planters' Club, because it at least gave her a roof over her head and two square meals a day.

Marigold lived in a world of fantasy. She talked of her third husband suddenly appearing in Darjeeling and claiming conjugal rights. She rattled off names of Darjeeling celebrities who had tried to seduce her or proposed marriage to her. In mixed company she used obscene four-letter words. Though born a Catholic she referred to church goers as 'God botherers'. Despite the succession of husbands she claimed to have had, she had strong views on philandering and adultery. 'They should be lynched; adulteresses are worse than whores.' She surrounded herself with pets. At one time she was sharing her rooms with nine dogs, a pair of geese and a crow with a broken wing. Larry the crow became a great favourite. In winter she put on him a sweater she had knitted herself. Indrani tells of a cold evening when she went to see Marigold in her room. Her entire menagerie was there with Larry sulking in a corner.

'What is the matter, Larry?' she asked.

'I'm cold,' croaked Larry.

'Wear your sweater.'

'I already have it on.'

'Then come near the fire.'

Larry hopped closer to the fire.

Once Marigold was about to leave a cocktail party—she loved parties and was partial to gin. When pressed to stay, she pleaded, 'He is very domineering.'

'Who is very domineering?' asked Indrani.

'Jethu,' she replied. Jethu was the oldest of her Tibetan apsos. When Marigold Wisden died on 17 September 1983, she left behind twenty-two dogs, three cats and a pair of geese. Larry had predeceased his mistress. The other pets were adopted by her friends. The geese found a new home in Indrani's Glenburn Tea Estate. The local Catholic cemetery refused to receive Marigold Wisden's mortal remains. She was cremated with Buddhist rites and her ashes scattered on the hillside.

◆

Ower-Johnston and Marigold Wisden were a few of the now almost defunct English lot who decided to stay where they had lived all their lives rather than return to cold, foggy, wet old Blighty.

GLIMPSES OF AGRA

Agra has many other monuments besides the Taj, of which at least three are amongst the most important examples of Mughal art: the Red Fort and its palaces, the mausoleum of Emperor Akbar at Sikandara and the tomb of Itmad-ud-Daulah. There is also the deserted city of Fatehpur Sikri forty-two kilometres west of Agra, which many people consider the most bewitching of all ruins to be seen anywhere. When the visitor has 'done' the four 'musts' of Agra, he could visit the ancient European Cemetery, the industrial estate at Dayal Bagh and its ambitious marble temple designed to rival the Taj. And when the visitor has had his fill of mosques, palaces and mausolea he may lose himself in the medieval Kinari Bazaar and the winding lanes that take off from it; he will see the handiwork of Agra's master craftsmen: exquisite inlay in marble and miniature Taj Mahals; enamel and metalware; leather, carpets, and dhurries. The gourmet whose palate is acclimatized to Indian food may sample the two delicacies for which Agra is famous: its succulently sweet translucent petha (white pumpkin cooked in sugar syrup) and crispy, spicy dalmoth.

Agra has two other places of importance: it is the birthplace of Mirza Asadullah Khan Ghalib (1797–1870), the greatest poet of the Persian and Urdu languages. His tumbledown house in the bazaar is a place of pilgrimage for the literati. It is also the birthplace of the most celebrated exponent of classical music, Ustad Faiyaz Khan (1886–1950) and to this day the centre of the school of singers of the Agra Gharana.

THE NAME

There are many legends about the origin of the name Agra. Scholars believe the site of the present city was the southeasterly outpost of early Aryan settlers; they called it Aryagraha—the abode of the Aryans. With the passage of time the two words were telescoped into one: Agra. Ancient Hindu texts refer to it as Agraban—the woods of Agra.

Ptolemy calls it simply Agara.

Emperor Shah Jahan tried to rename the city Akbarabad in honour of his father but the old name Agra came back into its own.

THE BUILDERS OF AGRA

Not much is known of the earliest history of Agra; it is believed that it was occupied by Rajput tribes till Mahmud of Ghazni ejected them and plundered the city in 1131 CE. Later, it was apparently re-occupied by the Rajput and Jat tribes of the neighbourhood. Three centuries later, the Afghan Sikandar Lodi decided to make it the seat of his government and built a fort and a city which was named after him, Sikandara. All that remains of the Lodi city are a few ruins. Sikandara is on the Delhi-Agra road, eight kilometres north of the present city and noted for the tomb of Akbar.

The Mughal Babar overthrew the Lodi dynasty in 1526. Most of the four short years of his life in India were spent in Agra. He laid out gardens along the banks of the Yamuna (the exact location is still disputed) and when he died in 1530 his body was first interred in one of these gardens before being transported for final burial to Kabul.

Babar's son Humayun (1508–1556) had a very chequered career and had to spend most of his years in exile. He was not able to contribute much to the building of India.

Humayun's son Akbar (1542–1605) was one of the greatest monarchs in the history of our country. He extended the empire of his forefathers and he was a just and able administrator who made no distinction between subjects of different faiths. And he was a great builder. Although unlettered, he was an enlightened patron of the arts; at his court were 'nine gems', the most distinguished men of his time including the musician Tansen; the brothers Abul Fazl and Faizi who were men of learning and helped the emperor formulate his religious policy; Raja Todar Mal who organized the revenue system which endures in India to this day. Akbar married women of different faiths and races—amongst them a Rajput princess who was the mother of his son and successor Jahangir, an Armenian Catholic and a Turkish Sultana Istamboli Begum. The palaces of these wives and the houses of his distinguished courtiers can be seen at Fatehpur Sikri and Agra.

Akbar made Agra his capital. He demolished the remains of the old castle called Badalgarh and, on its ruins, raised the present Red Fort. He also built Fatehpur Sikri which for ten years became a rival capital—and then the fort at Lahore where he had to spend some years to suppress a revolt in his northern territories. Akbar returned to Agra (but not Fatehpur Sikri). He started the construction of the mausoleum at Sikandara in his lifetime; it was completed by his son, Jahangir. All of Akbar's buildings were made of red sandstone.

Jahangir (1569–1627) was not a great builder. He did however make additions to the Red Fort. His favourite wife, Nur Jahan, more than made up for her husband's lack of interest in building. She raised a mausoleum for her parents on the banks of the Yamuna. Itmad-ud-Daulah is the best example of a monument all in white marble with pietra dura inlay. It undoubtedly inspired Jahangir's son Shah Jahan and the craftsmen he employed.

With Shah Jahan (1594–1666) the Mughal dynasty reached its zenith in power and creative achievements. What Akbar had done in sandstone, Shah Jahan outdid in marble. He quarried the white rock at Makrana near Jaipur and sent for semi-precious stones from wherever they could be found. A massive building programme was started in Delhi and Agra. He built the palaces and mosques in the Red Fort; his daughter, Jahanara, built the great Friday mosque, Jama Masjid, in the city, and all the experience of the architects and the craftsmen was pooled to raise the queen of all monuments, the peerless Taj Mahal. Shah Jahan was indeed the greatest builder of all time.

Shah Jahan's son Aurangzeb (1618–1707) neither had the breadth of vision of his great-grandfather Akbar nor the lavish generosity of his father. He was a stern monarch, austerely Muslim in his private life and uncompromising in his attitude towards other faiths. He disapproved of 'waste' on expensive buildings. Aurangzeb's successors paid the price of his bigotry. Hindu militant races—the Marathas, Rajputs, Jats, and the Sikhs rose in revolt. Muslim satraps set up independent kingdoms. Foreigners began to invade the country from all sides. The Persian, Nadir Shah, sacked Delhi (1739), massacred its inhabitants and took away the peacock throne, and the Koh-i-noor diamond; the Afghan, Ahmed Shah Abdali, invaded India nine times, ransacked Delhi and

Agra and other rich cities. In one of these marauding expeditions he used 28,000 elephants, camels and mules and 80,000 horses to carry away the loot. The Rohillas joined in the looting and the Jats stripped the palaces of Delhi and Agra of their gold and silver and precious stones; the Marathas helped themselves as well and whatever remained in the way of precious or semi-precious metal or stone was taken by English vandals who had occupied Delhi and Agra in 1803. What we see today in Agra is but a shadow of what had once been.

THE TAJ MAHAL

The Taj Mahal—crown of the palace—is named for Mumtaz Mahal, the regal title of the wife of Emperor Shah Jahan. The mausoleum was first known as Taj Bibi ka Rauza—the burial place of the Lady Taj—and then shortened to Taj Mahal.

Arjumand Bano, the daughter of a nobleman, was nineteen when she was married to Prince Khurram (as the emperor was then known) who was twenty-one at the time. Although she was the second wife of her husband who, as was customary with royalty of the time, married or maintained many other wives and concubines, Arjumand Bano (Mumtaz Mahal) remained her husband's favourite. She accompanied her husband on all his military campaigns and, when he fell out with his father, shared his misfortunes for seven long years. When Emperor Jahangir died in 1627, Prince Khurram destroyed all his other rivals and ascended his father's throne with the title Shah Jahan—King of the World. Mumtaz became his chief adviser and keeper of the royal seal. Later she gave up interest in matters of state and devoted herself entirely to works of charity—looking after widows and orphans and providing marriage expenses for girls of indigent families. This period of domestic bliss lasted only three years. In 1631 she was with her husband at Burhanpur when she was delivered of her fourteenth child and took seriously ill. Before she died, she entrusted her husband's care to her eldest child, Jahanara Begum. She made her husband promise that he would raise over her grave a mausoleum worthy of the love that she had borne him in the eighteen years of their married life. After her death Shah Jahan was so grief-stricken that within a few days his hair and beard turned completely grey.

A poet wrote:

His hair was grey but not with years
Nor grew they white in a single night
As men's would from sudden fears
Ah! Cantankerous grief his heart did blight.

Mumtaz was first buried at Zainabad Gardens in Burhanpur. Six months later her coffin was disinterred, brought in solemn procession to Agra and once again given a temporary resting ground in a garden on the banks of the Yamuna. Shah Jahan then issued orders for the building of the mausoleum. Innumerable designs were presented to the emperor. He selected one made by Ustad Isa Khan Effendi, an Indian of Turkish origin in the employ of the Mughal empire. Effendi had to make a model in wood before final approval was granted. An army of 20,000 labourers, masons, stonecutters and jewellers was assembled. Marble was brought from Makrana; sandstone from Sikri, semi-precious stones from the mines of India, Afghanistan, Persia and Central Asia. In the absence of mechanical devices, a 3.2-km-long sloping ramp was laid in order to carry building material to the dome that was designed by Ismail Khan.

It took twelve years to complete the central mausoleum. Mumtaz Mahal's remains were given their final burial exactly below the central point of the dome. A replica of the tomb was built on the floor above so that people could pay homage to her without disturbing the peace of her real resting place. The surrounding buildings—a mosque towards the west, a mosque-like structure in the east to provide the balance (appropriately called Jawab—answer), the high wall which encloses the 1,700 square metres of garden and the massive three-storeyed gateway took another five years to build. Then came the tombs of other members of the royal family and the ladies-in-waiting, the gardens and the mosques. These took yet another five years, making a total of twenty-two years to complete the project. According to popular legend, the twenty-two little domes on top of the entrance gateway mark the twenty-two years of construction. The emperor was very pleased with the building and composed the following lines in its praise:

Radiant like the garden of heaven.
Full of fragrance of paradise as if wrought in ambergris
With their eyelashes the angels of paradise brush its threshold.

There is little doubt that Shah Jahan intended to build another mausoleum for himself. The placing of Mumtaz's tomb in the centre of the hall is proof of the fact that she was to be the sole occupant of the Taj. But we are not as certain about what the emperor had in mind for himself. It is popularly believed that he had intended to build a replica of the Taj in black marble across the river and link the two with a black-and-white marble bridge. The only evidence of this is the remains of a wall and a chhatri on the east bank of the Yamuna of roughly the same dimensions as the riverside wall of the Taj Mahal. Proponents of the black marble Taj theory claim to have found pieces of black marble at Mehtab Bagh—the moonlit garden. There is no way of verifying the truth of this legend because Shah Jahan was ousted from power by his son Aurangzeb and kept under house arrest in the marble palace he had built for Mumtaz in the Red Fort. He was looked after by his daughter Jahanara Begum and spent his last days in the Musammam Burj from where could see the Taj Mahal. He died on 22 January 1666, gazing fondly at his handiwork. The next morning his body was taken by boat and interred alongside that of his beloved queen from whom he had been apart for thirty-six years. The parsimonious Aurangzeb argued that he (Shah Jahan) would be happier beside his loved one rather than in an expensive mausoleum of his own.

◆

The Taj defies description. Visitors are known to be so overcome by its impact as to miss their step and severely injure themselves; others are known to be stricken dumb for several minutes. Some praise its beauty when the rising sun touches its minarets and dome with a soft pink; some prefer to see it dazzle under the glare of the noonday sun; and everyone loves to see it in the silvery light of the moon.

The Taj Mahal is not architecture as all other famous buildings are, but as Edwin Arnold said: 'the proud passion of an emperor's love wrought in living stone'. An unknown English poetess addressed the following lines to Shah Jahan:

> Sleep on secure! This monument shall stand,
> (When desolation's wing sweeps over the land,
> By time and death in one wide ruin hurl'd)
> The last triumphant wonder of the world.

◆

The massive walls of the Red Fort dominate the city of Agra. It is the creation of four successive emperors. Akbar demolished the old fort of Badalgarh and raised the ramparts of the new one. Jahangir built some of the palaces inside and the attached bastion Salimgarh is named after him. Shah Jahan built the royal palaces, the halls of audience and the mosques. Aurangzeb made minor additions.

The fort is triangular in shape with a kilometre-long base on the Yamuna and the other two sides meeting in an apex at the Delhi gate. It has a moat and two walls running right around it. The inner wall is over thirty metres high; there is enough space between the walls for parades and sports like elephant fights. The outer wall is two and a half kilometres long. It has four main gates—two opening on the side of the river, both of which are permanently closed; the Delhi Gate in the west, which is exclusively for the use of the soldiers stationed in the fort; and the Amar Singh Gate (also called Lahore Gate), which is for the use of visitors. The fort was designed by Mohammad Qasim Khan who was Akbar's harbour master. It took Akbar eight years (1565–73) to build it at an estimated cost of Rs 35 lakh.

Amar Singh Gate got its name from Amar Singh Rathore of Mewar. Amar Singh was a legendary warrior who served in the Mughal court under Shah Jahan. But he attracted the jealousy of fellow courtiers and when attacked by them he is believed to have jumped from the Agra Fort mounted on his horse, Bahadur. The horse died and a stone effigy marks the site where he fell. At one time Amar Singh Gate was a blaze of colour; today a few multi-coloured glazed tiles still remain. The road from the gate slopes gently upwards and is made of jagged flagstones to give elephants a better foothold. It emerges in an open space. Visitors will notice the six-pointed stars like the Star of David on the palace entrance. There is no satisfactory explanation for this emblem appearing on Mughal buildings. The popular theory is that it is a Hindu emblem symbolizing the six seasons.

To the east is a large stone cauldron and beyond it the bright red walls of Jahangiri Mahal, the residence of Jodha Bai, Jahangir's Rajput wife. The first object of attention is the massive stone cauldron, 7.6 metres in circumference and 1.4 metres high, hewn out of one rock. This was acquired by Jahangir in 1611. The use to which this 'bath' was put is not known. The emperor's name and the year of acquisition are inscribed. Since the year was the same in which Jahangir married Nur Jahan, it has been assumed that it was a wedding present from Jahangir to his bride.

Jahangiri Mahal or Jodha Bai's palace was built by Akbar. It is an excellent example of the blending of Hindu and Muslim styles of architecture; its walls are decorated with figures of parrots, ducks, peacocks and some fabulous creatures taboo to the Muslim artisan, who was forbidden by his faith to create the likeness of an animate object. The highly ornate brackets and the air-cooling ducts between walls one and a half metres thick deserve notice. The roofs were at one time painted; all that remains are a few indistinct signs and a small patch renovated on the orders of Lord Curzon to show what it once was. Little remains of the green-and-blue glazed tiles that decorated the outer walls. From the roof of the palace, a splendid view can be had of the meandering river and the Taj Mahal.

At Khas Mahal, we move into the marbled world of Shah Jahan. He built this private (khas) palace in 1637. Its marble work is worthy of attention, particularly the use of translucent slabs in the windows. The Khas Mahal suffered badly at the hands of vandals and was only partly restored by Lord Curzon. The Diwan-i-Khas—hall of private audience—is once again, the work of Shah Jahan. A Persian inscription inlaid in black marble mentions the date of its completion—1637. This audience chamber consists of an outer and an inner room connected by three archways. The twin columns of the Diwan-i-Khas with their black fluting and delicately curvaceous floral bases are worthy of attention. So also are the marble window screens of the inner chamber and the red carnelian inlay.

The palace, its courtyards and baths were designed for the ladies of the harem. The Angoori Bagh (Grape Garden) has no vines now but only patches of lawn between the fountains. Alongside it is the Sheesh Mahal (Hall of Mirrors), which was in fact the royal bathroom. When the attendant lit a torch, the flame was reflected in the many mirrors, illuminating the room. The stones in the wall are of varying thickness and produce sounds of percussion instruments when tapped. The baths lead onto the Musamman Burj, the octagonal tower which overlooks the river. It was here that Shah Jahan spent his last days, gazing at the Taj. A crystal in one of the marble pillars catches the reflection of the Taj Mahal. The octagonal tower, a form reproduced in many buildings, is a particularly fine piece of craftsmanship.

Near the Musamman Burj is a rectangular bench of black stone. This was hewn out of a meteorite which fell at Allahabad. It was brought to Agra on the orders of Emperor Jahangir. When the British attacked the fort in 1803, a cannonball fell on the slab and damaged one corner.

Next on the itinerary is the Macchi Bhavan (Fish Pond) where tropical fish were kept for display. The surrounding walls and roof appear to be the work of Hindu craftsmen. Two emblems that constantly appear are the sun and the incense burner.

From the Macchi Bhavan a passage leads to the Nagina Masjid, a small marble mosque for the use of the ladies of the royal household. Beside the mosque is the Meena Bazaar, the shopping centre for ladies, and above it a marble pavilion from which the emperor—the only male to enjoy the privilege—could view the buying and selling in the arcade below. The Moti Masjid (Pearl Mosque) is a couple of hundred metres away to the north. It is the largest marble mosque in the world. This mosque is also the handiwork of Shah Jahan and took seven years to build.

The biggest building in the Red Fort is the hall of public audience, the Diwan-i-Am. The red sandstone hall of pillars was, as could be guessed, built by Akbar; the marble balcony inlaid with semi-precious stones where the emperor took his seat and the adjoining rooms for the ladies of the harem were built by Shah Jahan.

◆

Across the river Yamuna is one of the most exquisite examples of Mughal craftsmanship—the first experiment in building in white marble with pietra dura inlay and hence a forerunner of the Taj.

Itmad-ud-Daulah, whose real name was Ghias Beg, was the father of Jahangir's wife Nur Jahan (and grandfather of Mumtaz Mahal). Nur Jahan's affection for her parents is evident from the care she took in building their last resting place; it took her six years (1622–28) to complete the mausoleum.

We enter through an imposing gateway and see the squarish mausoleum with its four squat minarets and a pavilion on top. It reminds one of a music box made of mother-of-pearl.

A close examination of the building will show the recurring themes of a cypress tree, a wine flask and jugs—symbols more appropriate for Jahangir than Itmad-ud-Daulah. Note also the delicate chikan-work in the marble arches, a feminine touch. The tombs inside are a little disappointing in the choice of stone. Both are of dark-brown marble with black. Here too it is apparent that the mausoleum was first meant to enshrine only the remains of Nur Jahan's mother (whose tomb is in the centre); her husband was laid beside her for reasons of economy, or sentiment. Nur Jahan's other relatives, including her brother Asaf Jah and his wife (the parents of Mumtaz Mahal), are buried in the adjoining chambers.

The replica of the tombs on the floor above and the marble screen which encloses them will delight the connoisseur of art. A flight of stairs (Mughal stairs are of the most uncomfortable dimensions) takes one to the platform on which the tombs are situated. Here the craftsmen have excelled themselves; the floral fluting around the tombs, the inlay of multi-coloured stones and above all the latticed screens without a joint anywhere compel admiration.

Itmad-ud-Daulah has an airy baradari with a fine view of the river and the city on the other side. The lower stories of the baradari are flush with the stream; the upper stories are for those times when the river is in flood. Despite the proximity of the tombs, the bon vivant Jahangir used the pavilion for his bacchanalian parties. Alongside the baradari is an old waterworks: the Persian wheel which drew up the water from the river and fed the channels that criss-cross the garden.

◆

About a mile upstream from the tomb of Itmad-ud-Daulah is the Ram Bagh—the earliest example of a Mughal garden of which the famous Shalimars of Kashmir and Lahore are but copies. This was laid out under the orders of Babar in 1528 and for a time became his favourite place of recreation. It was called Bagh-i-Afghan or Aram Bagh, later corrupted to Ram Bagh. Since the design came from Afghanistan, the local inhabitants also called it Kabul Bagh. Ram Bagh is for lovers of solitude. It is a lovely garden with well laid out lawns, ancient flowering trees and fragrant bushes, gaudy butterflies and flocks of peafowl. Here amidst the greenery, the fountains and the Yamuna flowing by, Babar drank his heady Shiraz wines and listened to the lute. Little of Babar's garden now remains—a baradari on the river bank, a few water courses and slabs of marble cut in zig-zag pattern to create ripples when the water ran over them.

◆

Akbar's tomb at Sikandara is most likely to be the first monument that visitors coming from Delhi will encounter. The gateway to the mausoleum is the most imposing one you can see anywhere: a massive Mughal archway of red sandstone inlaid with white marble and four slender minarets rising in perfect geometrical proportion. The gateway is believed to have been constructed by Jahangir in 1613.

The tomb is laid in a vast garden of sixty hectares where roam herds of blackbuck and deer, red-faced rhesus monkeys and black-faced langurs. The eastern and western ends also have large gates; the northern gate suffered at the hands of vandals and is in the process of renovation.

The central mausoleum is a four-storeyed building of which the first three are red stone and the fourth is white marble. Sikandara is obviously a copy of the Panch Mahal at Fatehpur Sikri. The real tomb is in the catacomb below. Above is a replica with the ninety-nine names of God and the words 'Allah-u-Akbar' (God is great) along with the motto of Akbar's religious creed, Din-i-Ilahi—'Jalla Jalaluhu'—and great is his glory.

There are a few monuments near Sikandara which will catch the eye of the visitor driving down from Delhi. A few hundred metres north of Sikandara on the eastern side of the Delhi-Agra road are the remains of the baradari built by Sikandar Lodi in 1495. This was expropriated by Jahangir who, in 1623, erected the tomb of his mother Mariam Zamani on the same site. On the outskirts of Akbar's tomb a few metres west of the entrance is the beautifully preserved red sandstone Sheesh Mahal. On the other side of the road is a red effigy of a horse. It is said to be the grave of Akbar's favourite Arab stallion and beside it a human grave, presumably of the syce.

◆

Forty-two kilometres west of Agra is the deserted city of Fatehpur Sikri. During Akbar's reign it was a sister capital and more populous than Agra. Now it is just an impressive—perhaps the world's most impressive—abandoned city. A magnificent metropolis on a hilly eminence in the midst of a vast expanse of khaki unrelieved by the slightest protuberance anywhere, Sikri is India's Pompeii.

Fatehpur was a small insignificant town inhabited by a community of stonecutters who took the raw material for their trade from the hillock on which they lived. To this town came a mystic, Salim Chishti, who spent many days meditating in a grotto. The stonecutters were won over by this man and built a mosque over his grotto. The emperor heard of Salim and, being desirous of a son, came to ask for the holy man's blessing. According to legend, Salim's six-month-old son sacrificed his own life and his spirit was reanimated in the womb of Akbar's Hindu wife, Mariam. For her confinement Akbar built a palace (Rang Mahal) close to the stonecutter's mosque. When a son was born, the emperor named him Salim after the mystic. Soon after, he decided to shift his capital to the town.

The building operations began in 1569. The availability of building material, stone masons and the enthusiasm of the monarch contributed to its quick elevation and by 1574 Akbar was holding his court at Fatehpur Sikri. But the construction of the walled city with its innumerable palaces and mosques took fifteen more years to complete. An English traveller, Ralph Fitch, who happened to visit the city wrote: 'The King hath in Agra and Fatepore…100 elephants, 30,000 horses, 1,400 tame deer, 800 concubines: such other store of ounces, tigers, buffles, cocks and hawks, that is very strange to see. He keepeth a great court...Agra and Fatepore are two very great cities, either of them much greater than London...'

Akbar lived in his new capital for only sixteen years. Troubles in the northwest compelled him to shift to Lahore, and then he returned to Agra instead of Sikri. The shortage of water at Sikri undoubtedly contributed to its downfall. Within a few years, the palaces, mosques and mansions of the omrahs were deserted and became the haunts of wild beasts: leopards and hyenas prowled in the palaces; jackals howled in empty courtyards; the hoot of the owl reverberated through the corridors and bats made their nests under the eaves. Only once again did a Mughal king deign to honour Sikri. This was in the April of 1719 when Muhammad Shah sat in state on the peacock throne and had himself crowned Emperor of India.

(*Undated*)

WHY I LOVE DELHI

There are seven reasons why I love Delhi. There are many more reasons why I loathe having to live in it. By strange coincidence there are seven old cities of Delhi. I love all the seven—or whatever remains of them. More than the seven, I love the eighth, New Delhi, in which I have spent most of the years of my life and where I expect to be buried when I die.

Let me elucidate. A city without a history has no character. The older it is, the more loveable it becomes. You can have your Canberras and your Calcuttas (a mere 300 years old) but give me Athens, Cairo, Baghdad, Rome, London or Paris—cities that have antiquity and unique personalities of their own. Delhi is one of the oldest of the old cities of the world. There had to be good reasons for my ancestors to make Delhi their home and the country's capital in preference to other available sites, to raise forts, palaces and places of worship strong enough to last several centuries. If you happen to come to Delhi by air during daylight hours (unfortunately most international flights land and take off between midnight and 4 a.m.) you can get a good bird's-eye view of all the old seven cities and the eighth new city of Delhi now clustered together in one mega metropolis stretching fifty kilometres from end to end. You will easily spot the Qutab Minar, Delhi's Eiffel Tower, Big Ben and Statue of Liberty. This twelfth-century seventy-three-metre victory tower made of marble and sandstone stands amidst ruins of temples much older than itself. You may also be able to spot the remains of what were once the battlements of an older city which included these temples. You may catch a glimpse of extensive ruins of the fourteenth-century city, Tughlaqabad, stretching eastwards, and a couple of kilometres beyond it the river Yamuna. Most planes coming in from the north and the west circle over this river as they lower their landing gear to make for the runway of the Indira Gandhi International Airport. While coming in to land, you can get a view of ancient forts, palaces, mosques and mausolea rising amidst huddles of bazaars as well as modern multi-storeyed skyscrapers and attractive villas standing in spacious gardens. Within a minute or two you get a panoramic view of the history of Delhi—some monuments dating back to a hundred years before the birth of Christ, others in the process of being constructed.

It is nice to live among a people who have a sense of belonging and pride in their city. A city with a peripatetic citizenry who live in it without being emotionally involved with it are not worth knowing. Delhi wallahs have pride of belonging in ample measure. That is the second reason for my loving it. Although the city was swamped by outsiders in the summer of 1947 (when India became free) and today more than half of its residents are the first generation of Delhi wallahs, they too have by influence of older families begun to love the city of their domicile. Many poets have sung praises of this city; an inscription in one of its marble palaces claims in letters of gold that it is paradise on earth. Its most famous poet, Ghalib, who lived in the nineteenth century and saw the British take it over from the Mughals, recorded in a memorable couplet what the city meant to him:

I asked my soul what is Delhi?
It replied: the world is the body
Delhi is its soul.

My third reason for loving Delhi is that it is the greenest capital city in the world. It has more trees to the square kilometre than any other. There is not a time of year when some tree or the other is not in full flower: silk cotton, flame of the forest, coral, siris, jacaranda, gulmohar, laburnum, lagerstroemia. From Christmas to Easter, when the skies over Delhi are a lapis lazuli blue and the air cool and balmy, Delhi's innumerable parks present a veritable riot of colours. The abundance of trees and the river attract a large variety of birds. The Delhi Bird Watching Society has listed over 600 distinct species identified every year. Unfortunately only one of these, the magpie robin—also known as dayal or shama—has any pretence to being a songbird; the rest just chirp or scream or chatter away incessantly. But they are in such vast numbers and so ubiquitous that you are surrounded by them wherever you go. There will be mynas on the pavements of the most congested bazaars and on the platforms of railway station; parakeets and common mynas coming to roost on the trees in Connaught Circus or any of the avenues leading out of it make such a racket as to drown the roar of traffic. You can never get away from the cawing of crows and the chirping of sparrows. And all through the long summer days you can hear the barbets calling and the koels' loud coo-oo come through thick foliage. Delhi is an ornithologist's paradise.

Delhi is a very pleasant place to live in. If you are an old resident, as I am, paying old rents, it can also be the cheapest as far as housing is concerned. Also, if you happen to be a civil servant, the government provides you with furnished accommodation at rates less than one-tenth of what it may cost you in the open market. But if you are an outsider, the exorbitant rates demanded from you are likely to make you feel unwelcome. Delhi's five-star hotels are beyond the pockets of most Indians unless they are on an expense account. But even our most expensive hotels cost no more than average middle-class hotels in Europe, Canada or the United States. But one thing you can be sure of is that you will get much better personal service than you'll get elsewhere. There are also dozens of cheaper hotels, hostels and private lodging and boarding establishments. Delhi caters to the millionaire as well as the hippie on a shoestring budget. That is my fourth reason for liking it.

A unique feature of Delhi's housing is that your address will reveal your economic, social and bureaucratic status. Everyone knows where he or she belongs. New Delhi's various nagars (townships) are divided according to the salary and place in the bureaucratic hierarchy. You start from neecha (low) nagar, and slowly move up the ladder to an ooncha (high) nagar, from a single-bedroom tenement, to a two bedroom flat, to a small bungalow with a tiny garden to a mansion with three acres of lawn. If after knowing where a Delhi wallah lives, you are still in doubt about his social status, all you have to do is to tactfully ask him if he belongs to any club and what games he plays. If he is a member of the Golf Club, whether or not he plays the game, he belongs to the elite. That goes for the Riding and the Hunt Club as well. It is there that he rubs shoulders with the diplomatic corps and with other wogs known popularly as 'koi hais'. A shade below these clubs is the Gymkhana—one of the oldest British-style clubs with bars, ballroom floors, billiards and card rooms, a good library, tennis and squash courts, a pool and, on winter mornings, a military band to help you digest indigestible food. It is no longer as pucca as it used to be and caters to plebeian tastes, even showing Hindi movies. There are dozens of other clubs but they don't count when it comes to social snobbery. The only exception is the India International Centre adjoining one of Delhi's loveliest parks, the Lodi Gardens. It is not a sporting club but a venue for Delhi's intellectuals to socialize. Besides a well-equipped library it is the venue of conferences, seminars, dance and music recitals. As with the other clubs, the waiting list is over 5,000 applicants long. However, you don't have to be a member to attend any of its programmes. And there are a lot of generous bores who will invite you to tea or coffee if you are willing to listen to them grind out their pet obsessions.

Another plus point in favour of Delhi is its food. There are few cities in which you can eat as well and for as little. Of course, if you want to pay through the nose for your food, Delhi provides for that too in many of its fancy five-star hotels with their French, Italian, Chinese and Polynesian restaurants. A bottle of French, German, or Italian wine will cost you ten times more than in its country of origin. But as you're in India, it would probably be better to sample Indian cuisine. This can be as good and perhaps better in a wayside dhaba for a fraction of what you would pay in a five-star restaurant.

The great thing about living in Delhi is that if you know the ropes you can get at least one good meal with good wine free of charge every day. We have over 120 embassies, high commissions, legations and consulates. Every one of them celebrates their national days and throws parties to welcome a new ambassador or bid farewell to him when his tenure is over. It is not difficult to get into the circuit of diplomatic parties. What you have to do is sign the visitors' books maintained by them, including those maintained by various agencies of the United Nations. Foreigners are eager to show off their local contacts. Allow them to do so by accepting their hospitality. They don't expect to be invited back. If you have the nerve you may even gate-crash parties without an invitation card. No one asks any questions.

And Scotch flows like the waters of the Yamuna in flood. The lines of E. Flower on life in Bloomsbury apply to life in Delhi.

It is a succession of parties for sponges and bores
With traffic jams outside, they turn up in their scores
With first-rate sherry flowing into second-rate whores
And third-class conversation without one single pause.

The final reason for loving Delhi is that it grows on you. The longer you live in it the more difficult it is to get away from it. There are innumerable people who would rather continue living in Delhi than go elsewhere on promotion and better prospects. There was the celebrated court poet, Sheikh Ibraham Zauq, who, though reduced to poverty, refused a tempting offer from a raja of Hyderabad. He wrote:

Though love of poetry be at its height
In Hyderabad of today
How can I tear myself away from these lanes?
How can I leave Delhi and go away?

If there are seven reasons for loving Delhi, there are more than seventy for hating it. They can be summed up in three words—nothing really works. In the heat of summer taps run dry, air conditioners die on you, lights go off without warning, telephones go dead. It is a heavily polluted city. During winter mornings smog spreads over the city; flights are delayed or cancelled. Traffic is chaotic. Buses and trucks belch smoke, three-wheelers rattle like machine guns. And every driver honks his horn for the sheer joy of honking. We are a noise-happy people. But you soon get used to the noise and the dirt and the frequent breakdowns in essential services. That's the magic of Delhi.

(*Undated*)

THE INDIAN WAY

MORNING STAR AND STUD BULL

What makes some people succeed where others have failed? Too often success is ascribed to luck, too seldom to the one quality that more than intelligence, circumstances or personal magnetism leads to it—single-mindedness. A dogged round-the-clock pursuit never fails.

I saw an instance of this the other day in the person of Obaidullah Khan, block development officer of Malhargarh in Madhya Pradesh, and his band of village-level workers. During the days I was in their company, I failed to excite their interest in anything apart from the narrow domains of their work. No art, no literature, no interest in the fauna (except pedigree bulls); no knowledge of the flora (except foodgrain and corn crops). Not even in gossip. With them it was roads, sanitary wells, latrines, schools, seed stores all day and then around the hurricane lantern the same in reverse order—seed stores, schools, latrines, sanitary wells and roads.

I left Malhargarh in the very early hours of the morning. It was a dark night and the stars sparkled beautifully, particularly Venus, the morning star, which shone like a large luminous lamp of quicksilver on the eastern horizon. Then followed a few moments of enchantment that come to one perhaps once in a lifetime. Straight ahead of us at the end of the big road the grey dawn broke. Above it rose a finely pared crescent moon—the last before the moonless night. I had never seen the moon, the morning star and the dawn together. I decided to interrupt the animated discussion of my companions on the respective merits of varieties of stud bulls. They looked at the scene for a minute or two without making any comment. Then a thin scraggy cow ambled across the road. Mr Obaidullah Khan remarked triumphantly: 'We are no longer in my block. See the state of that cow—the new breed sired by our stud bulls is much fatter.'

(*1957*)

VISITING A LUNATIC ASYLUM

I have been trying to analyse the reasons which impelled me to spend the better part of a day visiting a lunatic asylum when there were so many more important things to do. Given the choice, I would still rather visit a mental institution than see a good play or the best film. Here is drama full of tragedy but the actors wear masks as if at a carnival; and it is so human that you sometimes forget which side of the stage you are—actor or spectator.

Hitherto I have only visited one mental home: the famous one at Ranchi formerly meant only for Europeans. It has beautiful gardens in which the different wards are located. Dr L. P. Verma, the head of the institution, is obviously keeping up the place as it ought to be kept and is deeply involved in his work.

Two impressions stand out in my memory. The first was that the male patients were more cheerful and willing to work than the female—who seemed to mope more and be more melancholic. The other was that a large number of patients seemed utterly normal; I mistook several for hospital staff. The dividing line between sanity and insanity is apparently extremely thin. This was proved to me personally.

Just before leaving I ran into an old school friend. I had lost contact with him and had no idea he had become a mental patient. He was very pleased to see me and complained bitterly of the lack of good company. 'Now I will have somebody to talk to,' he exclaimed with satisfaction. 'Which ward have they put you in?'

(*1957*)

THAT EXAMINATION FEELING

Officially the season is spring. The yellow mustard fields, the laziness in the air, and the perfume in public parks all proclaim the fact. But if you look carefully at the flora and fauna in public parks, you will discover a phenomenon that proclaims the fact much more unmistakably than anything else. And this is the sight of a harassed-looking youth pacing up and down agitatedly, book in hand. If it is not too long ago that you have been a student yourself, you will realize at once that the season is the examination season. And you will recognize the phenomenon at once as 'an examinee preparing for the forthcoming exams'. His lips move as he reads words, sentences, chapters, made meaningless by constant repetition in an effort to learn them by heart. When he is tired of pacing up and down, he sits cross-legged on the ground, and rocks back and forth as he reads aloud. The rocking is really a technical device. It provides an accompanying rhythm to the words as they are pronounced aloud, thus helping to fix them in his memory.

The scene is repeated in hostel rooms, buses, laboratories, and homes all over the country. It will continue to be repeated until our system of examinations is changed fundamentally. February, March and April will continue to be nightmarish months (despite the gaiety of Holi) for all those who are embarked upon the doubtful business of getting themselves a degree.

Every few years there is talk among educationists of doing away with such an arbitrary system of assessing merit and work. Our schools, colleges and universities continue to turn out students whose degrees have very little connection with the years they have spent working for those degrees, or with their real worth.

A well-trained and keen mind is of no avail if its owner is a nervous type who cannot muster all his wits together in the crucial, all-important three hours, which is the normal duration of an examination paper. At the same time it is possible for the holder of a brilliant academic record to be a person of poor intellectual stature but have more than an average presence of mind.

There seems to be perfect unanimity about the fact that the prevalent system of examinations encourages feats of memory rather than the exercise of intellect and the analytical powers of the mind. Nor is there disagreement about the need for a drastic change. But we tend to fall too easily into a smug way of thinking where the mere recognition of a need and its constant reiteration become a substitute for action. The very people who have expressed dissatisfaction with the system have the power and the responsibility to take the necessary steps.

(1957)

TRAPPINGS OF POWER

Some years ago Miss Nancy Mitford introduced a new concept in the English language based on the vocabulary used by the upper class as distinct from that used by others. Telling U usage from the Non-U became quite a pastime in England. Did you say: 'Can I use the telephone?' or 'Can I ring up?'. Did you ask for a serviette or a napkin? Did you ask to be shown the WC or the lavatory? And so on.

We Indians do not have any usage of speech by which we may recognize a person's class. Most of our so-called upper class speak English and, unless they have been educated in England, speak it exactly as if they were speaking the language of their region. They use the same stress, accent and inflection of voice, accompanied by a generous variety of gestures—positively Non-U by English convention. Even when we speak our own languages, there are no distinctive patterns of speech for what we might call the U Class in India. But speech is not the only thing. And it is of very little import when it comes to identifying the class that matters today—the people in power. Our division is P and Non-P with their recognizable trappings.

Mr Nehru has made reference to the trappings of power in disparaging terms and denounced some of them as remnants of the British Raj. Peons in scarlet robes, flags on motor cars and armed sentries patrolling platforms as VIPs slumber in their saloons are all probably remnants of the Raj. But there are other practices which are pure Swadeshi products of our Ps which the British Us would do well to emulate.

◆

The most celebrated P practice is concerned with the number on motor cars. There is something positively U about a man who drives a vehicle with No. 1 on its number plate. It has none of the vulgar ostentation of the flag and yet it puts its owner in a class by himself. As the number increases the importance of the owner decreases. By the time it reaches four figures both vehicle and occupant cease to have any class significance whatsoever. If the choice is between riding in a Rolls Royce with an undistinguished number plate or in a dilapidated Baby Austin with No. 1—the Austin would win each time.

The allotment of car numbers has been the privilege of collectors of districts and most confer the distinction of being No. 1 upon themselves. At important conferences in state capitals, one can see a dozen or more number ones. When the collector moves to a higher post, he expects to be compensated for the loss of a distinctive number plate by a flag or a sentry. It may happen that an elevated status may find the bureaucrat between the unique number plate class and the flag-sentry class; then there is trouble.

One such case happened in a northern state when a collector on promotion refused to part with his No. 1. His intrepid successor proceeded to hang the identical honour on his own car. As fate would have it, the two cars were involved in an accident. Fortunately the officials were not on speaking terms and considered it non-P to report the accident to the police. Their wives prated at some length on the merits of the case and then agreed to take it to the supreme tribunal of the town—the mofussil ladies' club. There the matter rests, still unsettled but in eminently P circles.

(*1957*)

VIP BALLY-HOO

The performance was by one of the best Bharatanatyam dancers in the country. The theatre was the capital's best auditorium. It was made of red sandstone and marble and had alabaster walls to silence the echo, and subdued lights to produce a twilight effect. The audience was also of the best of society. Large limousines flying the flags of many nations drew up one after the other. The Indian tricolour was conspicuous by its absence. In the hall, too, the foreigners outnumbered the Indians. There was a galaxy of ambassadors in their black and white, their wives in elegant strapless gowns. The khaddar caps, sherwanis and dhotis of our VIPs were missing. But the hall was only half-full and the notice at the ticket office said all seats had been sold.

The curtain rose punctually at 6 p.m. The Indian VIPs had apparently scheduled to leave their homes at that hour. They began to pour in during the first item. They blocked the gangways and demanded to be shown their seats (not their places). They called for the programme wallahs (and, being VIPs, had no small change, only ten-rupee notes). So instead of Bharatanatyam we saw the broad backsides of our VIPs. When the lights went up, the hall was nearly full and had a fine display of turbans and khadi caps. Some seats still remained vacant.

The curtain went up on item two—this had been advertised as the best in the repertoire of the artist. She started with superb grace and it was obvious that she had put in many years of hard work to master the technique. She created that silent communication between performer and audience that held both in an ecstatic spell of magic. The silence and the spell were broken by the arrival of yet another VIP. His voice boomed across the hall: 'Oh, it has started already!' He was obviously hurt that they had not waited for him. A host of young men with squeaky shoes piloted him to his seat. Another lot followed with the programmes; a third group asked him if he would like something to drink. And finally a fourth gang enquired if he was all right. The second item was thus dedicated to this very VIP. The lights went up for the interval.

The first part of the third item was similarly ruined by people returning to their seats after refreshing themselves. Most of the latecomers were again our own countrymen. Then we came to the last item—a dance form never before performed in the city. Once again the danseuse cast her spell over the audience. The dance moved to its climax. Apparently, only the Indian VIPs knew that the performance was coming to a close. Many of them got up and began to move across the rows and up the gangways. Young men with squeaky shoes came to escort them and whispered their sycophantic enquiries about how they had enjoyed it. When the curtain came down the hall was half-empty again. Only the foreigners remained to applaud the superb performance. The danseuse took one disgusted bow and vanished.

Outside the theatre the limousines were lined up once more. But this time they did not only display flags of foreign nations; there were a large number of Indian tricolours. And they were ahead of all the others.

(*1958*)

DIDN'T OUR PRIME MINISTER SAY...

I saw the policeman outside the gate when I threw open the windows of my bedroom to let in the sun. The sight of a policeman still makes me nervous. I went out and asked him respectfully whether I was wanted for any offence. 'No,' he replied sourly. 'The governor is to pass this way. I am on duty.' I could understand his sourness. It was cold in the mountains and the hour was 7 a.m.

When I went out for a walk I saw the whole route lined with policemen: one every couple of hundred metres. They were all there waiting to salute the governor when he drove by. I gathered that there was no danger to the life of this august official. As a matter of fact, neither the policemen nor any of the passers-by knew his name.

The governor passed. A pilot car went in front, another one loaded with armed constabulary followed. But the policemen stayed on. 'He has to return in the evening,' explained the man at my gate. I do not know at what hour the governor returned, but I saw the policeman still outside the gate when I shut my windows against the cold night air and went to bed.

Didn't our prime minister say that this sort of thing is not right?

On my way back to my hometown, I happened to find myself travelling on the same train as a minister. None of the passengers would have been aware of the privilege but for the fact that at every station, a policeman emerged from the servants' compartment and mounted guard on the platform outside the minister's air-conditioned coach. This constable carried a rifle with a bayonet stuck in it. The crowd at the stations watched this demonstration of power with awe.

Didn't our prime minister say people in power must not do such things?

When I came to Delhi, a big international conference was on. I believe the idea was to tell the visitors that we were a poor people who meant to improve their lot by hard work if they got the wherewithal and the know-how. Apparently it was decided the best way to do that was by arranging banquets where several hundred guests were entertained to many courses of exotic food and imported beverages. Expensive cigars and choice cognac are proverbially good for sales talk. But I wonder how we can talk of economic distress when our breath exhales Havanas and Napoleon brandy.

Didn't our prime minister say...

Well…

(*1958*)

HANGED BY THE NECK TILL YOU ARE DEAD

All this while I have been advocating the abolition of the death penalty. After sifting through the criminal record of the serial killer Raman Raghav and noticing the insouciance with which he heard the sentence 'to be hanged by the neck till you are dead', I am beginning to have second thoughts. What can society do with a man like him? If he is insane in the medical or psychological but not in the legal sense of the term, should he be fed, clothed and taken care of for the rest of his natural life at the expense of the state?

I had many occasions to visit condemned prisoners' cells in Lahore jail. There were about ten constructed in the shape of a V, every corner visible from one point. Several warders kept watch over the convicted men; at night a powerful searchlight played over them. They had to urinate and defecate under the public gaze. They had no cords in their pyjamas nor did any of the utensils in the cells have sharp edges lest they cheat the law by taking their own lives. The ghastliest part of the business was the time it took between the passing of the sentence and its execution. The period between the verdict of the sessions judge, its confirmation by the high court and the rejection of the appeal for mercy could be anything from six months to two years. During this period a condemned man would, every week, witness one of the others in the neighbouring cells meeting his parents, wife, children and other relatives for the last time and a day or two later being led out to the scaffold. Most men when their time came to die were already half-dead out of fear and anxiety. (Curiously enough, under the shadow of impending doom, they ate more and put on weight.) If Arthur Koestler is right, many are dead before the noose is tightened round their necks and the floorboards fall away.

There is another legend about execution by hanging: that death is instant. It is not. At least two magistrates who witnessed executions as a part of their duty told me that the condemned men often die not due to the snapping of the spinal cord caused by the fall but by strangulation; the executioner has to go down into the pit and pull their dangling legs to finish them off. (The magistrates sickened at the sight and took to their beds for a day.) I personally know of one case where a man was hanged twice but did not die. This was a Sikh constable, Atma Singh, sentenced to be hanged for the murder of a fellow policeman. The first time the rope snapped. It was quickly tied together and the poor man put back on the scaffold. The second time the knot gave way and a very dazed but alive Atma Singh walked out of the pit. The sentence was thereupon commuted to one of transportation for life. In due course Atma Singh found himself in a criminal lunatic asylum suffering from what would appear a very sane hallucination. I met him in jail twenty-three years ago. He was an enormous man. Nearly six feet tall, corpulent and as powerful as a grizzly bear. 'Yes, I killed a man,' said Atma Singh 'but they've hanged me not once but twice. What more does the sirkar want to do to me?' In the asylum an inmate who called him mad was rewarded by a whack on the head with a brass ladle which bashed in his skull. Atma Singh was again sentenced to die. This time he got away on the plea of insanity. For all I know he is still alive.

(*1969*)

MR BUMBLE: THE LAW IS AN ASS

Early in August I received a notice initialled by a gentleman describing himself as the principal postal appraiser informing me that a parcel containing seven copies of *Playboy* magazine addressed to me had been seized on the grounds of obscenity. I was also 'required to show cause, in writing, within ten days...why penal action should not be taken against me'. And I was informed that if I failed to do so the case would be adjudicated, as it were, ex parte.

I did not show cause either in writing or in person and no action was taken against me. I have little doubt that the principal postal appraiser and the assistant collector of customs are wrangling between themselves about who has the prior right to enjoy this so-called obscenity. More likely, having shared the joys in turn, they've sold them to some dealer who in his turn is offering them for sale at more than three times their marked price. Anyone can buy *Playboy* and its compendium of naughty jokes at any pavement stall in any big city in India.

How can guilt conceivably attach to an innocent person who is sent something as a gift? If I were to post copies of *Playboy* to the principal postal appraiser or the assistant collector of customs, would they be guilty of receiving obscene literature? How idiotic can one be!

However, I cannot claim to be an innocent receiver. When I was in the United States I became a *Playboy* addict. It had excellent articles and short stories by the most renowned thinkers and novelists of our time—Russell, Mcluhan, Ginzberg, Wilson, Malamud, Mailer, etc. It also has girlie pictures, risque jokes, and Rabelaisian bawdiness. I do not object to any of these. On the contrary. The copies seized were posted by me in the States to myself in India. I am doubly guilty as the sender and the receiver. Please sir, principal postal appraiser or assistant collector of customs, have me arrested and jailed.

May I let you self-appointed censors of our morals in on another secret! A few days ago I ran into R. K. Narayan at Palam airport. You may not know it but RK is our most distinguished novelist today. And what do I discover! He not only receives and reads *Playboy*, he *writes* for it. The July issue has a piece by him. He received $2,500 for this very short short-story entitled 'A Breath of Lucifer' and has been asked to write more. (Incidentally, RK's admirers have presented him with an air-conditioned Mercedes Benz. Envious authors, please note.) Please, Mr PPA, may I share a cell with RK? And may we have our seized copies back to while away the dull tedium of prison life?

I hope some Member of Parliament will undertake to rectify this sorry state of affairs about the law and practice (not the same thing) of controlling obscene literature. I, for one, am against any law on the subject. I am convinced that it is impossible to define obscenity and there is no reason to waste one's energies in trying to do so. Writing cannot be labelled clean or unclean, only good or bad. Pornography, according to Nabokov, is the 'copulation of clichés', not human beings.

Our censors may learn something from international experience. Currently there is a 'Sex 69' exhibition taking place in Copenhagen. The Danes have made pornography a lucrative export business. That I think is disgusting. However the organizers admit that since Denmark abolished censorship its internal sales have dropped rapidly. But exports (sexports is the better word) to countries with rigid laws have rocketed. Says one of the organizers: 'We find from our mail that people in countries where anti-sex laws are strictest are our best customers.'

The moral is plain: abolish censorship and you will see that people will soon be bored with pornography. Our experience with prohibition should be a pointer. As soon as you proclaim something illicit, it becomes all the more fascinating.

(*1969*)

GENTLEMAN GOONDA

In Delhi I ran into a demonstration outside the Congress office on Jantar Mantar Road. I could hear Zindabads for Indiraji and Hai Hais for 'Golgappa'. The police stopped me and warned me that if I took my car any further, I might well be murdabad myself. I parked my vehicle at a safe distance and edged my way through the police cordon into the demonstrators. The old syndics were having a rough time. But who were these patriotic slogan-shouters? Where had I seen these faces before? Of course! At most demonstrations in Delhi... Yelling anti-Maoist slogans outside the Chinese Embassy, anti-Pakistan slogans outside the Pakistani High Commission, throwing stones at the US Embassy (which is carefully designed to be out of reach of a human propelled missile).

I recognized a Sardarji whom I had seen everywhere—including weddings, diplomatic cocktail parties, official receptions. He is a kind of professional cheerleader at all demonstrations in the capital. You can hire him and his gang in the same way you'd hire a band for a wedding. It is Rs 6 per head per demonstrator (Rs 100 for the leader) plus a free bus ride to the site of demonstration; and, if you want a few brickbats hurled, a supply of stones; iced beer and Coca-Cola are much appreciated by the shouters.

I know the Sardarji well. Two years ago, he organized a gherao of my house. Give him credit for having a cool nerve. He came with a forged invitation and partook of the repast I had laid out. At the same time his boys smashed up windowpanes and electric bulbs and assaulted many of my guests: one, a well-known Congress leader, suffered a broken wrist. He has a good public relations set-up. Next morning some papers (mainly of the left wing) wrote that despite the provocation by the organizers of the function and the police, the demonstration had been entirely peaceful.

I did have an occasion to ask the 'gentleman' why he had treated me in this manner. He apologized and said that it hurt him very much to have to do this to a fellow Sardar, but business is business and one must fill one's belly. He assured me that if I ever needed his services I should not hesitate to get in touch with him. A perfect goonda gentleman if ever there was one. I am told that every large city has its quota of this nouveau aristocracy of thugs.

(*1969*)

INDIAN TEHZEEB AND EUROPEAN ETIQUETTE

Both tehzeeb and etiquette are outdated concepts. One rarely hears any comments on saleega (can't think of an English equivalent) in the manner of speech. But foreigners often complain that we Indians lack manners. We don't say 'please' and 'thank you', our behaviour in public places is inconsiderate towards others and we are loud-mouthed. I am inclined to agree with the verdict, with the caveat that like the French we attach more importance to courtesy than to deportment. A Frenchman will kiss a lady's hand and pay the plainest looking girl the handsomest compliments. An Indian will touch another's feet when he would really like to kick him on the posterior, and shower words of praise on the least praiseworthy.

However, encounters between Indians and foreigners and their attempts to outdo each other in effusions of goodwill can often be amusing. I recount two incidents from my past.

A French lady was dining with a Sikh family consisting of many brothers who looked very much alike in their turbans and beards. The hostess introduced the eldest and the youngest, and, having nothing better to say, asked the visitor who she thought was the younger of the brothers. The French lady scrutinized the two from all angles like a connoisseur examines a work of art. Then she placed her finger on the younger man and explained with the necessary hesitation. 'I zink he is ze younger. But very, very little, only by about seex mons.'

When the hostess explained that the process of creation took a little longer in India, the guest was embarrassed. She was French and a Frenchwoman is expected to know the facts of life better than women of any other country. 'Mais oui oui,' she explained, recovering her composure. 'What are a few months this way or that, but we should always be polite, tojours la politesse n'est ce pas?'

The Americans have an altogether fresh approach to the problem of human relationships. Good manners and courtesy are charmingly old-worldly but they get one anywhere. One has to get around a person, and to do that one should know the other's name (and use it as often as possible), know office problems and interests, discuss them and generally flatter his ego into utter submission. The technique can misfire. I recall meeting an American lady who had risen to dizzy heights of social success by mastering her Dale Carnegie. Before she met me, she had taken the trouble to find out something of my antecedents and consulted the Encyclopaedia Britannica on the Sikhs. She communicated this information to me. Having fed my vanity and aroused my interest she lapsed into an indifferent silence—broken by two sentences she repeated alternately at suitable intervals. The conversation proceeded somewhat as follows:

'I've been reading about your community, the Sikhs. Violent lot, aren't they? I wonder why?'

I explained how virile people are often violent and Sikhs were a very virile race.

'How nice.'

It wasn't nice at all, I continued, because they could do so much that was constructive. The Sikh peasant wasted a lot of energy in being violent.

'I wonder why?'

Family feuds, odd notions of honour, sometimes just to crack a bald skull for the fun of it.

'How nice.'

It wasn't nice at all, I insisted. Marxists believe that the ultimate cause of crime is poverty and here was India's richest peasantry with the highest incidence of violence.

'I wonder why?'

I went over the business of family feuds and vendettas again. I also explained that the Sikh peasants did not stoop to anything as low as petty pilfering or robbery. But when it came to fighting, they were like the Irish. 'Would you believe,' I said in a tone of horror, 'that of every ten chaps hanged for murder in the Punjab at least nine will be Sikhs.'

'Oh, how nice.'

(*1978*)

THERE IS SOMETHING ABOUT A WALL

What a lamp post is to a dog, a wall is to the Indian male. The block of apartments I live in has a long wall. It demarcates our block from the main thoroughfare and a bus stand. Every bus disgorges dozens of passengers who quickly divide themselves between paan chewers and pissers. One lot cluster round the paan wallah's booth; the other line themselves against the wall, turn their beatific gazes heavenwards and unzip their trousers. They make little noise but a lot of stink. If I were a Mughal prince living in Mughal times, I would practice archery on their privates. However, living in an epoch of democracy wherein the nauseous effluent has attained the status of amrit, all I can do is to grumble. My friend Sri Chand Chhabra, now president of the municipality, is a man of action. He is determined to make New Delhi the cleanest, greenest and most beautiful city in the world. He has an incredible passion for fountains but has very strong views about humans spouting water as and where it pleases them. To prevent further fouling of our environment he has had installed an iron railing about a yard from the wall. I do not think the railing will daunt any pissers, au contraire, I expect the eruption of a new sport to be named 'hit-the-wall'. Only the middle-aged or those with enlarged prostrates may be daunted by the distance. However, as the old lady said as she pissed in the sea, every little helps. All power to Chhabra's railing against the wall. But let me tell him that the only way to prevent people from pissing is to put up pictures of gods and goddesses at strategic points. We are a superstitious people and would rather piss in our pants than insult our deities.

I channelize my wrath against public urinators by delving into the literature on the subject. Apparently the word 'piss' was quite respectable and used as a synonym for urine because of its echoic-onomatopoeic quality. After 1760, the word came to be associated with drunkenness, bragging and sycophancy. A pub became a piss factory (a pub in a London suburb was named The Pisspot); to be drunk was to be pissed; or so drunk as to open a shirt collar to piss; gin mixed with hot water came to be known as piss-quick. A braggart became one who pissed more than he drank or a piss-fire because he talked as if he could put out a conflagration by urinating on it. A flatterer was one who pissed down one's back. Something that was never likely to happen came to be known as goose pissing. However the most appropriate use of the term could mean both generosity as well as niggardliness: to piss on a nettle was to be miserly, to piss money against a wall was to indulge in squandermania. And so on.

I am not sure whether the remark attributed to Clemenceau about Winston Churchill's oratory was meant as a compliment or otherwise. He said 'Ah! Si je pouvais pisser comme il parle'—I wish I could piss the way that man talks.

(*1979*)

HUMILIATION AS PUNISHMENT

A year ago some women caught pickpocketing had the words 'jeb katree' (pickpocket) tattooed on their foreheads by the Punjab police. It was a criminal act and the policemen responsible for it were punished. But the idea was a good one. I believe that the most appropriate punishment for some crimes is public humiliation. Only, care should be taken that persons penalized are first pronounced guilty by a judicial authority: the police can only charge persons with offences, not judge them. And the penalty imposed should not maim the offender for life. If those women were convicted of pickpocketing by a magistrate, instead of sending them to jail, he should have been empowered to sentence them to carry placards reading 'I am a pickpocket' and be paraded at places where they committed thefts and around the localities where they lived. Thus humiliated, they would not repeat their crimes.

Such powers are available to judges in many states in America. Shoplifters are often made to stand outside department stores from which they stole goods wearing them on their persons with placards reading 'I stole this cardigan, muffler, bra, etc., from this store'. Statistics show that people thus subjected to public humiliation are less likely to repeat their crimes than those fined or sentenced to imprisonment.

There is one other misdemeanour for which public humiliation will prove a more salutary deterrent than imprisonment or a fine. This is the molestation of women in streets, buses and trains—or what is known as eve-teasing in India. In this case the public has to be more spirited than it is. Instead of leaving it to the victim to report the matter to the police and then face interrogation in courts of law, people who witness such misbehaviour should get together, catch hold of the culprit, give the fellow a few tight slaps and then, if necessary, hand him over to the police. The magistrates trying such cases should be empowered to sentence the guilty to stand at bus stands, outside railway stations or public thoroughfares for a few hours bearing placards reading: 'I molested a woman, I am sorry'.

I have written many times about changing the penalty for rape from long-term imprisonment (or death) to a mandatory sentence of surgical castration. A rapist should be deprived of his ability to repeat his crime. It will prove a far stronger deterrent than any other form of punishment. Men dread losing their manliness.

A more pressing need is to change punishments for people who take part in communal riots. Those who indulge in violence against another community may be arrested and sentenced to a fine and imprisonment. Unfortunately, they emerge as heroes in the eyes of members of their own community. It is imperative that communal violence is quelled swiftly and the guilty punished on the spot. For this, the administration should depute magistrates to set up courts at the site, hear witnesses and the police without the presence of lawyers and pronounce judgements at once. They should be empowered to order the flogging of culprits—not the savage leather thongs used during the British Raj but just a cane—but it should be carried out in full view of the public with the culprit's bottom exposed. Nothing deprives a man of the image of macho heroism than to have his buttocks exposed to public gaze. He becomes the laughing stock of the locality in which he lives.

(*2001*)

THE IMPORTANCE OF BEING IMPORTANT

It is great fun watching important people trying to make sure that everyone around them knows they are important. The game is better watched while travelling by train. People who go by air are mostly of some importance because they pay a lot of money to get plane tickets, and since they are strapped to their seats most of the time, they do not have many opportunities to show off their importance. Those who travel by bus are the lowest caste of travellers; they don't bother about each other and, like air travellers, remain affixed to their seats or stand in the aisles. Rail travellers come from different sections of society; they are freer than air and bus travellers to move up and down the aisle and display trappings of importance. I had the opportunity to see some of them in action the last time I travelled from Kalka to New Delhi by the Shatabdi Express.

Few people board the train at Kalka; all of them come from resorts sprinkled around Shimla. There was a strapping young man who helped me put my suitcase on the rack. I thought he had recognized me as somebody of importance. He had not; he was simply being kind to an old man. Then came a party of six—four men in flat round turbans, a lady in black silk salwar-kameez loaded with gold bangles and rings and her daughter in jeans and a T-shirt with her head demurely covered with a dupatta.

I recognized the leader of the group as I had often seen him on TV doing kirtan in gurudwaras. He carried a three-foot-long kirpan which he reverently placed on the rack above his seat. (Being an orthodox Khalsa he should have kept it in his hand.) He is not a top-class raagi but is very popular because he maintains a rapport with his sangat by frequently exhorting them, 'Bolo saadh sangat', and they respond with loud cries of 'Sri Wahe Guru'. I was impressed that the saadh-sangat of the Shivalik Hills had willingly paid six executive class fares to hear him sing. No sooner were they seated than several tiffin carriers were opened. Snacks were served on silver platters, tea in silver tumblers.

It was a very upper-class Guru ka langar. I noticed the young girl cross the aisle to speak to her father. She addressed him as 'papa', as any convent-bred girl would. It would have been more appropriate if she had called him 'pitaji'. Raagis, however popular, are not entitled to be papas or daddys.

The really important people board the Shatabdi Express at Chandigarh. They don't come rushing in like other hoi polloi, looking for their seats and grabbing places for their luggage. Their lackeys precede them, find their seats and place their baggage. They enter in state just as the train is about to leave. On this journey there were three such important personages. One was a full general. As he sat down, his orderly saluted him and departed. The general did not wish to talk to anyone. He opened a newspaper and appeared lost in its contents. The other was a portly Sardarji with his paunch jutting out six inches beyond health limits. The first thing he did after he took his seat was to take out his mobile and ring up his home in Delhi. In a booming voice, he said: 'We are leaving Chandigarh; tell the driver to bring the car to the VIP parking area.' We were in no doubt he was a VIP.

The third important person was the governor of some state. He was accompanied by his shrimati, a personal servant in spotless white turban and coat, and a tall young ADC in military uniform. All ADCs of governors look like handsome gigolos who add importance to their bosses. In addition, there was a railway police guard armed with an ancient carbine. He stood in the aisle questioning the credentials of everyone who wanted to go to the loo located at the end of the compartment. Neither the governor nor his shrimati had to tell other passengers that they were important.

At New Delhi railway station, a small procession of important people marched out towards the VIP parking area. The members of the raagi jatha were not in this procession. But they scored over other VIPs by being received by admirers who garlanded them and raised their voices, 'Boley So Nihal! Sat Sri Akal!'

(*2002*)

HOW A RAPIST SHOULD BE PUNISHED

Some weeks ago *India Today* had a lead story on rape. The cover page highlighted the detail that in India a woman is raped every 54 minutes. 'Sexual crimes are on the rise in our cities.' As a matter of fact, the incidence of rape and crimes against women are much higher and increasing by the day both in urban and rural areas. A majority of cases do not get reported as common people have no confidence in the police or criminal courts and do not wish to expose the victims of such crimes to publicity. The magazine's team of researchers also revealed that 75 per cent of rapists are married men, a substantial proportion of them relatives or friends of the victim's family. This does not cover incidents of gang-rape. Besides adducing data on sex-related crimes, the researchers had little to offer by way of solutions. They quoted R. S. Gupta, Delhi's commissioner of police, who had said that if girls dressed modestly and did not expose too much of their bodies, the incidence of rape would be reduced by half. This is as silly a statement as I have ever heard. And even sillier was the deputy prime minister's statement that rapists should be sentenced to death. In most advanced countries, even murderers are no longer executed; to hang rapists would be a retrograde step.

We need not indulge in horrendous stories on the lives of victims of rape. Pinki Virani's story about Aruna, a nurse in Bombay who was in a coma for decades after being raped, while her rapist—having served his sentence of imprisonment—walked free is enough to keep you awake for many nights. We have to take a common sense approach to the problem.

Rape and molestation of women take place all over the world; their incidence is much higher in male-dominated societies than in societies where women matter as much as men. India is still a male-dominated patriarchal society in which women are regarded as lower than second-class citizens. The situation in Pakistan is much worse; there violence against women is more prevalent than in India. Only recently a woman was gang-raped with the sanction of a tribal council. We too have had cases where caste panchayats have been behind the rape of women belonging to another caste to settle old scores. It will take time for the man-woman power equation to be balanced.

In advanced societies, rapists are treated as psychopaths needing medical treatment. In backward societies like ours, they are more often normal people who suddenly feel the urge to expend their lust on unwilling females. Lust can be an expression of love; it can also be an expression of hate, revenge or misdirected masculinity. Whatever be the motivating factors, it is a serious offence against the dignity of women and deserves suitable punishment.

First, we must see that it is the offender and not the victim who is exposed to publicity and public disgrace; with us it is the other way round. Victims of rape get much more unwelcome and often unsympathetic media attention. This has to be reversed.

Another necessary step is to legalize prostitution—whether carried out in brothels or by call-girls—provided the sex workers are adults and have not been forced into the trade. The more you try to put down prostitution, the higher will be the incidence of crime against innocent women. You may find the idea repulsive but ponder over it and you will realize there is merit in the argument.

A radical change must be brought about in the punishment for crimes against women. We have blindly followed laws which punish such crimes with imprisonment and fines. Neither is enough of a deterrent to men committing them. We should re-introduce our age-old methods of exposing rapists to public disgrace before suitably punishing them. Courts should be empowered to order them to be taken to the localities in which they reside, be stripped and lashed. Nothing can knock the machismo out of a man faster than being humiliated in front of his friends and neighbours. And finally, the most appropriate punishment for a rapist is not being sent to jail for a long period or hanged (as has been suggested in various quarters), but to be deprived of his manhood. The sentence of castration should be made mandatory.

(*2002*)

BIRTHDAY CELEBRATIONS THAT LEAVE A BAD TASTE

At the time and place I was born (now in Pakistan), no one bothered about birthdays. No records were kept and not even the Hindu and Sikh families had horoscopes cast for their children. It was only after my parents migrated to Delhi and my father had to fill in my date of birth in the school admission form that he put in a date which came to his mind. It was some years later when I had to take birthday gifts for boys and girls that I started celebrating my own, on a made-up date. By the time I finished school, I finished with birthday parties as well. Sometimes friends sent me greeting cards or rang me up, nothing beyond that. We celebrated the birthdays of two of our ten gurus, just as Jains celebrated that of Mahavira and Buddhists that of Gautama Buddha, and as Hindus celebrated the birthday of Lord Rama, Muslims of their Prophet and Christians their Jesus.

Our leaders, if they celebrated their birthdays, did so in their homes with members of their families and also friends. No one ever dreamt of making them public events at public expense. Ever heard of Bapu Gandhi cutting his birthday cake? Or the anglicized Nehru throwing a party for his supporters? Or Rajendra Babu, Radhakrishnan, Gurudev Tagore, Azad Zakir Hussain, Sardar Patel, Netaji Subhas Chandra Bose, Indira Gandhi, Rajiv Gandhi or any of the stalwarts of the past generation celebrating their birthdays? No, the public celebration of birthdays of public figures at public expense is a phenomenon of recent years. Do retired actresses, schoolteachers and librarians who have made good in politics really think that their birthdays are of any interest or importance to the common people? No, they laugh at them. So do their chamchas or chamchis, after they have gorged themselves on chocolate cake, pakoras, mithai and chaat. These netas do not know the word sophistication nor the difference between culture and crass vulgarity.

(*2003*)

A MATTER OF POLITICS

THE STORY OF NINE MILLION HUMANS AND 300 CRORE RUPEES

It was the winter of 1947 and late in the evening. The sky was overcast and a fine drizzle fell on the deserted street. A cold wind blew and chilled my bones. I wrapped my thick overcoat closer to my body. The boy who sat huddled alongside the wall of the shop hugging a bundle of newspapers was wearing a cotton shirt and pyjamas. He was barely ten years old. He was a Sikh but had no turban to cover his topknot nor shoes on his feet. He shivered in the cold. I could hear his teeth rattle.

'Give me the evening paper,' I said and handed him a rupee note.

He stood up and handed me the paper. Then he began to undo the knot in the hem of his shirt in which he had tied up his change. He was a delicately built child with light brown hair. His long eyelashes curved up towards his eyebrows like a film star's. It was obvious he came from a well-to-do urban family.

'Keep the change,' I said in as gentle a manner as I could. I expected him to get embarrassed with gratitude. Instead, he turned on me like an angry baby cobra. He snatched the paper out of my hand and flung the rupee note on the ground. 'You think I am a beggar!' he hissed indignantly. He picked up his bundle of papers and disappeared into the night.

That little Sikh boy symbolized the indomitable spirit of the people of the Punjab. Five million of them were compelled to leave their homes, lands and shops in Pakistan a few months after Partition. These five million included the landed gentry, some of whom owned estates of the richest canal-irrigated lands of India yielding almost a lakh of rupees a month. After Partition they contented themselves with a few miserable acres of thorn and shrub without any irrigation facilities. There were eminent lawyers and doctors with well-established practices who had to rebuild their homes, libraries, laboratories and clinics in strange towns and cities. There were petty tradesmen who had to start their small businesses from scratch. Above all, there was the peasantry which had once more to clear jungles, drain marshes and turn the sod on virgin lands. One saw schoolgirls abandon their books to ply tongas. One saw erstwhile owners of industry hawking goods on the streets. They grumbled a little—but never was a hand stretched out to ask for alms.

Do you know how much our Punjabis lost in this exchange of population?

Our people who came out of West Pakistan left 21,448 square kilometres of land. People who left India and went to Pakistan left behind 15,580 square kilometres acres of land. So we were short by 5,868 square kilometres of land. Our loss in residential property was even worse. Our people left behind in Pakistan property worth Rs 500 crore. Property left by migrants to Pakistan was worth less than Rs 100 crore i.e. less than a fifth.

To this day Pakistan has not paid a single anna to compensate for the difference.

The people of the Punjab have, however, rehabilitated themselves by their own resources and the generous help given to them by their government. The tragic tale of the Punjab is over.

EAST PAKISTAN

The story of refugees from East Pakistan has not ended. It is like a serial where one instalment outdoes the previous one in sordidness. Hitherto 4 million Bengalis from East Pakistan—from Khulna, Barisal, Chittagong, Dacca and all other districts—have crossed into India and they continue to come. The author of this sad serial is the government of Pakistan. For one, it has not been stable—it has had six prime ministers in ten years and each shake-up in the government weakens the administration and causes more nervousness in the minorities. For another, despite their promises to look after the minorities, harassment continues without redress. People never give up the security of their homes, lands and incomes unless there is danger to their lives. And the 4 million Hindus of East Bengal have done just that: given up the security of their homes, trades and lands to come to the congested cities of West Bengal. In some months the flow of refugees reached the figure of 55,000 per month. The Pakistanis accused India of seducing these people with offers of money. If they only paid a visit to Calcutta today, they would know what nonsense that is. The city's parks and pavements are full of refugees. At Sealdah railway station there have been as many as 10,000 people cooking, eating and sleeping on the platforms and approaches. Even today it presents a scene of indescribable filth and squalor.

The refugee problem of Bengal is unlike the one in the Punjab. The migrations in the Punjab were finished once and for all when all the non-Muslims were ejected from West Pakistan. Our government at least knew what it was up against. The migration of Hindus from East Pakistan continues. Of the 12 million Hindus in 1947 only 8 million remain today. And even now they keep coming over, sometimes in trickles of twos and fours; then suddenly in the thousands. We cannot plan ahead, and each wave of immigrants causes a crisis. In the Punjab, the movement was a two-way traffic. Refugees who came to India found lands and homes—however inadequate—left by those who left India. In Bengal it is one-way traffic—from Pakistan to India. (Ours is a secular democracy wedded to Mahatma Gandhi's principles of keeping India the home of all religions and races without any discrimination—so our minorities are safe and happy in their homes.) West Bengal was densely populated and now its capacity to take refugees has reached bursting point. To add to these difficulties, there is the reluctance of the Bengalis to settle in areas other than those where Bengali is spoken.

BIG SLICE OUT OF PLAN

Amongst the greatest achievements of our government in the ten years of its existence is the resettlement of refugees from Pakistan. And it has done so without putting out the begging bowl to any foreign power or agency. Almost all the 5 million refugees from the Punjab have found homes and means of living. The same process is taking place in Bengal now. Today, there are 350,000 displaced persons living in 211 camps. Many thousand others have been put to work in hydro-electric projects, digging canals and making roads provided for in our Five-Year Plan. There are 351 settlements for refugees in the state.

New townships, new schools, colleges and technical training centres have sprung up everywhere.

Anyone travelling in West Bengal today will be struck by the enormous amount of work done in rebuilding new cities and adding to the old ones. He will also be struck by the enormity of the task that still remains to be done. He will see miles of khaki-green tents in which live families waiting to be given permanent homes and work. If he goes to the jungle tracts of Dandakaranya which link Bengal, Bihar and Orissa, he will see bulldozers clearing forests and new townships going up.

All this has taken a heavy toll on our development programmes. We have already spent Rs 300 crore on these resettlement schemes. In addition, we continue to spend Rs 3 lakh every day for the immediate needs of the refugees in West Bengal.

One has mixed feelings on the subject of refugees. On the one hand there is the feeling of pride in the great achievement. On the other, one of sorrow: how much bigger would our economy and prosperity have been if we did not have to spend so much money and energy on the rehabilitation of displaced persons.

(*1957*)

NOT WANTED IN PAKISTAN

Religious hatred is history's legacy to both India and Pakistan but while India fought against it, Pakistan fanned it. This has resulted in the flow of refugees—Hindu, Buddhist and Christian—from Pakistan into India ever since Partition. And for the first time since 25 March 1971 Pakistani Muslims have also been forced to seek sanctuary in secular India. Why? The present migration is on a much larger scale than all the previous ones put together. The manner in which they have been expelled has shocked the conscience of the world.

◆

'Why did you leave Pakistan?'

She wrapped her migration papers in a piece of cloth and put them back in her steel trunk. 'Why don't you ask all these people on the platform?' she said at last. 'Why don't you ask the millions of others who have come away? Why pick on me?'

Her voice was charged with emotion. She broke down and began to sob.

'I asked you only because you are the latest arrival here. You lived in Pakistan all these years; what made you come away now?'

Sarvamangala Devi had been most eager to speak to me when I came on to the Petrapole railway station platform. She had edged her way through the crowd and rapidly narrated her tale of woe. How her widowed daughter had been killed in the riots one year before Pakistan had been formed; how she had brought up her two-year-old orphaned grandson; how, as the boy grew older, his future began to worry her and the years grew heavy on her; how she grew desperate with anxiety and decided to come away; and how she found herself stranded at the first railway station on the Indian side, barely 100 metres from the Pakistan border—with no friends or relatives to look after her and no money to proceed anywhere. The platforms of Petrapole railway station had been their home since they had come to India, and her grandson's earnings from beggary their only means of livelihood.

'Did the villagers bother you? Was there any danger to your life or to that of your grandson?' I asked her gently.

She dried her tears with her hand and brushed back her short, tousled mop of hair. 'No! The Muslim villagers were kind, very kind. God bless them! They even gave us money to come this far. It was the outsiders and small officials who kept bothering us. They took whatever they wanted from our houses and no one listened to our complaints. When we went to the police station they said, "You go to India. There is no room for Hindus in Pakistan."' She looked up at me and added bitterly. 'It seems there is no room for Hindus in India either!'

Sarvamangala Devi continued her tale. She agreed she had stayed on in Pakistan for many years—she would have stayed on for the rest of her days if the other Hindus in her village had also stayed. But one after another they began to disappear, till only two of them were left—she, a sixty-year-old widow, and her grandson, a boy of thirteen. Then she too packed her belongings and came away. 'If I had died there, my boy would have been left alone in the world,' she sobbed.

She broke down once more and hid her face in the hem of her sari. Other refugees eagerly took her place and began to tell their stories. They came from all parts of East Pakistan; from distant Chittagong and from neighbouring Khulna. Most of those at the Petrapole railway station were from Barisal or Dacca. They had left on different dates and for different reasons.

Some had been victims of riots; others had had their womenfolk insulted. Some had been summarily dismissed from their jobs; others were refused renewals of trading licences. Some had their harvests stolen or their cattle lifted; others just felt nervous about their future and decided to go while the going was good. The one common theme which was repeated like a refrain was that whenever they had taken their grievances to the police or the courts, they had been turned back without redress.

HISTORY'S LEGACY

This was in 1957. I went to Petrapole again in 1964. And for the third time last month in June 1971. Each time the object was to find out why so many were leaving Pakistan.

Our leaders, Mahatma Gandhi and Jawaharlal Nehru, believed that the people of India were one people; and they were against communal separation. Opposed to this viewpoint was the Muslim League which believed that the Muslims were a distinct nation with the right to a state of their own.

Mr Jinnah, the founding father of Pakistan, in a speech delivered in London on 13 December 1946, said: 'The differences between Hindus and Muslims are so fundamental that there is nothing that matters in life upon which we agree... It is well known to any student of history that our heroes, our culture, our language, our music, our architecture, our jurisprudence, our social life are absolutely different and distinct...'

For many years the Congress refused to concede this on the grounds that Hindus and Muslims were of the same race, spoke the same languages and lived so completely mixed up in towns and villages that no partition of the country on religious grounds was possible. The demand for a separate state for the Muslims, however, gathered support from large sections of the Muslims. With it grew communal bitterness which burst into frenzied rioting, first in Calcutta in August 1946, where Mr Suhrawardy, a Muslim, was then chief minister. From Calcutta the rioting spread to the Muslim region of Noakhali (also in Bengal) where the Hindus were victims. From Noakhali it spread to Bihar where the Muslims suffered at the hands of the Hindus. In the winter of 1946–47 there was large-scale rioting in the predominantly Muslim areas of the NWFP and the Punjab. It was under the pressure of this widespread violence that the Congress Party agreed to a partition of the country.

PARTITION MASSACRES

Most frontiers follow courses of rivers or mountain ranges. Indo-Pakistan frontiers did not follow any natural boundaries. They were drawn with the sole object of separating predominantly Muslim areas from non-Muslim ones. The communities were so inextricably mixed up all over the subcontinent that, despite the tortuously zigzagging lines, those charged with dividing the country failed and did not satisfy either India or Pakistan. Forty-five million Muslims were left in India and 18 million non-Muslims in Pakistan. Since the division took place after a year of continuous communal rioting, the outcome was anticipated. In the north there was bloodshed, the like of which the country had never known. All Hindus and Sikhs (numbering over 5 million) were hounded out of Western Pakistan; about the same number of Muslims were driven out of northern India to Pakistan with equal ferocity. Thus did violence bring about a hurried exchange of populations and within a couple of months the intentions of those who drew the boundary lines to demarcate Muslim areas from the non-Muslim were fulfilled with a vengeance—at least in the Punjab. Immediately after attaining independence, the leaders of India re-affirmed their faith in the unity of the people of the country that was left to them. Nehru, as prime minister, outlined the policy of his government. 'So far as India is concerned,' he said, 'we have clearly stated both as Government and otherwise that we cannot think of any State which might be called a communal or religious state. We can only think of a secular, non-communal, democratic state in which every individual, to whatever religion he may belong, has equal rights and opportunities...that has been the ideal of the Indian National Congress ever since it was started sixty-five years ago and we have consistently adhered to it.'

The Indian government abrogated laws which, like the one of separate electorates, perpetuated communal distinctions. It outlawed bodies which preached hatred against other religious communities. It abolished communal institutions like separate schools, colleges, restaurants, etc. And despite the fact that a majority of the Muslims in the country had supported the demand for Pakistan, it tried to win the loyalties of the 40 million Muslims who stayed on in India. Their proportions in the services were strictly maintained and complaints of discrimination thoroughly scrutinized. Muslims became ministers in the central and state governments, governors of states, ambassadors, and generals in the army, and were entrusted with key jobs like any other Indian. The result was that not only did the exodus of Muslims, which had started in 1947, cease but over a million of those who had fled in the wake of the riots came back and have never again left Indian soil.

PAKISTAN'S POLICY TOWARDS NON-MUSLIMS

None of these things happened in Pakistan for the simple reason that with the Pakistan government the distinction between the Muslims and the Hindus was an article of faith, the basis on which the state itself was founded. Since Pakistan was to be a homeland of the Muslims, they were provided with jobs and trades at the expense of the Hindus whose representation in the services fell to less than a quarter of that due to them by virtue of their numbers. Pakistan became an Islamic state and, despite assurances that Islam preached unity and equality of mankind, it did not prevent non-Muslims from being relegated to the position of second-class citizens.

As most Hindus had opposed Pakistan up to the day it was formed, they were treated with vindictiveness. Instead of being given a chance to rehabilitate themselves in the new atmosphere, their leaders who had subscribed to the ideals of Gandhi and Nehru were promptly thrown into jail. This discrimination percolated down to lower levels where petty officials began to harass Hindus out of spite or for gain. Unsocial elements—particularly Muslim refugees who had come from India—joined them. Soon, there were no Hindus or Sikhs left in West Pakistan. The government's discriminatory policy towards its Hindu minority had to be directed against the Hindus of East Pakistan.

THE TWO BENGALS

The boundary line dividing Bengal made even less sense than the boundary in the northwest. Of the total Hindu population of Bengal, as much as 42 per cent was left in Pakistan, including some areas like the Chittagong Hill Tracts where they numbered more than 90 per cent. The new frontiers also played havoc with the economic life of the province. Jute mills were left on the Indian side; jute lands in Pakistan. Practically all the industrial and mineral resources came to India; most of the agricultural lands went to Pakistan. Well-to-do Pakistanis were cut off from the educational, social and cultural aspects of life which was centred in the metropolis of Calcutta. They described the division as 'the territorial murder of Pakistan'. Although Bengal remained peaceful at the time of partition, there was an understandable nervousness among the minorities on both sides. They remembered the old riots, and stories of happenings in the Punjab were not calculated to engender peace. On the Indian side, the Gandhi-Nehru policy of winning over the Muslims was put into effect and the very people who had a year before violently supported the demand for Pakistan were rehabilitated as good Indian citizens. Even a man like Suhrawardy, whose name had ugly associations with the riots of 1946 when he was chief minister, went back and forth from Calcutta to Dacca with impunity and finally settled in Pakistan a year later (having failed to satisfy Indian income-tax authorities). In the case of East Pakistan it was not easy to meet the demands of the middle-class Muslims without getting middle-class Hindus (who were better educated and therefore held better jobs as lawyers, doctors and businessmen) to quit. They also owned most of the land and employed Muslims as their tenants.

HINDU EXODUS

The first move was naturally against the propertied middle-class and men in the professions. Hindus in service were sacked in large numbers. (To this day when guarantees of a 23 per cent representation have been given, there are fewer than 5 per cent Hindus in Pakistan government jobs.) Their properties in the cities were seized by declaring them as intending evacuees. The first to leave Pakistan was the Hindu upper middle-class. Most of them had contacts on the Indian side and could look forward to picking up professions and trade in their new surroundings. This was an unfortunate move because most of the leaders of the Hindus came from this class.

The ejection of the well-to-do did not make enough room. East Pakistan is among the most densely populated areas of the world, with 992 persons per square mile. Dacca has 1,700 to each square mile. The next move was against small landowners and tradesmen. This was done through attempts at forcible conversion and violence. Anti-Hindu riots flared up in Khulna in December 1949 and spread to Barisal a month later. The Hindu peasantry, deprived of its leaders, fled in abject terror. In the month of March 1960 alone, over 75,000 were admitted to Indian refugee camps. Since they had been subjected to violence, they meted out violence to the Muslims on the Indian side, and before the government could stop them, a two-way traffic of refugees started across the border in the way it had taken place in the Punjab in 1947. At a meeting between the prime ministers of India and Pakistan it was agreed that the governments of their respective countries 'shall ensure the minorities throughout its territory complete equality of citizenship, irrespective of religion, a full sense of security in respect of life, culture, property and personal honour, freedom of movement within each country and freedom of occupation, speech and worship, subject to law and morality'. The refugees were invited to go back to their countries. They were promised restoration of their homes and properties. This time it was a one-way movement—of Muslims from Pakistan to India; one million of them came back to their lands and homesteads. The Hindus waited for the Pakistan government to take steps which would ensure the return of their property and safety of life. They waited in vain.

The next big spurt came in the middle of 1952. Economic conditions in East Pakistan deteriorated and crimes against the person and property of Hindus increased. About 200,000 of them crossed into India.

THE LAST STRAW

In the next two years (1954–56) a steady flow of between 6,000 and 10,000 Hindus left Pakistan for India every month without Pakistan doing anything to stop them. Early in 1955, the figure shot up again to over 30,000 a month. This time because of the agitation in connection with the safeguarding of Bengali against Urdu, the officially recognized language for all of Pakistan. Once more the two governments came together and the Pakistanis agreed to take several steps to check the outflow of Hindus. Quite obviously nothing was done because the migration continued unabated. Whatever Pakistan's ministers or officials did was soon vitiated by the constituent assembly when it declared Pakistan an Islamic state. This was the last straw which broke the Hindu cow's back.

The figures of migration reached the highest ever. During some of these months, figures reached a record of over 56,000 per month. West Bengal could not stand the strain of this inflow. It had no more land to settle the migrants on; no trades to put them in; no jobs to offer;

no money to feed the enormous population in the transit camps. The city of Calcutta teemed with refugees living in parks, on pavements and in public buildings. The scene at Sealdah railway station, where many detrained, became one of indescribable filth and squalor; over 10,000 people cooking, eating, sleeping, copulating, giving birth and dying on its platforms. The Pakistan government alleged that India was seducing migrants with offers of money. Until 1957 over 4 million East Pakistan Hindus migrated to India.

THE 'BIHARIS'

Seven years after my first encounter with Bengal refugees in 1957, I was back at Petrapole to report on a new wave of refugees which had started pouring into West Bengal. In those seven years the pressure on land in East Pakistan had again become intolerable. The increase in population (3 per cent per annum) accounted for some of this. There had also been anti-Muslim riots in several cities of India, chiefly in Calcutta, Ranchi in Bihar and some towns in Madhya Pradesh. Thousands of Indian Muslims fled to East Pakistan. Most of them settled in the cities of Dacca, Chittagong and Khulna in compact colonies. Their language was Hindustani, not Bengali. They were isolated in their new homeland; they threw in their lot with other linguistic minorities like the Punjabis, Pathans, Sindhis and Muslims of Uttar Pradesh who were well established in businesses, the civil service, the police and the army. All of them came to be lumped together and described as Biharis.

Their numbers are not easy to establish. Mr Zainul Abedin, West Bengal minister for refugees and rehabilitation, estimated them at about half a million. Mr Hossain Ali, who defected from the Pakistan government and is the chief Bangla Desh representative in India, puts the figure around 2 million. The 'Biharis' did not participate in the movement for an autonomous Bangla Desh. They did not support Sheikh Mujibur Rahman's Awami League that was demanding an end to the economic exploitation of East Bengal and the loosening of its relationship with West Pakistan. After the sweeping victory of the Awami League in the general elections of December 1970 (they won 167 seats out of 169) tension between the Biharis and the Bengalis exploded into violence in many cities. The Biharis took a terrible beating. The Pakistani press and radio now claim that they suppressed the reports of these riots in order to prevent reprisals against Bengalis living in West Pakistan. (President Yahya Khan did not refer to them in his speeches. Only recently has the theory of retaliation for what the Bengalis did to Biharis been given currency.) As soon as Sheikh Mujibur Rahman was arrested and the Awami League outlawed, the Biharis came out into the streets to settle scores.

While the West Pakistan army first cracked down on the Awami League leadership and Bengali intellectuals, the Biharis' chief targets were Hindus—who had enthusiastically supported the Awami League. Thus began the recent exodus from Pakistan. Three factors make it different from the earlier emigrations. It is bigger than all the previous emigrations put together; over 6 million crossed over in the two and a half months between the end of March and mid-June of this year; it is the greatest migration known in the history of the world. It is obviously designed to rid East Pakistan of all its Hindus and perhaps Christians and Buddhists as well. And for the first time it also includes a very substantial number of Bengali Muslims.

THE FINAL EXODUS

Last June I was back in Petrapole. The countryside had not changed. Only the ninety-six-kilometre route was lined with the hutments of refugees. All the towns and villages that I passed were crammed; schools, colleges and other public buildings had been turned into shelters, ration depots and hospitals.

I stopped at many refugee encampments. Immediately crowds of semi-clad men, women and children surrounded me. I started with the same questions I had asked the refugees in 1957 and 1964. 'Why did you leave Pakistan?'

This time the answers varied: Pakistani soldiers surrounded our village, killed all the young men and told us that if we did not leave they would kill us too... Biharis burnt our homes and took our cattle... My daughter was raped in front of me and I was told that if I did not get out my mother would also be raped.

The story of Mandhari Dasi of village Bhuttia (in District Jessore) is worth telling. She was known in the neighbouring hamlets for her beauty. When her mother-in-law heard the sound of jeeps she told the girl to run and hide in the jute fields. The soldiers asked for her. They beat the villagers but got no information. At random they picked up six young men, including Mandhari Dasi's husband, tied their hands behind their backs and shot them.

At every encampment there were some people with marks of injury—a young Muslim showed me the scar of a bayonet wound on his chest; a boy held up his arm, it had been smashed with the butt-end of a rifle; women covered their faces and sobbed when they were unable to talk of what had passed with them. Some had the nipples of their breasts bitten off by their ravishers. For the rest, the answer was the standard one: when they saw or heard what Pakistani soldiers and Biharis had done they left because of bhoy—fear. In four days I must have heard that one word—bhoy—a thousand times. Fear indeed has many eyes.

Most of the refugees are landless peasants, petty shopkeepers or menial workers; fisherfolk, thatch-makers, potters, weavers, cobblers, ironsmiths or labourers. The holdings of those who had land were seldom more than three bighas (about 4,000 square metres). And this has been acquired and given away to others to win their loyalty. I asked everyone I interviewed whether they would go back to Pakistan. Some replied, 'Yes, when Bangla Desh is liberated.'

I passed truckloads of Indian soldiers and saw trenches along the road. Suddenly the car pulled up in obedience to the command to halt. We were at the checkpost guarded by the Border Security Force. I got out of the car and approached the sentry. 'You can't go further. That's Pakistan,' he said, pointing to a yellow building a couple of hundred metres away. 'The border is sealed.' He was a young Rajput and eager to talk. 'I was told that 100,000 refugees cross over from Pakistan every day. There is not a soul here.'

'The Pakistanis have blocked all the roads. But they come all the same—over fields and across rivers.' He was right—India's border with East Pakistan is about 4,000 kilometres long. At a few places it is demarcated by rivers, for the rest it is only white stones marking one paddy or jute field from another. The boundary runs over dense jungles and mountains through habitations of hillmen more conscious of tribal than national loyalties. There are no barbed-wire fences and on the Indian side only 70,000 men of the Border Security Force who also patrol the West Pakistani and Chinese borders. 'The papers say you have been trading shots with the Pakistanis.'

'Something goes on every day. The Mukti Fauj is always up to something.'

'You think there'll be a war?'

'That is known only to Yahya Khan and Indiraji.'

I turned back towards Calcutta.

LIKE ESKIMOS ENTERING AN IGLOO

I stopped at many refugee camps. All had been put up almost overnight. They were like rows of barracks made of massive tarpaulins stretched on bamboo poles and open on all sides. In each, there were several hundred families separated by no more than a bedsheet or a sari hung on a rope. Others were made of a few bricks piled on top of each other and covered with a chatai. You had to crawl in on all fours like Eskimos entering an igloo. There were many who had made their homes under trees or under the open sky. The lucky were ensconced in drain pipes stacked along the side of the road. Only the pipe-dwellers would be sheltered from the fury of the monsoons.

At Barasat I visited a hospital. The maximum capacity of 230 patients had been stretched to over 600. Every bed had one patient on top and at least two lying on the floor underneath. All verandas were crammed. Those who had died of cholera that morning were laid alongside in a corner with only their faces covered. In the clinic I saw a doctor pour in the remains of a white powder from a bottle marked 'cholera' into the open mouth of a woman. A few minutes later I saw her throw up and collapse in his arms. She was laid alongside the corpses which by now had a dead child with his eyes wide open lying beside them. The morning papers gave the official figures of death by cholera as 5,000. Another thousand or two had succumbed to dysentery or typhoid or fatigue. As I was leaving the encampment a Tempo van was being loaded with corpses; three adults and three children were piled on top of each other. The Tempo drove off leaving the women wailing on the road. Shahara Camp along Calcutta's Dum Dum Airport has more than 40,000 refugees under tarpaulin, tent, thatch and open sky. The camp is well below the level of the road and known to turn into a lake after a heavy downpour. I saw men and women defecating in the open and asked the social worker on duty why he did not forbid this.

'How can I?' he pleaded. 'The pit latrines are full. One small shower and all the nightsoil will be floating into the tents.' He covered his nose with his handkerchief. 'If the monsoon is heavy, there will be a real disaster.'

Back in Calcutta I called on officials dealing with the refugees. Mr Nirmal Sen Gupta, chief secretary of the Bengal government, exclaimed: 'For the last three months we have done nothing except feed, clothe and house refugees; other work has been suspended. In eight of our sixteen border districts the number of refugees is more than that of the local inhabitants. It is the same in Assam and in Meghalaya. Tripura has doubled its population in the last two months. This creates problems.

'At Barasat, Hindu refugees occupied a mosque. Local Muslims drove them out. There was a riot. The refugees are costing us one crore of rupees a day. We have no money left for anything else.'

NEVER SEEN SUCH 'BONYATA'

Mr Zainul Abedin, till recently the minister in charge of Refugees and Rehabilitation, spoke: 'Barbarous savages, uncivilized brutes who spared neither Muslim nor Christian, neither Buddhist nor Hindu. Never, never has the world seen such bonyata (the Bengali word for savagery).' He draws a graph of the refugee exodus rising from 25,000 in March to 200,000 a day in the last week of May. 'It is difficult to explain why,' he admitted. 'It is like a river. When the summer comes, snow melts on the mountains. It takes a few days before the flood gets to the lower reaches of the river. People living in the interior were subjected to violence. As they trekked towards the frontiers, other villagers joined them. By the time they crossed to India, it was like the bursting of a dam.'

'Why don't we seal our borders?' I asked him.

'How can we do it? Right now we at least patrol the 4,000 kilometre border. When it rains we can't do even that. Then they'll come like the monsoon flood.' In the afternoon I called on Hossein Ali. He is ensconced in a massive three-storeyed mansion which was once the office of the deputy high commissioner of Pakistan. The green and gold flag of Bangla Desh now flies on the mast. 'We are giving our liberation forces extensive military training. We'll throw out the Pakistani army,' he said with confidence. He is discreet and did not tell me how many are being trained, where and by whom. But I picked up the information. Fifteen thousand are undergoing regular army training; some are being put through a three-week crash course in guerrilla tactics—how to dynamite bridges and roads, how to handle hand grenades. The target is a 50,000-strong force in a few months.

'When will your forces go into action?'

'They harass the Pakistanis all the time. Go to any point of the border and you'll hear sounds of rifle and mortar fire. Our liberation forces will soon get the upper hand—Inshallah.' 'Inshallah,' I replied as I took my leave. General Jagjit Singh Aurora, head of the Indian army's Eastern Command, is a tall, strapping Sikh. I asked him bluntly whether India will go to war against Pakistan. 'Not a fair question to ask a soldier,' he replied looking into his glass of Scotch. 'But you tell me what are we to do when 5 million, by the time it ends it may be 90 million people, are forced on us? We can't look after them and the world doesn't give a damn and there is a civil war on our borders.'

It is a dismal prospect. When I went to make my last call, black clouds were spreading across the sky. I passed trucks bearing legends—UNICEF, War on Want, Oxfam, Ramakrishna Mission. I rang the bell at the Missionaries of Charity headquarters and was let in by an Indian nun. Mother Teresa is expecting me. She is a sixty-year-old Albanian woman who has spent most of her life in Bengal. There was a small crowd of people asking her for something or the other. While she was busy with them, my eye caught a framed prayer hanging on the wall. I took down some of it in my notebook. 'Make us worthy, Lord, to serve our fellow men throughout the world who live and die in poverty and hunger. Give them, through our hands, this day their daily bread, and by our understanding love, give peace and joy.

Lord, make me the channel of Thy peace, that where there is hatred, I may bring love; and where there is wrong, I may bring the spirit of forgiveness...'

I had got that far when she turned to me. 'Don't bother to take it down. I'll give you a copy of the whole text.' From her desk she fished out a slip of printed paper and wrote. 'God bless you, Teresa Ma.' I asked her about her work amongst the refugees. She smiled and told me that she had not been able to do very much for them. 'We have to look after schools and leprosariums and night shelters for beggars. Our hands are full.' But God will always find people to do his work, etc.

When I came out, a cool breeze was blowing and a fine drizzle was coming down. The monsoon was not far away.

(*1971*)

FREEDOM FIGHTERS OF BANGLA DESH

The Mukti Fauj came into existence spontaneously on the night of 25 March 1971 when the Pakistani army launched its campaign of genocide in Bangla Desh. It had only 10,000 trained men. Today it has become the Gono Bahini—a people's liberation army with over 150,000 men and women and many million more ready to take up arms. How did the iron enter the soul of the peace-loving Bengali?

On the morning of 12 November, a 7,000-tonne cargo boat, the *City of St Albans*, flying the British flag limped up the mouth of the river Hooghly towards Calcutta. It had seventy holes of different shapes and sizes in its steel plates spreading from the rim of its funnel down to the waterline and from stem to stern. The next day a local newspaper carried pictures of the vessel, with a story ascribing the damage to the newly acquired naval wing of the Mukti Bahini, the liberation organization of Bangla Desh. The state government immediately clamped down on the episode. No photographers were allowed to take pictures of the ship and all that other papers published was a brief official handout to the effect that the ship had been attacked somewhere off the coast of East Pakistan.

Many questions came to my mind. Was the ship carrying cargo to East Pakistan? What was the nature of the cargo? Where exactly was it attacked? In Pakistan territorial waters or on the high seas? Who were the assailants? If it was really the Mukti Bahini—as is generally assumed—how, when and wherefrom did it acquire a gunboat to carry out the assault?

Four days later I managed to get a pass to enter the Garden Reach docks where the ship was berthed. There were many curious dock labourers and clerks of the port authority strolling along the wharf and exchanging banter with mechanics suspended from ladders soldering plates with acetylene blow lamps. I joined one group counting the holes on the starboard side with unconcealed pleasure. 'Twenty-six!' shouted one man a little ahead of me. 'Must be as many on the other side, Joy Mukti Bahini!' I caught up with him and asked why he thought it was the work of the Mukti Bahini.

'Who else?' he demanded. 'It is either them or us. It is the same thing. Their victory is our victory; their defeat, our defeat.'

After some pressure and persuasion, the ship's agents in Calcutta gave me a permit to board the ship. Late in the evening I was in Captain Hines' cabin discussing the episode with him and his blonde wife, Rosemary Hines. The skipper, a rough, corpulent Scotsman, was evidently enjoying the sudden publicity he had received. 'I was on British telly last Sunday, you know! Of course I didn't see myself. And I am not supposed to talk about this business. Not till the official enquiry is completed. Our naval attaché came down from Delhi and inspected all the damage. I've told him all there is to say.' Then he proceeded to tell me all that had transpired.

The *City of St Albans* had just come to Calcutta to offload its cargo. On the afternoon of 11 October it had weighed anchor, gone down the Hooghly into the Bay of Bengal and turned towards Chalna, East Pakistan's second-largest seaport after Chittagong, to take on a cargo of jute. At 1.25 a.m. a gunboat (or boats) had come out of nowhere and peppered them from all sides. 'It was ten minutes of absolute hell,' said Rosemary Hines. 'I've been through this kind of thing during the last war,' continued the skipper, 'but if anyone says he is not frightened, he is a liar. It scared the daylights out of me. We turned tail and fled back to Calcutta.'

'The holes seem to be about the same size,' I suggested. 'You think they were caused by one weapon, like a pom-pom?'

'They are certainly not the same size!' insisted Captain Hines. 'I am no ballistics expert. But even I can say there were at least two kinds of explosives used. We've picked up some of the shrapnel and handed it over to our naval attaché.'

'Who do you think did it?'

'I haven't a clue! And I am not making any guesses for anyone.'

◆

Colonel Muhammad Ataul Ghani Osmany is the commander-in-chief of the Mukti Bahini. He is a slightly built man in his early fifties.

His snow-white handlebar moustache stands out against his swarthy complexion. He speaks impeccable English in the style of a Colonel Blimp. His speech is punctuated with Anglo-Indian military slang full of old boys, puccas and jolly goods. But there is nothing very jolly about him. He has a forlorn, melancholic look in his eyes. In the one hour I spent with him he did not smile even once. His eyes lit up when he talked of his 'epic' battles and the gallantry of his men. When he spoke of the atrocities committed by the Pakistani army against the Bengalis his eyes sparkled with hate.

Colonel Osmany is not easy to reach. Wherever he may be, he has only one address: somewhere in Bangla Desh. I was escorted to his shack late at night. He was sitting stiffly in his chair with a gas lamp hissing above his head. The table in front of him was bare. The bamboo walls of his shack had no calendars or pictures (not even one of Sheikh Mujibur Rahman). He shook hands very stiffly and did not waste any time. 'What can I do for you?'

I started off by asking him about the *City of St Albans*. Colonel Osmany had no doubts about the location of the ship or the ethics of attacking an unarmed ship or a neutral country. 'It was in our territorial waters,' he insisted. 'It did not have our permission and was trading with our enemy. If the world is so exercised about a miserable cargo vessel it is as well to remind it that when these West Pakistani savages were butchering innocent men and women and children, raping and looting, no nation thought it politic to tell them to stop. What had happened to international morality then, I ask you?' he glowered. I decided to drop the *City of St Albans* and turned to the origins of the Mukti Bahini.

The Bangla Desh Liberation Force is now eight months old. It came into existence spontaneously on the night of 25 and 26 March 1971 when the Pakistani army launched its campaign to exterminate what it considered to be Bengali secessionist elements. 'We had no intention whatsoever of raising an army before that,' said Colonel Osmany. 'I am a professional soldier brought up in the tradition that soldiers must not meddle in politics. I can tell you what I have not told anyone before: that as late as 19 March, when rumours of a Pakistani army crackdown were rife, Sheikh Mujibur Rahman asked me to make contact with senior Bengali officers and ask them to be prepared for all eventualities. I sent a secret circular through a trusted officer, Major Khaled Musharraf. I made three points: do not get embroiled in politics; do not allow anyone to disarm you; in the event of repression strike as hard as you can. If the Pakistanis had only limited their action against selected politicians, Bengalis in the army and the police might have stayed neutral. It was only when information got around that the Pakistani army was out to kill Bengali intellectuals and servicemen as well that we revolted to a man. The Mukti Bahini was manufactured overnight by the Pakistani Army.'

Colonel Osmany did not name any individual leaders but Mr Humayun Rashid Choudhry, who was Pakistan's deputy high commissioner in Delhi till 4 October when he went over to Bangla Desh, had told me that some weeks prior to the army action, senior Bengali officers had either been transferred to West Pakistan or assigned non-operational jobs and it was the junior officers who led the revolt. He named three: Major Usman Chuadanga, Major Khaled Musharraf (now lying injured in hospital) at Comilla and Major Zia, somewhere in the Chittagong sector. Bengali soldiers and policemen rallied round the young officers and within a few days they had an army of about 10,000 trained men. They picked Colonel Osmany, who had been elected to the national assembly on the ticket of the Awami League, to be their commander-in-chief.

The Mukti Bahini is composed of a number of distinct groups. The political leadership is provided by members of Sheikh Mujibur Rahman's Awami Party. Most of them are in their forties or fifties and though they are unfit to wield arms they try to monopolize decision-making by virtue of their having won 167 out of 169 seats in the national assembly in the election of December 1970.

The hard core of fighters is composed of men of the East Bengal Regiment, East Pakistan Rifles (a paramilitary force meant to guard the frontiers), the police, and ansars and mujahids trained as home guards to maintain peace in the cities. About 10,000 of these men survived the holocaust of 25 March. This hard core was, and is, non-political. Most have personal grievances stemming from discrimination against Bengalis in matters of promotions and postings. They might well have stayed neutral if the Pakistani army had left them alone.

A third group consists of volunteers enlisted by the Mukti Bahini (those rejected on physical grounds have banded themselves separately). The majority of this group consists of boys of between 15-20 years of age from high school or university. It is in this group that political ideology plays an important part. There are two communist parties, the pro-Peking, known after its aged leader as the Bhashani group and the pro-Moscow Communist Party of Bangla Desh, known as the Muzaffar group. Factory workers who have joined up have brought in their respective brands of trade union-oriented political outlooks. Last August, an attempt was made to forge a united front of radicals by getting up a Co-ordinating Committee of the Left—the CCL.

Yet another group composed of student leaders and their followers has recently come into existence. Its two prominent leaders are Tufail Ahmed and Fazlul Huq Moni. These groups undergo more extensive and rigorous training in the use of sophisticated weapons and hope to emerge as an elite force in Bangla Desh. They call themselves the Mujib Bahini.

THE TERRORIST TRADITION

I could not find out the total strength of the Mukti Bahini. Colonel Osmany refused to give me the figure. 'I prefer to call it the Gono (people's) Bahini. Every able-bodied Bengali is a soldier of the liberation army. Most other officials put the figure between 50,000 to 60,000, soon to be raised to 150,000. At one time it was a purely Muslim force. Today some 3,000 Hindus of Bangla Desh have joined it.'

Bengalis may not have made good mercenaries but they showed a natural aptitude for handling bombs, dynamite and pistols. During British rule, Bengali terrorists assassinated more Englishmen than all the other Indian terrorist groups put together. And most of them came from the region that is today East Pakistan or Bangla Desh. It does not take very much to change from an urban gunman or bomb thrower to a full-fledged guerrilla fighter.

West Pakistan's predominantly Punjabi and Pathan ruling classes continued to discriminate against Bengalis. Although they retained the East Bengal Regiment and Armed Constabulary, few Bengalis were promoted to senior positions. As late as 1970 there was only one Bengali lieutenant-general in the Pakistani army. No Bengali has ever held an equivalent rank in the air force or navy. Once when I was arguing the point with a Punjabi-Pakistani friend and reminded him that while the Eastern Wing had 56 per cent of the population of Pakistan, Bengalis never got more than 7 per cent representation in its armed forces, he snorted, 'So what! You don't pick your fighting men out of a herd of sheep. Do you expect these dal bhat eaters to fight?'

Moazzam Ahmed Chowdhury of Sylhet, a friend of Sheikh Mujibur Rahman, told me how the youth of Bangla Desh acquired the iron in their souls. 'You know we are a peace loving people. It is the savagery of these Pathans, Balochis (from Baluchistan) and Punjabis that turned us into fighting men. They did not even spare our women and children. Even a timid animal will turn around to protect its mate and its young. Hate makes people fight like hell.' There is certainly a lot of hate in the hearts of the men of Bangla Desh.

GHOSTS TO WEST PAKISTAN

'Tell those American friends of yours,' said Colonel Osmany to me, 'that what the Pakistani army did to our people on the night of 25 and 26 March was worse than a hundred My Lais. We will not rest till we have totally exterminated them. Their corpses will rot in Bangla Desh; we'll send their ghosts to West Pakistan.'

The freedom fighters have steadily increased in numbers and fighting potential. Two months after its birth the name was changed from Mukti Fauj (army) to Mukti Bahini (organization). Fauj is an Urdu word, Bahini is Bengali. The change in nomenclature also indicated the expansion of a purely land-based guerrilla army into one with armed boats operating in rivers, frogmen who began to sink Pakistani ships with limpet mines. Group Captain Khondarkar was appointed air marshal of the Bangla Desh air force. To date, although they have quite a few pilots, they have no aircraft or an air base. Mr H. R. Choudhry said they would soon be acquiring fighter planes and air strips. 'Where will you get your planes from?' I asked him. He replied with a studied smile.

The Mukti Bahini has many training centres along the Indo-East

Pakistan border. For security reasons the precise locations of these camps were not divulged except for the standard reply. 'Somewhere inside Bangla Desh.' The same vagueness was observed on the organization and the methods of training. 'You can take it from me that it is not patterned after the guerrilla organization in Vietnam,' said Colonel Osmany. 'In the earlier stages I trained my men along conventional army lines and fought traditional style battles. We hoped foreign powers would intervene, stop the unequal fight and tell the Pakistanis to get the hell out of Bangla Desh. When that did not happen and the Pakistanis brought in four and a half divisions (80,000 men) equipped with tanks, heavy guns and tankers, I decided to change my tactics. Early last May I reorganized my forces into decentralized guerrilla bands and changed the technique of fighting from pitched battles to commando-style ambush. We had to concede some ground but we succeeded in forcing our enemy to scatter his forces over a vast, hostile countryside. We cut his lines of communication. We harass him all the time. We kill over a hundred a day; they take planeloads of coffins every day to West Pakistan. Only yesterday, one of my young commandos attacked a convoy near Comilla and brought in a load of arms with Chinese and American markings.'

A visitor to the training camp only sees boys in vests and lungis, drilling with staves or wooden rifles. No one is allowed to examine real weapons. When I asked them from where they acquired their weapons, the reply was always the same: 'Soldiers and policemen brought them when they came over to the liberation side; others we captured from the enemy. We also buy them from friendly sources with money sent over by Bengali communities settled in foreign lands.' When I asked Colonel Osmany how limpet mines and gunboats could reach Bangla Desh, he simply looked into my eyes and waved his hands: 'I cannot tell you anything about that.'

The training period varies from a few weeks to six months, depending on the nature of the task assigned. It does not take very long to learn how to derail a train or plant a mine on a road. It takes longer to learn how to fire a mortar or a Sten gun or swim underwater to attach a limpet mine.

The claims of the Mukti Bahini's achievements are difficult to verify. 'Up to the end of September we had killed 25,000 Pakistani soldiers, sunk 21 ships, destroyed over 600 bridges, and culverts and totally dislocated rail, road and river communication.' Colonel Osmany claimed. 'You can check for yourself. Few trains run in Bangla Desh and shipping in Chalna is non-existent. We will soon put Chittagong out of commission.'

The Indian Institute for Defence Studies and Analyses puts the figure of Pakistanis killed in Bangla Desh at about 6,000. The Pakistan government's attempts to play down the activities of the Mukti Bahini backfire and give currency to the exaggerated claims made by the Free Bangla Desh Radio and newspapers published in Calcutta. There are however two fairly reliable sources of information: Bengali crew (lascars) on ships coming from East Pakistan ports, and correspondents of foreign radio, television and newspapers who have sporadically been allowed out of Dacca to see things for themselves. Lascars have confirmed stories of damaged ships. In the third week of September the British tanker *Teviot Bank* was seriously damaged at Chalna. Immediately thereafter another British vessel, *Chakdina,* was hurt and forced to return for repairs to Calcutta. Lascars reported seeing two Pakistani steamers, a coastal tanker and many barges lying half-submerged in Chalna. On Pakistan's Independence Day (14 August) the *Ohrmazo* was attacked in Chittagong.

DISLOCATION OF TRADE

In the last two months (October and November) Mukti Bahini commandos have stepped up their activities. On 9 October, a bomb exploded in the West Pakistan-controlled Habib Bank in Central Dacca, killed five men and injured another thirteen. The next day, a few blocks away from the Habib Bank, a building housing the World Bank had one of its floors wrecked and a jute godown gutted. Bangla Desh observers in India assess that in peacetime, transport of goods was 38 per cent by rail, 34 per cent by road and 28 per cent by river. Today rail and road is below 10 per cent of the normal volume and river transport is completely dislocated. Jute which was East Pakistan's chief foreign-exchange earner is now transported by coolies. Industrial production is down by 35 per cent. Tobacco production is down by

40 per cent. Eleven tea plantations near the border have closed down; others are producing 25 per cent of the normal. All this is ascribed to the Mukti Bahini which has been paid a backhanded compliment by the *Pakistan Observer* of Dacca as 'a pitiless perpetrator of death and destruction...creating a sense of unreality with their hit-and-run raids and creating an atmosphere of chaos and uncertainty'.

The evidence of the success of the commandos is that they can take parties of Indian pressmen and photographers in and out of Bangla Desh at will.

My last appointment was with Bangla Desh's foreign minister, Khondarkar Mushtaq Ahmed. When I arrived in his personal assistant's room I found it full of visitors. In one corner, a party of Soviet journalists was being briefed on the genesis of Bangla Desh. They were poring over a map indicating areas liberated by the Mukti Bahini. 'How much is under your control? How much with the Pakistani army?' asked the interpreter translating the questions.

'It is very difficult to be precise,' replied the interpreter. 'Where the Pakistani army is present physically they are in control. The rest is ours. At night all they control are the barracks they sleep in. Our boys avoid direct confrontation with them. They have tanks and airplanes. Our boys have only rifles, hand-grenades, Sten and machine guns. As soon as we obtain heavy armour we shall take them on in the open field. It won't be very long now.'

A DIFFERENT JIHAD

The briefing was over. The leader of the Soviet party delivered a short speech on the ultimate but inevitable victory of democratic forces. After much handshaking and bowing the Russians took their leave shouting 'Joy Bangla Desh!'

Khondarkar Mushtaq Ahmed is a dapperly dressed man, reputed to be the most influential of the cabinet of Bangla Desh. When I entered his room he was rolling a cigarette for himself. 'It is the holy month of Ramzan,' I reminded him. 'You should be fasting.' He smiled. 'I know and today it is Shab-e-Barat (commemorating the day of the Prophet's brief ascent to paradise). But during a jihad (holy war) the faithful are given dispensation from fasting. This is our jihad for liberation.'

We discussed the reaction of foreign countries to the Bangla Desh movement. He took my hands in his and said: 'My friend, we will never forget what India did for us in our hour of trial. We know you are feeding and housing 10 million of our people. Free Bangla Desh will repay this debt by forging bonds of eternal friendship with India.'

'Nations are not known to have very long memories,' I remarked. The foreign minister was stung to eloquence, 'Have the Americans forgotten how France helped them in their war of independence? We will no more forget our gratitude to India than learn to jump over our own shadows.'

(*1971*)

SALAAMS TO AUNTYJI

My friends who have been to theatres of war tell me stories of fraternization between our men and the Pakistanis. They say that during lulls between hostilities gifts of mithai were exchanged across the firing line along with plenty of bawdy but friendly abuse. I have seen this spirit of camaraderie between the soldiers of our two countries who man our border outposts; siwayyan sent by Pakistanis on Id, halwa sent by Sikhs on Guru Nanak's birthday. Once when I was on the ceasefire line near Baramulla, I asked a Canadian UN observer going to Pakistan to shake on *my* behalf the hands of the Pakistani picket a few hundred metres away. A few minutes later the Canadian returned bringing back a packet of Pakistani biscuits and a message of goodwill.

The best true story of this kind that I heard was from a man who is today Pakistan's ambassador to a South American country. He told me that in the short encounter between Indo-Pakistan forces in Kashmir in the autumn of 1947, his brother, a lieutenant in the Pakistan army, was reported missing, believed to have been killed. His comrades said that they had seen him fall as a platoon of Sikhs charged them with drawn bayonets. The family made frantic enquiries and, after waiting for some days, resigned themselves to his loss and had prayers for the dead recited in their home. On the following Id, the young lieutenant walked back into his home. He had been captured by a Sikh who had been in school with him and often visited his home. 'What will Masiji (Auntyji) say if she heard I had kept you from her! Give her my salaams.' He escorted his friend to the ceasefire line and let him go.

(*1972*)

'Do you still believe that there is no alternative to Mrs Gandhi?' Morarji Desai asked me when I accosted him at Palam Airport. It was an embarrassing question loaded with the suggestion that there was an alternative, perhaps right before my eyes. I stood my ground and reaffirmed that I still believed that she was our best bet. I put the question back in Morarji's court: 'You tell me if we have any choice.' Morarji Desai began to expand on the theme in his precise, passionless voice. His argument ran somewhat as follows: 'But for India's ancient and deep-rooted faith in democracy, our democratic institutions would have crumbled under the strain to which they have been put in recent years.' He went on to enumerate incidents of corruption and misuse of power. 'Where has the Rs 60 lakh in the Nagarwala Case gone? Do you know that Bansi Lal is perpetrating the worst form of tyranny in Haryana? You press people say nothing about it.'

I admitted that I did not know what had happened to the money in Nagarwala's case but I knew that the pace of development in Haryana was faster than in any other state of India and that whenever Bansi Lal interfered with the freedom of the press we took up cudgels against him.

Morarji bhai continued: 'Do you know that they have tantric rites performed against me? A lakh of rupees was spent on these rituals. People who performed them told me and tried to get me to do the same. But I don't believe in such things.' I replied that neither did Mrs Gandhi—she had said so to me in exactly those words. This was the twentieth century and only the sick in mind went in for that kind of hocus-pocus. Morarji bhai gave me a condescending smile. Our conversation ended as admirers demanded his attention. 'You think it over again; the country is going through a terrible time,' were his parting words.

I thought over it as I had been told to do. We were indeed passing through the grimmest time in our history. I was reminded of Rumi's lines:

Wherever you look there is the din of tumult,
Wherever you go there are candles and torches,
For tonight this world is heavy and in travail
Striving to give birth to an eternal world.

The values of yesterday are at a discount; those of tomorrows to come are still undefined. Which of the many men and women who are forever finding fault with Mrs Gandhi's leadership has a better grasp of the situation, a plan of action to get us out of the morass in which we find ourselves? Who has a clearer vision of the future?

In every country there is a small segment of society which makes up the leadership pool. In India it is minute. The alternatives can be counted on our fingertips. The first and perhaps also the final requirement of a leader is acceptability—who do the people want? 'The question "Who ought to be the boss?"' said Henry Ford, perhaps the greatest industrialist of his time, 'is like asking "Who ought to be the tenor in the quartet?" Obviously, the man who can sing tenor.'

Is there any doubt in anyone's mind that, as far as acceptability is concerned, the only person the people still rely on is Mrs Gandhi and no one else? The Institute of Public Opinion, which regularly conducts a poll on her, reports that it has touched the lowest point since she became prime minister. These public opinion polls are notoriously fallible. (A similar poll carried out three years ago on the chances of the ruling Congress and carefully timed to be released on the eve of the elections proved to be grievously wrong.) Besides, the question posed by the pollsters is usually limited to assessing Mrs Gandhi's popularity, seldom to finding out who, if anyone, would be more acceptable.

These analyses couched in academic verbiage are about as reliable as the prognostication of palmists, astrologers and gossipmongers. Most of them are cooked up in Delhi. And you don't have to be in the capital for more than twenty-four hours to realize that political scandals, forecasting changes in the Cabinet, guessing who's the great favourite of (and who is in disfavour with) 'Madam' are the chief preoccupations of the Delhi wallahs. It is in the secretariat, coffee houses and clubs that all the gossip is spawned and passed on after being liberally sprayed with mirch-masala as coming from the horse's mouth. There is seldom any truth in anything one hears in New Delhi.

I also conduct a regular one-man poll during my travels across the country. I hear much criticism against the government, but rarely is Indira Gandhi held responsible for it. My favourite question to the people I meet is: 'Who do you think will make a better prime minister than Indira Gandhi?'

None has yet given me a name. Most of them reply: 'She's okay, but it's the others…'

One can assume that at the moment the people do not consider anyone fit enough to replace Indira Gandhi as prime minister and, if she were to seek a mandate, she would win it hands down. Her image as an able, astute and incorruptible leader remains unsullied.

Indira Gandhi has been prime minister for nine years. She has had lot to contend with. When she took over, the economy of the country was going down; the Five-Year Plans had gone awry; the rupee was not worth its metal content; the Sikhs were clamouring for a Punjabi Suba, the communists (chiefly Naxalites) were in violent revolt and her own party was split into factions and some of her colleagues were eagerly awaiting an opportunity to oust her. The elections of 1967 showed how low the stock of the Congress had fallen: it lost over 100 seats in Parliament and was left with a slender majority of 40. Many states fell to the Opposition.

Within three years Indira Gandhi was able to turn the tide. In the 1970 elections she won 356 seats, 120 more than before. Two years later she pulverized the Opposition in the states by winning for her party 1,926 of the 2,529 seats contested. It was as clear as the light of day that the people did not vote for the Congress Party—they voted for Indira Gandhi.

Although economic conditions have deteriorated and the popularity of the ruling Congress has declined, it has not diminished the stature of Mrs Gandhi in the eyes of the people. As a nation we are like that—we do not vote for anything as nebulous as a party, we vote for a person who inspires confidence.

The enormous concentration of power and the virtual absence of anyone of the same stature has often compelled her to seek the counsel of people who have no political standing.

Whenever someone has been brought to her notice as an expert in a particular field she has given him a chance to prove his mettle (Ashoka Mehta, Triguna Sen, V. K. R. V. Rao, Nurul Hasan, T. A. Pai). And when he failed to deliver the goods she did not let personal sentiment stand in her way and sacked him without ceremony. Reason and judgment, wrote Tacitus, are the two qualities required of a leader. Reason and political judgment Indira Gandhi has in full measure.

All this, however, does not apply to the party she leads, nor to many of her colleagues. The Congress party's method of collecting funds—arm-twisting would be a more apt description of the tactics adopted—are unethical and have generated a lot of ill-will. The association of self-seeking businessmen and self-promoting politicians will in the long run bring ruin to any party.

The ruling Congress has more than its share of either kind. It has been well said that there are two kinds of leaders: those interested in the flock and those interested in the fleece. As would become a good shepherdess, in order to preserve the health of her flock, Indira Gandhi must curb the rapacity of the wool-gatherers who wield the shears in her name.

(*1974*)

Her passport has been seized, her farmhouse searched; she has been served with a notice to get out of her house; her telephones are tapped, she and the members of her family are shadowed wherever they go. She has been arrested twice in two years and has spent nights in a police lock-up and in jail. Her younger son, Sanjay, has also been jailed and is currently defending himself in thirty-five criminal cases filed against him. He has been ordered to appear in courts in distant cities on the same day.

The widest publicity has been given to the wildest charges involving all members of the family for crimes ranging from theft, forgery, maintaining accounts in foreign banks to arson, mayhem, murder. People who stood by her continue to be harassed; those who betrayed her have been forgiven and rewarded. This is the fate of one who presided over the destinies of India with great distinction for eleven long years.

Forty-eight Commissions of Enquiry have been instituted against the Gandhis and their supporters. An array of senior civil servants and the police have been pressed into service to collect and sift material to formulate charges. The government-controlled media, a subservient press and journals that thrive on scandal continue to churn out the most fanciful tales of horror fabricated by politicians and gossipmongers. This mountain-heap of calumny is yet to yield its mini-mouse of truth.

It is time we the common people of India asked our government and ourselves: is this fair? If the only justification of these indefensible acts of persecution is to hark back to what happened during the Emergency (most of it yet unproved) does it not amount to political vendetta?

The foundations of this edifice of calumny were laid through a whispering campaign begun during the last years of Jawaharlal Nehru's life. Whispers became a gabble, and gabble turned into loud-mouthed scandalmongering. No member of the Nehru-Gandhi family was spared. Jawaharlal was painted as a philanderer; Indira as a vain, cunning, unscrupulous woman of modest abilities but vaunting ambition. On more than one occasion George Fernandes described her as a 'congenital liar...a woman whom I had first thought of as having a one-dimensional mind but later discovered to have no mind at all'. Raj Narain made her into a sick person suffering from 'tidal waves of hysteria'. Little was known of her elder son, Rajiv, except that he was a pilot but the wildest speculations were made about his attractive Italian wife, Sonia. Sanjay came as God's own gift to the gossipmongers. He was said to have been a wayward boy who flopped at school and stole cars, a youthful debauch with an inordinate passion for money and power. When he married Maneka Anand, the Anand family was also put into the grinder of the gossip mill.

Who are these gossipmongers?

Just about all the educated elite who frequent clubs, cocktail parties and coffee houses: men and women who look upon character-assassination as fundamental a right as free speech. However, when gossip gets into print it becomes libellous. The law of libel in our country being what it is, rarely can a person in an important position afford either the time or the money to engage in a prolonged contest of mudslinging which may go on for several years. Consequently our press has learnt to act on the simple rule: avoid libelling people who do not matter, they may prosecute you. But libel people in public life to your heart's content, they will do nothing.

Pressmen also know the safety valves. They know they are safe if they quote defamatory statements made in Parliament. They know they can get away by quoting speeches made by senior politicians or by resorting to the formula 'it is reliably learnt', or by liberally inserting the word 'alleged' in their text.

Some journals deserve special mention for their role in blackening the name of the Gandhi family: the *Indian Express, The Statesman,* the *Hindustan Times* (a dramatic volte face after March 1977), *Blitz, Current, Sunday, India Today, The Organiser, This Fortnight, Onlooker, Mother India*—there must be dozens of others in our many languages. There have also been several important books on the Emergency and quickie biographies of the Nehru-Gandhi family—the authors of these books incluce Kuldip Nayar, Janardan Thakur, M.O. Mathai, Uma Vasudev, Rajinder Puri, Vinod Mehta, D.R. Mankekar, C.S. Pandit, Zareer Masani, Arun Shourie, Nayantara Sahgal, K.T.J. Mohan, K.A. Abbas, Promila Kalhan, J.B. Kulkarni—and several others. Some of these books are readable because they employ the simple technique of mixing fact with fantasy and innuendo.

Journalists turned authors have made a quick buck while politicians have exploited the murky atmosphere created by gossip to gain political leverage. The wilder the statements they made, the more publicity they got out of them. Of this team of Nehru-Gandhi baiters the star performers are George Fernandes, Raj Narain, Jyoti Basu, Kanwar Lal Gupta, Ram Jethmalani, Subramanian Swamy and H.V. Kamath. The list could be extended upwards to include L.K. Advani, Atal Behari Vajpayee, Charan Singh and even the self-styled Gandhian upholder of truth, Morarji Desai. All of them have at one time or the other expressed opinions on members of the Gandhi family which they must have known to be untrue or vastly exaggerated.

There may be some excuse for members of the Janata Party for their ill-tempered and irresponsible outbursts because they suffered imprisonment or exile during the Emergency. But there is little that can be said in favour of those who were pillars of the Emergency regime who now indulge in vituperation against the very people they once fawned over: Jagjivan Ram, Karan Singh, T.A. Pai, Devakanta Barooah, Brahmananda Reddy, Inder Gujral, Chandrajit Yadav, Ambika Soni.

THE GENESIS

The campaign of slander began openly as soon as it became clear that Mrs Gandhi would have to get out of office. At first the rumour was spread that instead of bowing to the will of the electorate she (at the instigation of Sanjay) had asked the army to take over. The canard was promptly denied by the defence services chiefs. Then it was circulated that the family had chartered aircraft to flee the country to live in comfort on the millions they had stashed in foreign banks. When gossipmongers discovered that neither Mrs Gandhi nor anyone of her family had the slightest intention of fleeing from India, a third canard was floated that she was busy destroying all evidence of her misdeeds.

Dhanik Lal Mandal stated that before she left office, Mrs Gandhi had 700 files consigned to the flames. This allegation if true could have been easily proved by questioning officials of the ministries concerned and by examining registers in which the numbers and locations of files are recorded. This was not done because there was no truth to the story. The conflagration of files was born out of the fumes in Mandal's sick mind.

And immediately there was a clamour for a Nuremberg type trial—equating Mrs Gandhi and her supporters with Adolf Hitler and his Nazi henchmen. It is strange that while the Janata government had no qualms about withdrawing criminal prosecution against George Fernandes and his colleagues for admitted acts of sabotage (see C. G. K. Reddy's *The Baroda Dynamite Conspiracy: The Right to Rebel*) that endangered the lives of innocent people, it lost little time in instituting a succession of commissions to look into the various 'misdeeds' of the Gandhi family and their supporters. Dr P. Koshy was appointed (23 April 1977) to go into the allegations about the deliberate maltreatment in hospital of Jayaprakash Narayan while he was in custody; Justice J.C. Shah was appointed (19 May 1977) to examine charges of excesses during the Emergency; K.K. Das (21 May) to examine misuse of the media; Justice Grover (23 May) to investigate charges against Devraj Urs; Justice Mathur (25 May) to examine the affairs of Maruti. The month of June 1977 was equally fruitful for retired-unemployed judges and civil servants: the Chellappa Commission was constituted to find out whether Sanjay Gandhi had sat in the pilot's seat in December 1976; Jagan Mohan Reddy was asked to investigate the Nagarwala Case. The commission-appointing spree continued into July and August 1977: a commission to prove family planning excesses in Delhi; a two-doctor commission to probe the causes of Ram Manohar Lohia's death which had taken place ten years earlier in 1967. Then followed a series of arrests: P.C. Sethi, Nandini Satpathy, Yashpal Kapur, Bansi Lal (who was publicly humiliated by being handcuffed and marched through the streets), Zail Singh, N.D. Tiwari, S.C. Shukla, V.C. Shukla and hundreds of others. The spate of arrests climaxed with the arrest of Indira Gandhi on 3 October 1977. She was released unconditionally the next day because the magistrate found nothing substantial in the charges against her. The public furore created by the maladroit handling of Mrs Gandhi's arrest caused the Janata government to lose face and the spree of arrests was brought to a halt temporarily.

The publicity given to the proceedings of the various commissions of enquiry, particularly the Shah Commission, opened the floodgates of vicious propaganda against Mrs Gandhi's family and associates. Justice Shah himself did not observe the reticence one expected from a judge of his eminence while commenting on the evidence produced. For example, amongst the charges levelled was one which claimed that officials who had failed to clear consignments sent by a firm called 'Indira International' were harassed and arrested. Newspaper reports carried the story indicating that the company belonged to Mrs Amteshwar Anand, mother-in-law of Sanjay Gandhi. It did not. Nor had the name 'Indira' have anything to do with Indira Gandhi. The firm belonged to one Mrs Indira Dhodi, wife of a retired army colonel, and was named after her. The treatment of the custom officials was castigated by Justice Shah as 'man's inhumanity to man seems to know no limit at all'.

◆

Let us examine a few of the canards spread about Indira Gandhi in some detail. The one given widest currency is that she has a vast hoard of cash stashed away somewhere.

Gossip about people making money by unlawful means is readily believed in our country. And it has come to be accepted almost as an axiom that all politicians make money and all ministers amass vast fortunes. The sums involved get multiplied as gossip passes from mouth-to-ear-to-mouth. There are, however, a few names who even the most gossip-prone will concede as exceptions to the general rule that power and corruption are synonymous: Gandhi, Vinoba Bhave, Jayaprakash Narayan, Rajendra Prasad, Maulana Azad, Nehru. All of them had to deal with large sums given to them for social or political purposes but at no time did anyone suspect that they put any of it away for their personal use. This was particularly true of Jawaharlal Nehru. Apart from his considerable inheritance and his earnings from royalties there was that something about him which put him in a class by himself as far as money matters were concerned. He suffered a lot of corrupt colleagues and many friends he trusted and raised to high positions let him down by lining their own pockets but not a breath of suspicion ever tarnished his reputation. The same was true of his daughter, Indira Gandhi. She also inherited more than she needed to live in comfort and her standards of integrity were the same as her father's. Whatever else scandalmongers might have said about her, they could not cast aspersions about her greed for wealth. But they did not spare her for too long. She was young and attractive. So they concluded she must like the good things of life. They started a whispering campaign that as the prime minister's daughter she received gifts which instead of being turned in to the treasury she had kept for herself. Amongst them an overcoat of sable or mink worth a million dollars. (No such coat exists in the world.) Nobody saw the coat, nor has Indira Gandhi ever worn sable or mink at any time. But that was considered a minor detail. Anyone who has seen her up close knows that her saris are made of Indian cotton or handspun silk, that she wears no jewellery whatsoever except a necklace of rudraksha beads and on her wrist a Rs 150 HMT watch. Aha! said the gossipmongers, rudraksha can be very expensive and the beads she wears are worth thousands of rupees. And she had the import quota increased to get one for herself.

The last of these acts of perfidy was perpetrated very recently. Acting on the statement made by a farmer that he had seen treasure being buried in the grounds of Mrs Gandhi's farm at Chattarpur near Delhi, a posse of tax officials and policemen armed with metal detectors raided the farmhouse. They spent many hours examining every nook and corner of the little cottage and the surrounding farm land. They did not find a single coin.

◆

The list of men whose deaths gossipmongers have ascribed to Mrs Gandhi is seemingly endless. Whether they died in hospital or in road accidents, if they had the remotest connection with any member of the Gandhi family, their deaths were immediately ascribed to her machinations. Let's look at just a few cases.

Dr Ram Manohar Lohia, socialist leader, Member of Parliament, bitter critic of Jawaharlal Nehru and Indira Gandhi, died in Willingdon (renamed Ram Manohar Lohia) Hospital on 12 October 1967. At the time of his death, Lohia was an overweight fifty-nine-year-old man, who had high blood pressure, glaucoma and an enlarged prostate. He had been undergoing treatment for his various ailments in this very hospital since April 1967. He was finally admitted for surgery on 28 September 1967. He was an important enough man to be given the best medical attention available. As many as twenty-six specialists examined him and five surgeons were present at the time his prostate was removed. These eminent doctors included Brigadier Lal, Dr Durbari Lal, Dr Pathak and Dr R.K. Caroli. The operation was followed by profuse bleeding for three to four days and he had to be given several blood transfusions. An infection set in and more specialists were brought in for consultation. Following their advice, antibiotics and combinations of steroids were administered. Nothing could stop Lohia's rapid deterioration and he finally succumbed to uraemia.

Lohia's supporters including Raj Narain immediately accused the government, then headed by Indira Gandhi, of criminal neglect. When Raj Narain took over as health minister of the Janata government he not only repeated the charge but appointed (on 18 June 1977) a two-doctor committee consisting of Dr H.S. Bhat, urologist from Bangalore, and Dr K.C. Gangwal, professor of surgery from Jaipur, to report on the treatment and hospital conditions. The two doctors made their report four months later (30 October). They admitted that all the doctors and nurses involved in Lohia's treatment had not been available for examination nor were the records of much help. They were not even able to establish the identity of the chief surgeon who removed Lohia's enlarged prostate. From whatever evidence was available, the panel came to the conclusion that far too many doctors had been consulted, the surgeons did their job somewhat clumsily and far more attention should have been paid to the post-operation care than was done. All this was undoubtedly reprehensible. But a muddle of medical advice and incompetent nursing barely justified the insinuation that Lohia's death was caused by the government and that the doctors' neglect was 'criminal'. Nevertheless the *Hindustan Times* (9 November) carried the headline 'Former government's hand in Lohia death?'

◆

An equally fanciful story from which the Janata Party extracted the maximum publicity was an alleged plot to murder Raj Narain in March 1975, when he was pursuing his election petition against Mrs Gandhi. A Hindi journalist, Govind Misra, was arrested in the Allahabad High Court premises on 18 March 1975 when Mrs Gandhi had gone there to make her statement. Apparently a man called S. N. Irfan stated that Govind Misra had written a letter to him on 5 August 1977 that his target when he was arrested was not Mrs Gandhi but Raj Narain. It would appear that on the very day that Govind Misra wrote this letter he was murdered. This startling disclosure was made to the Parliament by Janeshwar Misra, Minister of State, on 14 August 1977. Why Govind Misra nor anyone else in the know could not divulge this fact for five months when the Janata Party had been in power and why the Janata minister waited till Govind Misra was dead to come out with this cock and bull story needs no elaboration. Needless to say, there was no follow-up because there was nothing to follow up on.

There are many examples as bizarre as the ones I've cited in which Mrs Gandhi's name was dragged in to discredit her. I will mention just one more—the famous Nagarwala Case.

Captain R. S. Nagarwala stole Rs 60 lakh from the State Bank of India on 24 May 1971. He was nabbed a few hours later and the money was recovered. He confessed to his crime and was sentenced (admittedly at unprecedented speed) to four years' imprisonment. He suffered a heart attack and was removed to a hospital where he died. His death was immediately attributed to Mrs Gandhi. Why? Because he might spill the beans and dead men tell no tales. The assistant superintendent of police P. K. Kashyap, who had investigated the case was killed in a car accident near Mathura on 20 November 1971 and his death was by the same 'logic' attributed to Mrs Gandhi. 'Was he murdered?' asked Rajinder Puri in his *The Wasted Years*. Having so planted the seeds of suspicion he left it to the reader to answer, 'Of course!' Mr

Puri went further. A relative of Nagarwala, aged seventy-eight, died in Hyderabad on 12 September 1972. Mr Puri states emphatically, 'He was murdered because of vital information in his possession.' The Jagan Mohan Reddy Commission which looked into Nagarwala's case examined several witnesses including Morarji Desai and L. K. Advani. Kanwarlal Gupta was quite sure that, 'He (Nagarwala) had been done to death…as also the police officer connected with the case.' However the judge could find no connection whatsoever between Nagarwala's death and the government of the time.

Indira Gandhi, it was alleged, had organized the death of JP while he was in detention. Sanjay Gandhi was accused of all manner of misdeeds, indeed none of her immediate family was spared.

The one redeeming feature of this campaign of falsehood against Mrs Gandhi and her family is that few people now believe that there is anything to it. This is as true in India as it is in the rest of the world. As an instance of what foreigners think of Mrs Gandhi let me quote a letter of the Zambian ambassador published in *The Times* of London (3 March 1978) when the hate Gandhi propaganda let loose by the Janata government was at its height.

> Mrs Gandhi is one of the greatest leaders by any standards and her eleven years as leader of the Congress and in office as the premier of one of the most populous countries in the world is a clear testimony of this. This is not a leader, and a woman at that, to be harassed. After her defeat in the last general elections there were distressing reports of harassment of Mrs Gandhi by the new government and its supporters.
>
> I was even thinking of writing to express my regret that India, which is widely regarded as a great democracy, should set such a bad example by ill-treating a defeated leader. I am glad, however, that the humble Indian voter has spoken for me loudly, judging the way Mrs Gandhi's splinter party is coming up in state elections. They have truly redeemed her and themselves. Ingratitude is fatal: it killed Julius Caesar.

The persecution of Mrs Gandhi should be a matter of concern to the people of India. It is not good enough to shrug our shoulders and say: they are small men, you should not expect any better from them. We are dealing with an ex-prime minister and her government of eleven years' standing. It may have committed 'misdeeds'. By all means bring the 'misdeeds' to book. But they should also bear in mind if these charges do not stick, they will be setting a dangerous precedent whereby every successor government will malign, persecute and prosecute its predecessor.

(*1979*)

JP—THE MAN THEY MOURNED BEFORE HIS DEATH

Most of the leaders who today heap words of praise on Jayaprakash had few kind words to say about him till he became a force to be reckoned with. They called him confused, muddle-headed, indecisive, inconsequential, reactionary. He is undoubtedly a chronic misser of buses but he is also the conscience-keeper of the nation.

Rumours of a young firebrand blowing up bridges and looting arsenals began floating around soon after the arrests of Mahatma Gandhi and other Congress leaders in the Quit India Movement in 1942. This was wartime and there was strict censorship on the papers. Even 'loose talk' could land a person in jail. Nevertheless, vastly exaggerated stories of terrorist activities in the eastern provinces continued to circulate in the Punjab, at the time ruled by the Unionist government proud of its loyalty to the British. Besides the loyalists, there were others who disapproved of the Quit India Movement and believed that India should first help the Allied Powers defeat the fascists and *then* force the British out of India. I subscribed to this school of thought and much as I admired people with the guts to do or die, I disapproved of what they were doing. Consequently, my emotional admiration for Jayaprakash Narayan was qualified by rational disapproval of his acts. My reaction to the news of his arrest was very muddled.

It was a bit of a shock to learn that Jayaprakash was in Lahore where I was then living. The massive walls of the Lahore Fort separated him from his countrymen. We discovered this when Pardivala, a socialist lawyer from Bombay, was arrested and brought to Lahore. His only crime was to have moved a petition of habeas corpus for the release of Jayaprakash Narayan. It was Pardivala who told us that Jayaprakash was being put through the third degree by the Punjab police. He had been beaten, kept awake for several days and nights, and made to sit naked on blocks of ice. He had withstood it all and refused to divulge anything against his fellow conspirators. All at once, whatever reservations I had about his politics, my admiration for his manly qualities swept them aside.

Another twelve years were to elapse before I got the chance to meet him. By then my admiration for him bordered on worship. Here was a man who had disagreed with Gandhi, spurned the chance of becoming deputy prime minister in Nehru's cabinet and had instead chosen the vagrant path of socialism. He had the courage to renounce the communists and was severely critical of the Congress party. He was forever championing lost causes! In the clamour made by sabre-rattlers for a tough line against Pakistan, he spoke up for friendship with Pakistan; in the chauvinistic denunciations of Sheikh Abdullah as a pro-Pakistani traitor, he acclaimed Abdullah as a patriot to whom India owed the accession of Kashmir; in an atmosphere fouled by killings and counter-killings in Nagaland, he was the only Indian who spoke up for the Nagas. He was rightly regarded as the conscience-keeper of the nation.

My introduction to JP came through David Astor, the owner-editor of England's prestigious weekly, *The Observer.* Like JP, Astor was a champion of unpopular causes. During the British Raj, he had supported Gandhi and Nehru; after India became free, he became critical of Nehru and lent support to JP. Under the influence of Guy Wint and Ursula Graham Bower, who had lived in Nagaland, he took up the cause of the Nagas and persuaded JP to look into their grievances. At the time, the Indian army had succeeded in squashing (as it later appeared, only temporarily) Naga insurgency and the Naga militant leader Phizo was on the run. I had known Astor since my university days; it was Astor who asked me to call on JP who was then in London.

I went to see JP as I was bidden. He was staying in Brown's Hotel. Brown's, though in fashionable Bond Street, was what might in Indian terms be described as a three-star hotel. JP occupied a small cubicle-sized room above the entrance. I had no difficulty in recognizing him as by now his photographs had appeared in all the papers and he had become a legend. My first impression of him did not change: he was a soft-spoken man of great charm; whether or not a person agreed with him, it was difficult to resist falling for him. I did. He asked me to help him look into the grievances of the Nagas and advise him on the course of action. I was flattered. Although I readily agreed to do so, I confessed that I knew nothing about the Nagas or their problems. I was told that I would be briefed by someone who would come to see me that evening. Perhaps I could give him a drink and a bite.

I was reading Ursula Graham Bower's book on the Nagas when my bell rang. I opened the door. It was a small, pale-skinned man with Mongoloid features, a scraggy goatee, and one side of his face bashed in from eye to cheek. Because of facial paralysis, he had difficulty speaking. It took me some time to realize that this was Phizo. At the time his whereabouts were unknown except to the British authorities, David Astor and to JP. (I was later pleasantly surprised to learn that they were also known to Indian intelligence. Mr Azim Husain, then acting Indian high commissioner, rang me next morning to ask me jocularly why I was entertaining 'our enemies'. It is possible that Azim got the information from my friend Evan Charlton of *The Statesman* who dropped in unexpectedly for a drink.) As I said before, communicating with Phizo was not easy. Besides the impediment in his speech, he was a very bitter man and accused the Indian army of all manner of diabolical acts—pillage, arson, rape and murder. I refused to believe him. Two days later he made a dramatic appearance at a public meeting and repeated the charges. *The Observer* devoted its front page to 'The Naga Rebellion'.

I called on JP to report my reactions. With him at the time was a tall, austere looking, grey-eyed man in a black coat and a clerical white collar. This was the Reverend Michael Scott. Scott was much loved by Indians for his championship of the blacks against the white racist regime in South Africa. I was somewhat agitated at what I believed to be the utterly baseless charges Phizo had made against our army. They heard me out in patient silence.

Back home in Delhi, I was again drawn into the Naga business. JP handed me a sizeable file containing allegations compiled by Michael Scott from his interviews with the Nagas. I was unable to make sense of them and suspected the atrocity stories to be very exaggerated, and said so to JP. However, by now our intelligence chaps were on my trail. A young IAS officer began to cultivate me and one evening, after grossly flattering me about my eminence as a writer, asked me bluntly whether I could let him see the documents that JP had given me. He followed up the request by suggesting that he could make the deal worth my while. When that did not work, he appealed to my sense of patriotism. In return I quoted E. M. Forster to him: '...if I had to choose between betraying my country and betraying my friend I hope I should have the guts to betray my country.' He was flabbergasted and took his leave. I reported the attempt to bribe me to JP. He simply smiled and said, 'How unnecessary! I have given a copy of the charges to Prime Minister Shastri.'

Not very long afterwards, Michael Scott, the same man our government had lauded for his pro-India role in South Africa, was declared persona non grata by the government because he had taken up a cause which it found inconvenient.

The Naga issue petered out. Plainclothesmen did not find it worth their while to waste time on me. Whenever JP came to Delhi (he usually stayed with J. J. Singh in Friend's Colony) I called on him. I took part in several seminars conducted by him. He made an excellent moderator—he was lucid, utterly objective and spoke in a manner reminiscent of the groves of academe. He had a better mind than any of our politicians, he was a man of impeccable moral character and there was never a breath of scandal about him. He was loved by everyone who knew him, but for some mysterious reason he did not make it to the top. He was neither a mahatma in the Gandhian mould, nor a raja of Nehru dimensions. He commanded more affection than awe, more respect than fear. Even his close friends like Minoo Masani spoke of him as 'indecisive'. Compliments paid to him were usually in negative terms: 'He is not assertive enough...he is too gentle...won't hurt a fly...can't tell a lie...trusts everybody...won't let down a friend who's betrayed him.' And so on.

I recall one meeting in Masani's house when he (Masani) was leader of the Swatantra Party and an MP; JP was sharing his analysis of the political scene in the country to an invited group of friends when Maharani Gayatri Devi, still ravishingly beautiful, came in. Seeing the chairs and sofas occupied, she sat down on the carpet beside JP.

JP paused for a long while as if his train of thought had been derailed. And then remarked in his usual soft monotone voice: 'This indeed is democracy! A maharani sitting at the feet of a commoner.'

I was in Los Angeles in 1965 when the Indo-Pak War broke out. It upset me very much because I had always (as I do today) given top priority to friendship with Pakistan. I never believed in the canards our newspapers published with sickening regularity about Pakistanis wanting to invade India; we were (as we are today) more than twice as powerful on land, sea and air than Pakistan. And having met President Ayub Khan I was convinced that the war could not be of his choosing. I was in a miniscule minority but felt sure that at least one man in India would see my point of view. On my way home, I broke journey at Hong Kong and, knowing that this would be my only chance of communicating with Pakistan, I wrote a letter to President Ayub Khan expressing my sorrow at the turn of events and appealing to him to call for a ceasefire. I also wrote an impassioned letter to JP suggesting that he lead a band of passive resisters, of whom I would be one, to offer satyagraha between the firing lines of the two armies. I arrived back in Bombay during a blackout.

My epistles were treated with the contempt they deserved. From my friend Manzur Qadir, who had been Pakistan's foreign minister, I learnt that President Ayub was vastly amused by my letter. Being laughed at did not bother me very much but to find that JP was not even amused hurt me deeply. He supported the Indian government's view that Pakistan had provoked the war and deserved what it was getting.

I should have known better. JP was not a pacifist. His main point of disagreement with Gandhi was that he believed in the legitimacy of the use of force in certain circumstances. It was his gentle manner, his sense of fairness, the ability to see an adversary's point of view, his close association with Vinoba Bhave's Bhoodan and Sarvodaya which had beguiled me into believing that he, like Gandhi and Vinoba Bhave, regarded ahimsa as paramo dharma. He did not. He was a krantikari.

I came closer to JP during the Bihar famine of 1967. Without warning I descended on him at Patna and announced that I had come to work as his private secretary. He was embarrassed. He did not want me as his secretary and did not really know how to make use of me. However, I stuck to him, saw him every day in his modest house in Kadam Kuan—the ground floor and courtyard had been given over to a school, two sparsely furnished rooms on the first floor were all that he and his wife Prabhavati had kept for themselves. Ultimately he decided that I should see things for myself, write about them and thereby generate sympathy and money for the work his organization was doing.

I accompanied JP and his wife to his farm in Sokhodeora, a few hours' drive from Patna. This was the first time I saw the two at close quarters over a stretch of days. They were said never to have known physical intimacy. Under Gandhi's baleful influence Prabhavati, without as much as consulting her husband, had taken a vow of celibacy. Somehow I refused to believe that this vow had been strictly observed. They had been together before Prabhavati had met Gandhi at Wardha. JP had been a strapping youth and made no secret of his liking for good-looking women. Even in her late fifties Prabhavati was a most attractive woman: fair, petite, animated and with a mischievous twinkle in her eyes. However, whether or not there was any truth to the notion that their relationship was purely platonic, they were very close to each other. When they were in company, they usually spoke to each other in their Bhojpuri dialect as if they wanted to be only with each other and exclude everyone else. She watched over him like a tigress watches her cubs. He was already in indifferent health: diabetic and with an enlarged prostate. He also suffered from chronic constipation. We had to stop many times for JP to empty his bladder. Prabhavati was always plying him with pills for something or the other, getting water or tea out of different thermos flasks she carried in a hamper, mixing Isabgol with his cup of milk, harar behera in his butter milk: it was ayurvedic, unani, homeopathic, allopathic—everything. But above all it was the loving, fussing Prabhavati who gave JP the real touch of healing.

At Sokhodeora I was with JP from dawn to well after sunset. Sarvodaya workers and villagers would assemble round his little cottage in the early hours. He would hear them out and speak to them till Prabhavati summoned him indoors for his breakfast of buttermilk and fruit. He then left the ashram by car or jeep to tour afflicted villages. Everywhere it was the same story—wells dried up, granaries empty and hungry children wailing for food. He gave what he brought with him, listened to their tales of woe by the hour. I found it very exasperating to see a man of action, as true a karmayogi as I had ever met, wasting his time listening to old women's woes. What an efficient executive would have done in five minutes, JP took fifty minutes to do. It drastically reduced his effectiveness. But he was beyond changing. He returned to Sokhodeora long after the scheduled time for lunch. There were always more people waiting to see him. He could not hurt them by refusing to listen to them. It went on till the irate Prabhavati drove them off without ceremony and took her husband indoors. The nagging went on through the meal till he wearily retired for his siesta. Prabhavati snoozed in a chair outside to prevent anyone disturbing her husband.

The afternoon was spent in the same way: touring villages, talking to villagers, giving them succour in cash, grain and words of hope. Then back to Sokhodeora to instruct Sarvodaya workers. It was only after dark that the two were left alone.

And these were the most rewarding moments of my all-too-brief association with them. We sat round a table with a hurricane lantern, the stars twinkling overhead. Jackals wailed in the wilderness and their howls mingled with the weird cries of villagers driving them off their fields. I had my Scotch—neither JP nor his wife had any hang-ups about what anyone ate or drank—and JP reminisced about the past for my benefit. There was a brief interruption to listen to the news and to eat the vegetarian meal that Prabhavati had cooked for us. They invariably walked to my shack, saw that my bed had been made, the mosquito net hung, and a flask of drinking water put on the table. By 10 p.m. Sokhodeora was fast asleep save for the dogs baying at a late moon and the villagers shouting abuse at wild pigs that raided their fields.

It was during these evening sessions by the light of the hurricane lantern that I got an inkling of the strained relations between JP and Indira Gandhi. JP was virtually the only leader of national importance who was devoting himself to famine relief operations;

his popularity amongst the people was ever increasing. The state government was very grudging in its appreciation of his work. Mrs Gandhi visited Bihar twice and both times met JP. Twice she promised to appeal to the people to help JP and both times did not do so. Did she resent JP's growing popularity? JP did not say so in so many words but the number of times he brought up the subject left little doubt in my mind that he thought so. (This was confirmed years later, when JP openly broke with her and launched his Total Revolution. In an interview I had with her, she lashed out: 'Who made JP a leader? What following has he in the country? It is you newspaper people who exaggerate his popularity...')

My contribution to relieve the hunger of the people of Bihar did not go beyond writing a series of sob-stuff articles for *The Statesman* which brought in some cheques to JP's organization. But the contact made in those few days lasted many years. I even toyed with the idea of working on his biography and at his insistence wrote to Dr H. Passim, an American professor who had borrowed JP's papers but had done nothing about them. The project came to an end with a brusque and rude note from Passim saying that the papers were his private property and I should stop pestering him. Apparently Passim was waiting for the day when JP became prime minister of India and his biography would ensure Passim handsome royalties.

I resumed contact with JP when he launched his Total Revolution. Though at the time I held no brief for Mrs Gandhi or her government, I made no secret of my total disagreement with a revolution which took the form of gheraoing (and at times assaulting) elected members of legislatures. But so unpopular had Mrs Gandhi's government become that JP's movement gathered strength. When he came to Bombay, I had the privilege of bringing him and Prabhavati for lunch to meet editors of the *Times of India* group of papers and journals. He looked very sick and Prabhavati had her usual hawkish eye on what he ate and how long he stayed. The next day I travelled with him from Bombay to Poona. Prabhavati was not with us so I had him all to myself and took the opportunity to ask him about his past. We were constantly interrupted by admirers coming to greet him. At every station there were crowds to pay him homage. By the time we reached Poona, he was exhausted by his visitors and by my ceaseless stream of questions. But for me it was a most rewarding train journey. He spoke with great candour, even naming girls with whom he had had affairs in his younger days. He attributed his poor health to the rough time he had had in the United States and the Indian doctor who had performed a very clumsy operation to remove his tonsils.

The gathering he addressed in Poona that afternoon was not as large as the one he had addressed in Bombay two days earlier. But it was large enough—about 60,000 people. I had no doubt that this movement was assuming the dimensions of a revolt. I wrote about 'The Total Revolution' for the *New York Times,* criticizing it as anti-democratic. JP was very hurt and wrote me a long letter saying that I had misunderstood the purpose of the movement, which was aimed at wiping out the corruption that had fouled our democratic institutions. I published his letter in the *Illustrated Weekly of India* which I was then editing. But a breach had been made in our relationship which was not to be healed. I wrote to (and even personally warned) Mrs Gandhi that although I disapproved of JP's movement, she was underestimating the strength that JP had gathered. It was then that she made the comment questioning JP's popularity that I have quoted earlier.

I saw JP lead the massive procession in Delhi on 6 March 1975, with Charan Singh, Atal Behari Vajpayee, Badal, Chandra Shekhar and many other leaders in tow. Amongst the hundreds of thousands of marchers, I had no difficulty in identifying RSS volunteers and the Jan Sangh. They were among the cheerleaders and slogan-makers: 'Desh ka neta? Jayaprakash. Andher ka roshan? Jayaprakash. Sab mil key bolo. Jayaprakash.' Anyone gifted with a little foresight could have seen the shape of things to come. Indira Gandhi and JP, who should have been on the same side, fighting against this force of resurgent fascism, were busy destroying each other; the only outcome of their conflict would be chaos and the only beneficiaries of the chaos would be either these backward-looking elements of Hindu communal forces or the communists.

When Mrs Gandhi declared the Emergency I was not sure on whose side I was. While I strongly resented the arrests and detention without trial of thousands of men and women and the muzzling of the press, I felt equally strongly that JP's Total Revolution had richly contributed to bringing us to this sorry state of affairs. The fact that there was hardly a murmur of protest—on the contrary a vast majority of the people sighed with relief—was ample proof that the people did not regard the Emergency as an evil (as it was later made out to be). Schools, factories and shops opened; strikes, lockouts, gheraos, hooliganism came to an end. I was however saddened by the fact that a saintly, loveable man like JP who was in poor health had been locked up. I was also conscious of his feeling that in siding with Indira Gandhi I had let him down. However, when he was brought to Jaslok Hospital in Bombay, I went to see him. Dr Mehta, who was treating him, did not give him many days. I was not able to have the heart-to-heart talk with him which I desperately wanted. He was obviously very hurt but being assured of my affection and being a gentleman he agreed to see me. 'I will ring you up when I am better,' he promised both the times I called on him. He never did.

And then he rose from his sickbed to lead the Janata to victory and be acclaimed as the Lok Nayak and the saviour of the nation. I did not see him in that light. And, being temperamentally incapable of seeking contact with people in power, kept my distance.

I do not know how history will judge JP. All I know is that most of the people who today are heaping adjectives of praise on him thought little of him before. They exploited him, rode his bandwagon to power without having the slightest regard or affection for him. He is a good man, an honest man, an able man and a brave man. Leadership has been thrust upon him by men who were neither honest nor able nor brave so that they could become leaders themselves.

(*1979*)

THE MAN BHUTTO WANTED DEAD

Ahmed Raza Kasuri was the man Bhutto wanted to kill. He made eighteen attempts to have him killed. The eighteenth effort resulted in the death of Ahmed Raza's father, Nawab Mohammed Raza Kasuri. For the crime, Bhutto was hanged. Ahmed Raza was not a nobody as Bhutto described him but a somebody who became a thorn in his side. He is a youthful firebrand, a well-to-do landowner, an aristocratic rabble-rouser fired up with limitless ambition. We may hear a lot of him in the years to come.

He is a strapping, six-foot-tall man bursting with good health. A booming 'as-salam-alaikum' followed by a hearty shake of hand that makes you massage yours after he loosens his grasp. Patches of grey hair about the ears and glasses; dressed in a striped shirt and trousers with a cardigan thrown over his back. 'I am Ahmed Raza Kasuri, the man Bhutto tried to kill,' he says, introducing himself. 'And this is my mother, Begum Maimuna Bano. She is from the Loharu family, niece of Nawab Ismail Khan of Aligarh and a cousin of the governor of your Himachal Pradesh. She was in the car when Bhutto's assassins killed my father.' She is an elderly lady, her dark face framed in silver white hair and thick glasses and though she has lived among Punjabis all her life, prefers to speak in Urdu.

I met them in Kasuri's bungalow in Islamabad a few hours after Bhutto had been hanged in nearby Rawalpindi Central Jail.

Ahmed Raza shows me several albums of clippings of his stormy political career. While his mother serves us tea he takes me over the clippings. The tenor of his theme is to prove that he never was a nobody as Bhutto had pleaded in his defence but a somebody who had been the most powerful student leader in the country and someone who had helped Bhutto build up the People's Party of Pakistan; a man of substance and of blue-blooded aristocratic lineage recorded in *The Chiefs of the Punjab* (a kind of Debrett's Peerage) who later fell out with Bhutto over Bangladesh, the need to have a free press and his overbearing attitude and criminal misuse of power. The fact that Bhutto made so many attempts to have him eliminated was proof enough that he mattered.

'It was in my home in Kasur that the PPP was born and it was in my home that it was buried,' proclaims Ahmed Raza. He opens an album and shows me newspaper clippings of November 1967 when he was elected member of the convening body of which Bhutto was chairman. Kasuri was the youngest member of the body and was chosen because of his unquestioned leadership of the students of Lahore. There were pictures of him with Bhutto, leading a procession protesting against the Tashkent Agreement. Both men spent a fortnight in detention. There was another picture taken two years later (January 1969) showing Kasuri leading another protest march against the detention of Bhutto; another of Begum Nusrat Bhutto in Ahmed Raza's home in Kasur and one with the two of them atop a tonga leading a procession in Lahore.

Ahmed Raza was Bhutto's candidate in the elections held in December 1970 in which he defeated his nearest rival Arif, son of Mian Iftikharuddin by 60,000 votes to become the youngest member of the National Assembly.

Then the rift with Bhutto began. Bhutto envied the young man's growing popularity among the youth and his rapport with the newspapers for whose freedom he and the cricketer A. H. Kardar went on a hunger strike. Within a month he and Bhutto were quarrelling openly. Bhutto threatened to resign from the PPP and on 2 May 1971 both men expelled each other to set up rival PPPs.

'Bhutto did not like my being outspoken,' says Kasuri quoting his patron saint Bulleh Shah: 'Sach boldiyan bhambad baldae'—truth sets off a blazing fire. Then it came to insults. Bhutto told Kasuri to have his head examined; Kasuri returned the compliment by calling Bhutto mad. When the National Assembly was convened in Dacca, Bhutto forbade his party members from going to East Pakistan and threatened that anyone who went would have his legs broken and would only go on a one-way ticket. The only PPP member to defy him was Kasuri. He not only went to Dacca but appealed to Sheikh Mujibur Rahman to keep the nation united.

In July 1971, Kasuri denounced Bhutto for consorting with CIA agents on a visit to Tehran. In August 1971, in a Peshawar hotel, Bhutto's supporters assaulted Kasuri. It was Kasuri who exposed Bhutto's designs to break up Pakistan by suggesting to Sheikh Mujib that the two divide the administration of the Eastern and Western wings between them: 'udhar tum, idhar hum.'

Bhutto decided that Kasuri was a bloody nuisance. On 17 January 1971, an attempt was made on his life at Kasur in which he and his brother suffered bullet injuries. Further assaults and murderous attempts took place in Karachi and Islamabad. When Kasuri protested to Bhutto, the only reply he got was, 'What can I do?'

When Bhutto replaced General Yahya Khan to become ruler of Pakistan, the confrontation between the two men was extended to Parliament. Kasuri refused to sign the constitution proposed by Bhutto and refused to be party to the recognition of Bangladesh which he always regarded as an integral part of Pakistan. When the PPP celebrated its one year in power on 20 December 1972, Kasuri organized black flag processions. He was subjected to a murderous assault. There was no instigation. Kasuri was suspended from the National Assembly for three months.

In 1973, Kasuri further embarrassed the Bhutto regime by supporting provincial autonomy for Baluchistan. Later that evening members of the National Assembly returning home by foot were run over by an army jeep. One, Chaudhury Iqbal, was killed and four others injured. All those men were Bhutto's supporters. Kasuri, the man they wanted, escaped unhurt. Yet another attempt to kill him took place on 24 August 1974 when a burst of Sten gun fire missed his car. And the final attempt was on the night of 10-11 November in which his father died in Lahore.

(*1979*)

IN DEFENCE OF SANJAY GANDHI

I continue to be criticized for supporting Indira and Sanjay Gandhi. Of late the tenor of criticism has changed and most of the critics say that they are willing to accept Indira only if she drops Sanjay and express surprise at my pig-headed support for what they are sure is manifestly unsupportable. It seems that I have not put Sanjay's case as well I should have done. Let me try once again and at the same time put a few questions to my readers who are perturbed by the Sanjay phenomenon.

The most important question we have to answer is: what right had Sanjay to assume power and pronounce on matters of national importance when he was neither elected by the people, nor appointed by their representatives in Parliament to do so? Was it not entirely because he happened to be the son of the then prime minister, and she either pushed him or connived at his pushing himself to grab the levers of power?

In order to answer this question we should know when and how Sanjay metamorphosed from an unsuccessful car manufacturer into a politician. It began with an interview in Uma Vasudev's *Surge*, a tabloid which made fitful appearances on Delhi's news-stalls. Nobody knows why Sanjay chose this nondescript journal with no circulation worth mentioning to announce his political debut. My own guess is that it must have been because of Mohammad Yunus who was close to the Nehru family and to Uma Vasudev. He tried to help Uma with a story which would give a boost to the sagging circulation of *Surge*. In this interview Sanjay spoke of his plans for a better India (clearing slums, planting trees, limiting families, abolishing dowries, etc.). He also said some home truths about the erstwhile communists and men with dubious reputations in business who had infiltrated the Congress. The *Surge* interview was reproduced in several papers. The impact was far wider than one would have expected. It pitchforked Sanjay into the helm of affairs of the Youth Congress which had till then been little better than a papier-mâché organization headed by Sanjay's surrogate Ambika Soni. A small group comprising no more than a couple of dozen young men and women heard Sanjay summarize what he had said to *Surge.* He suggested that they spread their activities to the grass roots at the block level. He is no great orator, but he did provide talking points which became a kind of manifesto of the Youth Congress. A far more important factor in the elevation of Sanjay into political prominence was the machinations of Congress members of Parliament. Of the 350 odd belonging to the party there were about 50 whose past association with the CPI and continuing pressure had been a source of irritation to the more conservative majority. Sanjay's caustic references to communists in his *Surge* interview provided them with the mouthpiece they needed.

WHAT RIGHT HAD HE?

At the Komagata Maru Nagar (Chandigarh) Session in December 1975 the anti-communist Congress group saw with their own eyes that Sanjay drew large crowds wherever he went. It was at this session that plans to utilize his growing popularity (his mother had nothing whatsoever to do with it) matured. It is ironic that the first Congress leader to exploit Sanjay's crowd-gathering qualities was Devaraj Urs, chief minister of Karnataka. In January 1976 he invited Sanjay to address an anti-communal convention. Bangalore had not seen as large a crowd in many years—nor the neighbouring towns and villages where Sanjay and his wife Maneka were taken.

It became apparent to other Congress chief ministers and leaders that on their own they could seldom muster audiences of a few thousand, but if they could get either Indira Gandhi or Sanjay, the crowds swelled into the lakhs. If they wanted to project themselves successfully it would have to be through the mother or the son. Indira was not easily available, and using her would expose them to charges of chamchagiri. At that time Sanjay was more accessible and not subject to insinuations of being the means to get closer to the prime minister. Urs had set the Sanjay ball rolling. After Urs it was Siddhartha Shankar Ray of Bengal. In February 1976, Sanjay was Siddhartha's guest as a speaker at a meeting of the Chambers of Commerce in Calcutta. The crowds that greeted Sanjay were immense. Other chief ministers took the cue. Shyama Charan Shukla invited him to Madhya Pradesh, Tiwari to UP, Vengal Rao to Andhra Pradesh, Zail Singh to Punjab, Hari Dev Joshi to Rajasthan, Banarsi Das Gupta to Haryana. The point to bear in mind is that in every case what these chief ministers (and other Congress leaders) were after was to project themselves through Sanjay. Look up the proceedings of any of these mammoth gatherings and you will find that without exception Sanjay was billed to be the last speaker because his hosts had learnt by experience that as soon as Sanjay left, the crowds melted away.

Why did Sanjay attract such vast throngs of people wherever he went? The use of government machinery (commandeering of trucks, buses etc.) does not provide the complete explanation. Government machinery has always been used and abused to provide audiences for leaders, chief ministers and the like. But they rarely manage to muster captive audiences of more than 20,000 to 30,000. Gandhiji, Nehru, Indira and JP drew crowds with and without the official crowd-gathering machinery being put into operation. For some mysterious reason so did Sanjay.

There have been (and are) other sons of other prime ministers and presidents equally ambitious of acquiring mass appeal. There is Hari Krishna Shastri (Lal Bahadur's son) who became a member of the Lok Sabha; there is also President Giri's son who tried his damnedest to get into the cabinet; Kanti Desai makes no secret of his political ambitions. If Kanti Desai were to mount the rostrum of Ramlila Grounds, he would be lucky to have a few dozen cronies to listen to him; the numbers of hecklers and the police would account for more. Even Suresh (erstwhile MLA and Babu Jagjivan Ram's son) would perhaps do better—but for reasons other than political magnetism. There are also sons of chief ministers: Surinder Singh Kairon, Om Prakash and Jyoti Basu Junior—all ambitious men, but not one of them able to do more than win an assembly seat.

An even more striking phenomenon is that Indira Gandhi has an elder son, Rajiv—tall, handsome, well-spoken—but not even he rouses more than the passing interest of onlookers as he goes from airport to airport. To say that Indira Gandhi has chosen and built him up is neither true nor an adequate explanation of the Sanjay phenomenon. It will need a scholar of mass psychology to unravel the mystique that has been built round the name of Sanjay Gandhi. The common man sees in this young man something of Jawaharlal Nehru, something of Indira Gandhi and something of a go-getter who talks little, does more and gets things done.

It is strange that despite the calculated and massive propaganda let loose against Sanjay and the animosity he rouses in some sections, he continues to attract larger crowds than anyone else in the country, except his mother—larger than Morarji Desai, Jagjivan Ram and even Chaudhary Charan Singh without the pre-organized kisaan sammelans. Why?

INDIRA WITHOUT SANJAY

Now that there are clear signs of a pro-Indira upsurge, many Congress leaders have started saying that they will accept Indira only if she drops Sanjay. The chief spokesmen of this point of view are the very people who were the noisiest and the most active in utilizing Sanjay's popularity when it suited them: Devaraj Urs, Siddhartha Shankar Ray, Dev Kant Barooah, Chandrajit Yadav, and Rajni Patel. All of them have also been associated with the communist or the socialist parties which have little do with socialism except for mouthing Marxist jargon. The Indira-without-Sanjay stance has the full support of the Jan Sangh and the RSS who see in it the last chance to prevent Indira Gandhi's inevitable victory in any fair and free general election.

SANJAY PHOBIA

What exactly did Sanjay do to earn the odium that the press, radio and grapevine have magnified into such monstrous proportions? He gave the slogan: kaam ziyada, batein kam (work more, talk less). He is himself a man of few words. His campaign against dowry and in favour of planting trees was wholly for the good. So was the drive for cleaner cities and curbing the birth rate. It was not his objectives which were objected to but the strong-arm methods adopted to achieve them.

Sanjay gave the lead; the execution was left to the different ministries concerned. Not one minister of Indira Gandhi's cabinet has said that Sanjay, in any way, interfered in the functions of his ministry. If officials exceeded their powers they did so with the full knowledge and connivance of these ministers who now wash their sanctimonious hands of all responsibility. Did Karan Singh really not know that the sterilization programme was being enforced with more zeal than necessary? Did he not read the figures of sterilization that his officials sent him regularly every month? And having publicly stated that Sanjay never interfered with ministerial functions, with what face can he now say that he had nothing to do with forcible sterilizations, and that it was all Sanjay's doing?

There has been much public breast-beating about the demolition of slums around Turkman Gate and forced re-settlement in newly-built colonies. If the slum dwellers had really been upset about being forced into new settlements, how do we explain the strange phenomenon that in the general election, in which the Janata swept the Congress out of power, the only areas in which the Congress party was able to more than hold its own were in these new colonies built at the instance of Sanjay Gandhi?

The blackest mark against the Emergency regime was the indiscriminate arrest of people; some for settling old scores. Did Sanjay have anything to do with these arrests? As far as arrests in Delhi were concerned, we must accept the testimony of the late Kishen Chand, then lieutenant governor of the union territory. He was closely questioned on the subject by the Shah Commission. Although he made several allusions to 'higher-ups', not once did he name Sanjay Gandhi as having either told him or anyone else to arrest anyone.

The Sanjay phobia is a phenomenon of the self-styled intellectual and the so-called educated elite of our metropolitan cities, it has not infected the honest villager or the factory worker. I have little doubt that if under pressure from the former group, Indira Gandhi were to disown Sanjay, they would be the first to scream at the top of their voices: 'What kind of mother is this Indira Gandhi that she disowns her own son!'

(*1979*)

A MATTER OF POLITICS

'You have no understanding of Indian politics,' say some of my critics. It is a serious charge to make against someone who has been the editor of mainstream newspapers and magazines. I do my best to fill the gap in my information. I waste much time reading the same news and speeches in the daily papers. I even read all editorials and political commentaries by the tribe of sab janta wallah journalists. I cultivate politicians and lend both my ears to hear the words of wisdom they let fall from their lips. I study the manifestos of the different political parties and know whether or not they profess to be Marxist, liberal or conservative. I take the general knowledge test on Indian politics. I flop. The question paper they set me is not the kind I expected. There are no questions on the historical background, the class structure, the economic programmes or performance of the political parties which I had prepared myself for. The questions are about politicians, their shifting loyalties and the factions within the parties. All these I had believed to be trivial, with little bearing on politics. I was wrong.

Our political set-up is like our caste structure. As we have the four varnas, we have now four major political parties: Janata, Congress, Communist and Communist (Marxist). But, as in the case of caste, where it is not the varna but the gotra or the sub-gotra that matters, so too in our politics; it is not the party but the faction in the party you belong to that is important. You are Janata? OK. But which Janata are you? Charan Singh–Raj Narain's group or Chandra Shekhar–Madhu Limaye's or Babuji–Bahuguna's or Vajpayee–Nanaji's?—and so on. If you are Congress, then are you with Chavan–Reddy or Indira Gandhi–Tripathi–Urs? And so it is with every other party.

What makes it even worse is when every fortnight or so these combinations go through a radical change. By the time I think I have the entire picture of the different groups, I am told how silly I am. Don't I know that now Babuji and Charan Singh have patched up, Madhu Limaye and George have fallen apart, so and so has now softened towards 'her', D. P. Mishra is going over to the other side and Charan Singh and Morarji bhai have once again... I give up in despair.

In India, any understanding of politics has little to do with the comprehension of political principles and is entirely concerned with information on who is on the side of whom in a particular situation.

Another thing you must bear in mind if you wish to appear politically knowledgeable is to ignore facts you find unpleasant and indulge in wishful thinking. Three years ago when Jayaprakash's Total Revolution was at its height and JP was drawing mammoth crowds wherever he went, the government dismissed the movement as of no consequence and Mrs Gandhi herself said: 'Who made JP a leader?... It is you newspaper people who exaggerate his popularity. The crowds at his meetings are largely hired.'

Now the situation is in reverse. Suddenly Indira Gandhi has re-emerged on the political scene; newspapermen (many hostile to her) who covered her tour of Uttar Pradesh and Gujarat reported that the crowds that greeted her were immense. Some of them, including foreign journalists, interviewed people everywhere and found them to be enthusiastic supporters of the former prime minister. But now the Janata leaders are crying themselves hoarse saying that people who come to her meetings are either curious or hired. They argue that by merely making the headlines she will not become popular once again. I feel they are making the same error as Mrs Gandhi made in underestimating JP's movement. This is my personal reading of the situation. But I must admit that many people firmly believe that I do not understand Indian politics.

(*Undated*)

NOTES AND ACKNOWLEDGEMENTS

Many of the essays that appear in this volume are versions of pieces that first appeared in *Yojana*, the *Hindustan Times*, *The Tribune*, *New Delhi*, the *Illustrated Weekly of India*, *The Statesman*, and the *Times of India* to name a few of the publications that Khushwant Singh contributed to. As the majority of the pieces were taken from typescripts in the possession of the author's estate it has been difficult to accurately source the name of the publication in which the pieces first appeared. All the essays in the book have been used with permission from the author's estate.

Every effort has been made to trace copyright holders and obtain permission to reproduce copyright material included in the book. In the event of any inadvertent omission, the publisher should be informed and formal acknowledgement will be included in all future editions of this book.

NOTES TO INDIVIDUAL SELECTIONS

UNFORGETTABLE PEOPLE

BABA KHARAK SINGH

Baba Kharak Singh was born on 6 June 1867 and died on 6 October 1963.

NEHRU AS A WRITER

A typewritten manuscript, this is believed to have been written for All India Radio's External Services. Khushwant's encounter with Nehru in London probably took place when he was employed in the Indian High Commission as press attaché and public officer.

AMIR KHUSRAU

Amir Khusrau (1253–1325) is known as the 'father of qawwali' and popular lore credits him with the invention of the sitar and tabla.

PORTRAIT OF A SERIAL KILLER

Raman Raghav was one of India's most notorious serial killers. He was arrested by Ramakant Kulkarni, Deputy Commissioner of Police CID (Crime) in 1968. Sentenced to life imprisonment, Raghav died in 1995.

HUMAYUN KABIR

Humayun Kabir (1906–1969) was a politician, writer and philosopher.

THE ANGLO-INDIANS' DILEMMA

Estimates of the number of Anglo-Indians in India vary from 30,000 to 150,000.

LATA MANGESHKAR

Lata Mangeshkar's career began in 1942 and she has been singing for over seven decades. She is the second vocalist, after M.S. Subbulakshmi, to have been awarded the Bharat Ratna (in 2001).

FAKHRUDDIN ALI AHMED

Fakhruddin Ali Ahmed (1905–1977) was the fifth president of India (1974–1977) and the second president to die in office.

MOHAMMAD SLEEM

Mohammad Sleem represented India at many tennis tournaments including Wimbledon and Roland Garros.

AN EVENING WITH DEV ANAND

Dev Anand (1923–2011) was born Dharam Dev Pishorimal Anand in Gurdaspur district which is in present-day Narowal district of Pakistan. He was the recipient of many awards and honours including the Padma Bhushan in 2001.

BEING UNTRUE TO ONE'S SALT

M. O. Mathai (1909–1981) died in Madras at the age of 72.

MALCOLM MUGGERIDGE

Malcolm Muggeridge (1903–1990) was a British journalist and satirist.

JOHN MASTERS

John Masters (1914–1983) was an officer in the British army and a novelist who wrote about the British Empire in India. He died in Santa Fe, New Mexico.

MEMORABLE PLACES

MOONLIGHT IN BOKARO

The Damodar Valley Corporation operates several power stations in the Damodar River area. It has been generating and transmitting power since 1953.

THE ADIVASI ON THE IRON HILL

Jamshedpur was India's first planned industrial city and was founded by Jamshedji Nusserwanji Tata. It is home to Tata Steel, the country's largest and oldest iron and steel producing plant.

THE DOOMED VILLAGE

Construction of the Koyna Dam began in 1956 and was completed in 1964. The Koyna Hydroelectric Project remains the largest in the country.

THE INDIAN WAY

HANGED BY THE NECK TILL YOU ARE DEAD

Khushwant Singh's article on the serial killer Raman Raghav is on p 18 of this book.

A MATTER OF POLITICS

THE STORY OF NINE MILLION HUMANS AND 300 CRORE RUPEES

'Dacca' has been left the way it was spelt at the the time this piece was written.

NOT WANTED IN PAKISTAN

There are around 400 Pakistani Hindu refugee settlements in cities such as Jodhpur, Jaisalmer, Bikaner and Jaipur. Most Hindu refugees from Bangladesh have settled in West Bengal and the north-eastern states.

The spelling of place names (Bangla Desh, Dacca) have been retained as they appeared in the original article.

THE GOOD SHEPHERDESS

Indira Gandhi's finest hour came when she sent the Indian army into what was then East Pakistan to stop the genocide that was taking place in 1971.

JP—THE MAN THEY MOURNED BEFORE HIS DEATH

Popularly known as Lok Nayak, Jayaprakash Narayan was an activist and political leader, remembered chiefly for leading the opposition to Indira Gandhi in the 1970s and the people's movement called Total Revolution.

IN DEFENCE OF SANJAY GANDHI

Sanjay was popularly believed to be Indira Gandhi's favoured heir and son. Following his death in an air crash in 1980, Rajiv Gandhi became Indira's political successor. Sanjay's wife Maneka and son Varun are members of the Bhartiya Janata Party.

ALSO PUBLISHED BY ALEPH

99: UNFORGETTABLE FICTION, NON-FICTION, POETRY & HUMOUR

Khushwant Singh

99 collects in a single volume the finest pieces Khushwant Singh published over the course of a long and prodigiously creative life. The essays, extracts, stories and poems (one for each year of his life) have been chosen for their excellence or because they represent an aspect of the author's versatility and range. Some of the selections are well known. Others have never been published in book form.

This is the definitive anthology of the work of one of our greatest and most entertaining writers—it will offer the reader page after page of thought-provoking pleasure.

REVIEWS

'This is a book which must find a place in any personal collection or in a library anywhere.'—*Sunday Tribune*

'A book to be read and savoured... All in all, *99* is highly recommended. There could not be a better tribute to the memory of Singh nor a better set of leads for readers and scholars to pursue.'—*Indian Express*

'Whether you dip into it at random or read it cover to cover is immaterial. It will amuse you in parts, possibly horrify you, teach you a thing about Delhi, the Emergency, England and a lot of other things, places or events that historians are too boring to ever include in the textbooks they bequeath us.'—*Mid-day*

'Reading this volume is an experience in itself, for the range and very expanse. From Khushwant's pieces focusing on his early life in his ancestral village, Hadali, to those centring on the towering personalities of this era, to the ground realities facing this country, to the various aspects of nature, to the everyday living patterns and what life and death holds out...the list is long.'—*The Statesman*

THE FREETHINKER'S PRAYER BOOK

Khushwant Singh

Khushwant Singh did not believe in God. Yet he woke up before dawn to listen to Sikh hymns, recited the Gayatri Mantra, and knew large parts of the Bible and the Quran by heart. He liked being known as a dirty old man who delighted in malice, but was in fact fanatically disciplined and generous to a fault. He lived an extraordinary life—marked by contradiction, mischief, compassion, courage and wisdom (though he denied all these charges). Where did this unusual agnostic turn for inspiration and strength? *The Freethinker's Prayer Book* gives us some answers.

This eclectic and deeply personal collection brings together prayers and precepts by prophets, poets and philosophers, and Khushwant Singh's favourite passages from the seminal texts of the world's major faiths. The Bible and the Guru Granth Sahib speak to us from these pages, as do the Quran and the Vedas. The songs of mystics and saints like Kabir, Rumi and Teresa of Ávila mix with the verse of poets like Ghalib, Tagore and Keats. In the final section, Khushwant Singh shares some of his own life codes and those of the rebels and mavericks he most admires.

REVIEWS

'*The Frethinker's Prayerbook* may be a compilation credited to an agnostic, but it keeps the faith in the doctrine of life, and how to live it to the fullest.'—*Financial Express*

'This well-produced book is a beautiful collection of quotations that needs to be kept by the bedside, readily available to those who wish to reach out to read, feel and understand profound thoughts, most elegantly expressed.'—*The Tribune*

'This is a beautiful collection that touches upon many aspects of life—from the spiritual and emotional to the pure physical... If you choose to have a daily dose of inspiration, this book can go right onto your reading pile.'—*Deccan Herald*

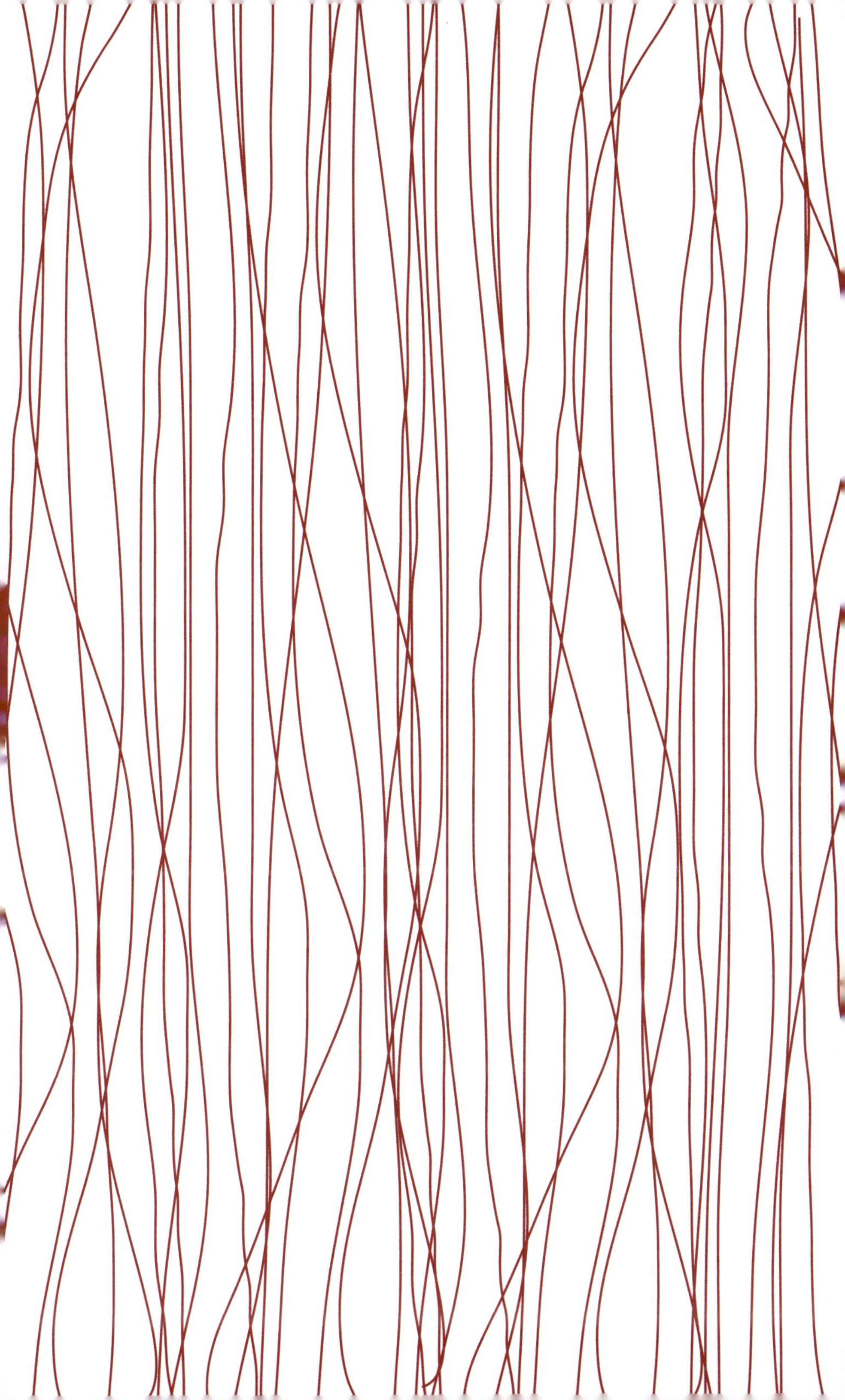

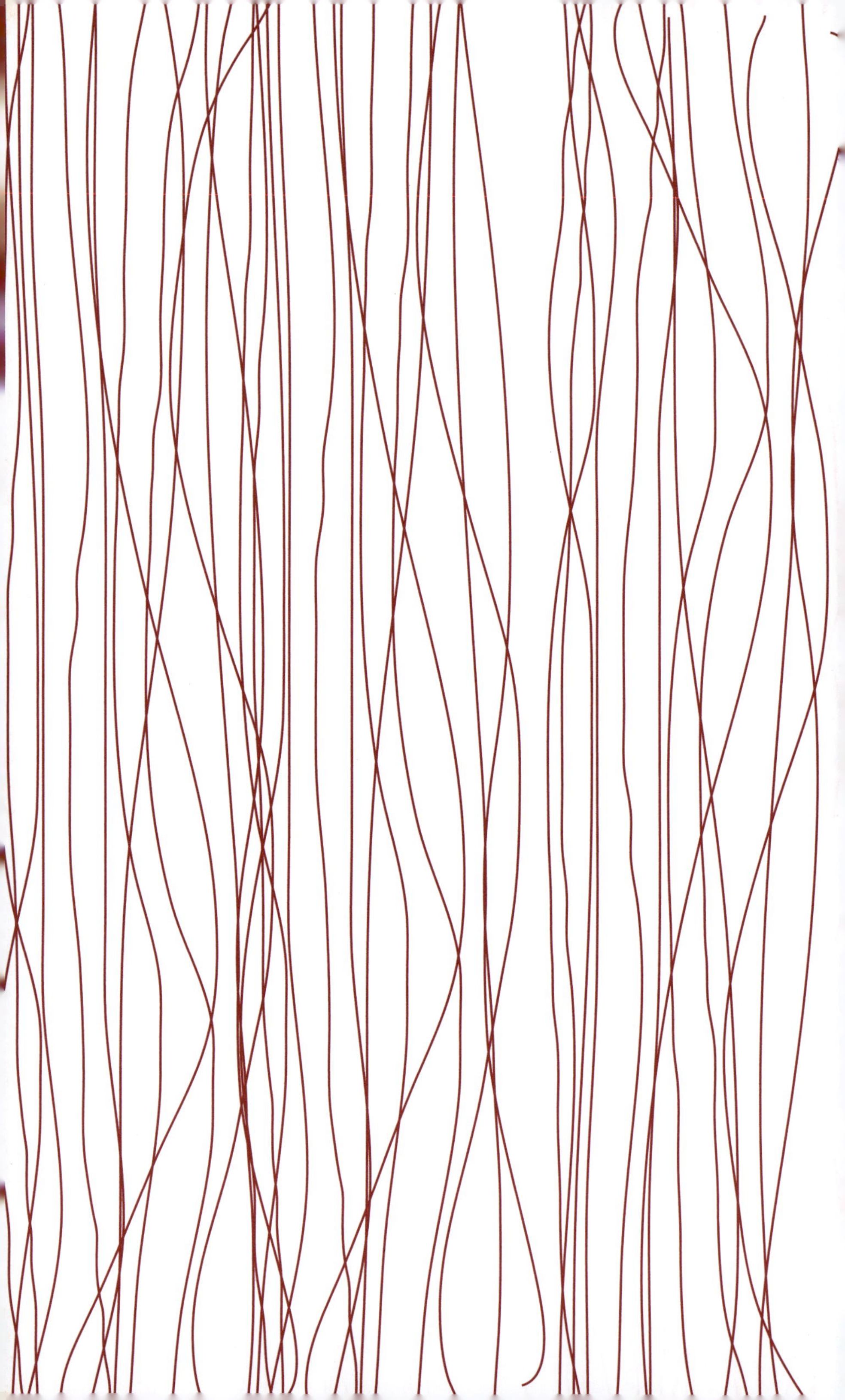